TWO PATHS TO UTOPIA

Two Paths to Utopia

*The Hutterites
and the Llano Colony*

by
PAUL K. CONKIN

GREENWOOD PRESS, PUBLISHERS
WESTPORT, CONNECTICUT

Library of Congress Cataloging in Publication Data

Conkin, Paul Keith.
  Two paths to utopia.

  Reprint. Originally published: Lindoln : University
of Nebraska Press, c1964.
  Bibliography: p.
  Includes index.
  1. Llano Colony (Secular community)--History.
2. Hutterite Brethren--History. I. Title.
HX656.L55C6 1983   335'.976361   83-16639
ISBN 0-313-24248-8 (lib. bdg.)

Reprinted with the permission of the University of Nebraska Press

Reprinted in 1983 by Greenwood Press
A division of Congressional Information Service, Inc.
88 Post Road West, Westport, Connecticut 06881

Printed in the United States of America

10 9 8 7 6 5 4 3 2 1

Foreword

We live in an age of growing revolt against community as a social ideal. This revolt may be against only a parody of community represented today (if not literally at least in the mind of critics) by the shallow and superficial mass conformity of suburbia. The most influential movements in art and philosophy are once again enshrining the individual, the arbitrary, the nonrational, and the unique. The anarchic forms or non-forms of contemporary art and the purposefully indefinable Nothingness of existentialism are cases in point. The widely caricatured organization man, the other-directed automaton, the soulless status seeker, and the well-adjusted man are objects of vindictive attack or growing pity. They have each, it seems, prostituted their humanity and lost their freedom to a nonhuman group. They have embraced a type of community and damned self. In religion, the social urge of Christianity in the early decades of the twentieth century has been replaced by a new orthodoxy of individual responsibility and irrational faith. These trends tend to obscure the very recent past, when the word community was still— despite its nebulous quality, its subtle and infinite suggestivity—the term most often used to symbolize the oldest and highest ideal in the whole history of man—the idea of a perfect society.

Beginning with Sir Thomas More, if not with Isaiah or Plato, the fictional pictures of a perfect social order, the utopias of Western man, have almost always idealized a cooperative or communal society, in which men voluntarily hold all things in common in order to secure peace and plenty. These utopias tend to glorify such virtues as humility, obedience, and cooperation, and such concepts as unity, equality, and conformity. But ideals change. They usually reflect, in reverse, the dominant fear of an individual or an age. In time of war, peace is the ideal of ideals; in time of depression, security. For the prosperous few of the West, want is no longer a pressing problem. Economic security is too commonplace to have the status of an ideal. But new problems exist, such as totalitarian ideologies, the subtle pressures of propaganda or advertising, forced collectivism under auspices either private or governmental, involuntary conformity in close-living cities or suburbs, an

v

inescapable but mediocre popular culture, and an all-pervading materialism. We now live in a type of community, a community of tastes, ideas, and values, but in each case so stereotyped, superficial, and shallow as to be oppressive and dehumanizing. This community, projected to an extreme, becomes the reverse utopia of *Brave New World* or *Nineteen Eighty-Four*. It calls forth its own ideals. Freedom once again becomes the supreme end. Status is attached to such words as quality, originality, nonconformity, uniqueness, personality. In an extreme projection, Nietzsche's assertive, irrational superman is more of a hero than the humble and cooperative citizen of Utopia.

Community, when defined as a social ideal, has two aspects. Descriptively, it means that the largest possible number of human concerns are held in common. Ideally, it means the attainment of the good life. But good, in this context, may mean either obedience to a higher law or the achievement of happiness and well-being, but rarely both. Thus, community demands that men share more things in order to be righteous or to be happy. The urge to full obedience has led to many varieties of religious communalism. The urge to achieve more human happiness has led to almost all reformist or socialist communitarianism. In practice, exponents of community have often stressed a common sharing in one sphere of life, such as property, and excluded others. Because of the modern interest in economic problems, community (or communalism) has most often been associated with common property, and only incidentally with a common creed, race, class, or language. Finally, in this secular age, the great community now is more often defined as a setting for human happiness than as a way of obedience.

Many advocates of a secular type of community hope only for some gradual, partial, and uneven achievement of an impossibly high standard. To them, the true community remains always an ideal, subject to greater clarity in definition and to expanded meaning. Some religious advocates of a future community see no hope, or at least only very limited hope, of achievement of the ideal until some future divine intervention and some more drastic overhauling of human nature. Thus they are willing to compromise, or even reject, the ideal in present practice. Some secular reformers believe that the glorious community is an earthly possibility, and that it will eventually encompass all mankind. They disagree on the best means for its early achievement, ranging from those who want to achieve it in small enclaves and thus demonstrate the correct pathway (communitarian reform) to the Marxists who want to use force to create a suitable environment for community before daring to move on to its actual achievement. Finally, there are the religious advocates who believe that a true community can, in fact must, presently exist among a regenerated and perfected minority.

The religious urge to community is the oldest. The proliferating communal sects of the nineteenth century simply carried forward a tradition that can be traced back through medieval monasticism to the first Christian Church, to the Jewish Essenes on the Dead Sea, and on to Hindu monasticism in India. In almost all religious communalism the object is perfect obedience to God or to some higher law. Whether asceticism is embraced or not, mere human happiness is rarely an object. Reform, at least in any secular sense, is always subordinate to the idea of separation from a sinful world. Common ownership of property is a secondary result of a higher religious dedication to complete brotherhood, and is not itself the major goal or even the most significant feature of religious communalism. The source of God's will may be some type of direct revelation or inspiration, the historic example of an earlier, more obedient people, or binding scriptural authority. An intense, personal religious experience is almost always present in the originators of communal orders or sects, giving an existential as well as an authoritarian or a rational foundation, but this experiential element rarely survives for more than two or three generations.

The Hutterite communities of the United States and Canada are today the oldest, the largest, and by far the most significant examples of Christian communalism. They are living demonstrations also of an extremely conservative and orthodox (not fundamentalist) type of Christianity that in our day is extremely rare. Their turbulent history provides abundant proof of the possible tenacity of total creeds, of the efficiency of a noncompetitive economy, of the strength and durability of a classless society, and of the effectiveness of careful and prolonged indoctrination. Their present colonies are living demonstrations of the advantages or disadvantages of community life. It is ironic that, depending on the point of view, they can be equally well described by passages drawn from either More's *Utopia* or Huxley's *Brave New World*.

The secular urge to community flowered in the nineteenth century. In the United States two great outbursts of secular communitarianism occurred, one before and one after Marx. Both were inspired by utopian ideals. The first movement centered on the ideas of Robert Dale Owen and Charles Fourier; the second on the diluted, idealistic Marxism of

Laurence Gronlund and Edward Bellamy, who sponsored the appealing dream of a coming cooperative commonwealth. Unlike orthodox advocates of Christian communism, the secular evangels of complete cooperation rejected any idea of prolonged separation from a sinful, capitalist world; almost always they wanted, through demonstration and example, to convert the world to their perfected institutions; and they rejected any concept of a nonearthly paradise. Insofar as liberal Christians were attracted to socialism and were able to espouse a purely earthly kingdom, they too joined in the quest for the cooperative commonwealth, in part merging the two communal traditions.

Among the many attempts to establish perfect, secular communities in America, a few, because of the individuals or the ideas involved or because of widespread publicity, captured the imagination of the whole country and therefore have a distinct and significant place in our history. New Harmony and Brook Farm were the preeminent examples. Yet both were short-lived and notably unsuccessful. Other communities, founded by more obscure men and lost either in the literal wilderness of nineteenth-century America or in the equally protective wilderness of twentieth-century apathy and sophistication, were much more successful and endured for many more years. Llano del Rio, the most successful American attempt at secular communitarianism, and nearly the last, was born in the twentieth century, yet was virtually unknown during much of its twenty-five-year existence. Established in California in 1914, the Llano colony migrated to Louisiana in 1918 and remained there until its final liquidation in 1939. Its history, heretofore largely unrecorded, reveals in great detail the perplexing, ultimately insoluble dilemmas of all utopian reform. Juxtaposed to the successful Hutterites, Llano pointedly illustrates the radical contrasts between the two main pathways to community.

Contents

Part One

*THE BRETHREN KNOWN
AS HUTTERITES*

I. Jakob Hutter's New Kingdom of Righteousness

The Hutterites have developed the most complete, nonmonastic community life in the Western world. Their completely classless and fully communal colonies have existed for over four hundred years and, with more than 140 communities today, represent the largest and most successful type of Christian communism ever developed. Their community life is inseparably connected with their religious beliefs, for the Hutterites, almost alone among Christians, insist that the Church of Christ is a total community of believers, with community defined in the most consistent and thoroughgoing manner. To them, the words Church and community are inseparable and almost synonymous. To be a Christian is to live completely in community with other Christians. Thus, to understand the Hutterites, it is necessary to review their early history and their virtually unchanging beliefs. In few cases in human history have ideas and beliefs been so enduringly significant, or even determinant, in the lives of a people. Rarely have economic considerations or environmental conditions meant so little.

The Hutterite faith developed out of the religious revivals that accompanied the Protestant Reformation in Switzerland and the western part of Austria. The formative period lasted only from 1525 to 1536, when Jakob Hutter, the first strong leader of the brethren who would soon bear his name, was burned alive in Innsbruck. The Hutterites represent the final, most consistent development of one distinctive reform movement which began with Ulrich Zwingli's earliest reforms in Zürich in 1518. By 1525, just before the official birth of his Reformed Church, a group of more radical reformers, led by Conrad Grebel, Felix Manz, and George Blaurock, broke away from Zwingli over such hotly-debated questions as a State Church and infant baptism, both of which Zwingli accepted. From this break came the Swiss Brethren sect, which faced almost immediate persecution from both Zwingli and Roman Catholics, and which soon bore the label of Anabaptist because it began the rebaptism of its converts.

The Swiss Brethren were the fathers of both the Mennonite Church to the West, and the Hutterites of Eastern Europe. The Brethren quickly spread their ideas into neighboring German provinces and down the Rhine to the Netherlands, preaching their doctrine of a purely voluntary Church, adult baptism and membership, lay ministers, and complete nonresistance or pacifism. In the Netherlands a former priest, Menno Simons, became the Anabaptist leader and gave the name Mennonite to this branch of the movement. Much later, when his writings and influence had spread back to Switzerland, the survivors of the much-persecuted Swiss Brethren also adopted the name of Mennonites. Thus today, the various Mennonite and Amish (a later faction) sects are the largest surviving remnants of the early Anabaptist movement, although its influence has permeated many other Protestant denominations. The Hutterites are the second largest and, today, the purest survivors of this branch of the Reformation.[1]

Even before 1525 some Anabaptist doctrines had been espoused by Austrian reformers. The greatest of these men was Balthasar Hubmaier, a former university professor and Catholic theologian who preached at Waldshut, just across the border from Switzerland. As did other Anabaptists, he first questioned Zwingli's acceptance of infant baptism, and was himself rebaptized on Easter, 1525, carrying with him into the Swiss Brethren movement over three hundred of his congregation. Forced to flee by Austrian authorities, he was harassed by Protestants in Zürich and ended up in Nikolsburg, Moravia, in July of 1526. Here he established one of the largest, but also one of the most conservative, Anabaptist congregations in Europe. With the intense Anabaptist persecution that followed the Peasants' Revolt in South Germany, Moravia became a haven for many of the Swiss Brethren and, even more, for a growing number of persecuted converts from the Austrian Tyrol, which was already becoming a center of the new faith even in the face of bitter suppression. Although the congregation in Nikolsburg practiced adult baptism, Hubmaier, unlike other Anabaptist leaders, compromised on nonresistance

1. Charles Henry Smith, *The Story of the Mennonites* (3rd ed., Newton, Kan.: Mennonite Publication office, 1950), pp. 2–13, 85–89; John Horsch, *The Hutterian Brethren, 1528–1931 : A Story of Martyrdom and Loyalty* (Goshen, Ind.: The Mennonite Historical Society, 1931), pp. 2–4; A. J. F. Zieglschmid, "The Hutterites on the American Continent," *American-German Review*, IV (Feb., 1942), 21–22; David E. Harder, "The Hutterian Church" (unpublished M.A. Thesis, Bethel College, 1930), p. 111.

and even permitted his church members to serve as magistrates. This "half-way" faith invited faction after faction, but endeared Hubmaier to the local barons, who were practically autonomous and who welcomed the Anabaptist farmers for economic reasons. Baron Leonhard von Lichtenstein of Nikolsburg was even rebaptized, making mild Anabaptism virtually a State religion. Most opposed to Hubmaier were the Tyrolean refugees, who represented a more radical and stricter brand of Anabaptism and, in many cases, a lower economic class. Before any doctrinal clashes were resolved, Hubmaier was imprisoned and then burned at the stake in Vienna in 1528. Since his mild Anabaptist faith is close to the beliefs of many modern-day Baptists, he is much revered by their historians.[2]

A leader of one of the dissenting factions at Nikolsburg, and in one sense the founder of the Hutterites, was Jacob Wideman, an iron-willed minister who came from Bavaria to Moravia in 1526. He disapproved of war taxes, the use of the sword, and other practices permitted by Hubmaier and his successors in the big congregation. As a result he gathered his own group of stricter brethren, or *stabler* (men of the staff), and met separately for worship. His group reproached the larger church for not pooling its resources in order to aid the stream of poor refugees from the Tyrol, and thus Wideman's group attracted many of these pilgrims from Austrian persecution. In 1528 Baron Lichtenstein, with all good wishes, asked Wideman's faction to leave Nikolsburg if it could not attend the regular worship services. Wideman took his group of about two hundred to nearby Austerlitz, where they were welcomed by liberal barons who were in need of good tenants for their estates and who had earlier given religious refuge to the Picards (Hussites). On the road to Austerlitz, Wideman introduced what was to be the most distinctive doctrine of the Hutterites, a community of goods. After four stewards were selected, each member of the congregation freely piled all his earthly possessions on cloaks that had been spread on the ground. At Austerlitz the brethren continued this communism by setting up their first common household, or *Brüderhof*. Yet, at this early date, the practice of community property was not thoroughgoing or even clearly defined. It had been occasioned in part by religious conviction, but also in part by expediency.

2. A. J. F. Zieglschmid, ed., *Die Älteste Chronik der Hutterischen Brüder* (Philadelphia: The Carl Schurz Memorial Foundation, 1947), pp. 49–51; Horsch, *The Hutterian Brethren*, pp. 5–7; Smith, *The Story of the Mennonites*, pp. 46–55; Karl Kautsky, *Communism in Central Europe in the Time of the Reformation* (New York: Russell and Russell, 1959), pp. 173–191.

The detailed implementation, and the thorough and consistent religious justification, awaited better leaders than Wideman.[3]

From Austerlitz, the Wideman congregation sent happy reports back to the Tyrol and to South Germany. The Kingdom of God had been established. The Tyrolean refugees came in a steady stream, but instead of one kingdom they found at least three. Just after Wideman moved to Austerlitz, one Gabriel Ascherham had led a group of Anabaptists from Silesia to nearby Rossitz, establishing there a second, semicommunal *Brüderhof*. From this group (called Gabrielites after its founder), a small faction broke away in 1529 and settled in Auspitz, under Philip Weber (thus the Philippites).

In the Tyrol the strongest Anabaptist leader, after the death of George Blaurock, was Jakob Hutter, a hatmaker without much formal education, but with amazing talents in organization and leadership. In 1529, at the invitation of his elders, he and a fellow minister, Sigmund Schutzinger, visited Austerlitz to investigate the new mode of life. Hutter was so impressed that he joined Wideman's congregation in the name of his own Tyrolean flock, and rushed back home to help his people escape to Moravia. Many left under the supervision of Zorg Zaunring, who was selected as a special emissary by Hutter. Even before Zaunring arrived, the Austerlitz congregation became embroiled in an internal struggle that led, eventually, to the intervention of Hutter and to the doctrines and institutions that still distinguish the Hutterites.[4]

At Austerlitz, Zorg Zaunring joined Wilhelm Reublin, a Swiss refugee and an unending troublemaker, in a revolt against the policies of Jacob Wideman. They complained about the uninspiring preaching, the poor treatment of children, irregularities in discipline, the lack of tact on the part of Wideman, and, perhaps most important, about mismanagement of common funds. In one letter, Reublin argued that the elders ate and dressed better than the rest of the congregation, and that wealthy converts had their own little homes. When outvoted by Wideman's supporters, Zaunring and Reublin in January, 1531, led a minority group to Auspitz,

3. Zieglschmid, *Älteste Chronik*, pp. 52–53, 86–87; Harder, "The Hutterian Church," pp. 15–17; Smith, *The Story of the Mennonites*, pp. 55–56; Franz Heimann, "The Hutterite Doctrines of Church and Common Life: A Study of Peter Riedemann's Confession of Faith of 1540," *Mennonite Quarterly Review*, XXVI (Jan., 1952), 23–25.

4. Johann Loserth, "Jakob Hutter," *Mennonite Encyclopedia* (Hillsboro, Kan.: Mennonite Brethren Publishing House, 1955–1957), II, 851; Christian Hege, "Auspitz," *Mennonite Encyclopedia*, I (1955), 192; Harder, "The Hutterian Church," p. 18; Kautsky, *Communism*, p. 193.

where they established their own *Brüderhof*. Both the Austerlitz and Auspitz groups sent letters to Hutter, asking for his support. Hutter and Schutzinger came to Moravia in 1531, and decided in favor of the stricter Auspitz congregation. Hutter then returned to the Tyrol, leaving Schutzinger in charge at Auspitz, which was the fourth distinct Anabaptist settlement in the area, not counting the old congregation back at Nikolsburg.[5]

Even the Auspitz congregation did not escape factionalism. Ironically, under the stricter discipline of Schutzinger, both Reublin and Zaunring were excommunicated within two years, Reublin for expropriating common funds and Zaunring for too easily forgiving his wife of adultery. But Schutzinger was able to win the support of the Gabrielites and Philippites, thus uniting three small factions. Jakob Hutter returned to Auspitz in 1533, only to decry existing conditions and to begin two years of lasting reform. Under intense "spiritual dedication," he eliminated the last vestiges of individual property, family distinctions, and class differences, and enforced the new communism by rigid discipline. Elected as *Vorsteher* (head pastor or bishop) by the Tyroleans, he charged Schutzinger with negligence and had him excommunicated. At the same time he severed his congregation from the Philippites and Gabrielites, both of which had supported Schutzinger. This ended the factionalism at Auspitz. After persecution in 1535, the Philippites and Gabrielites either returned to their homelands or joined the Hutterites. Later the dispersed remnants of both groups would be converted. Neither the Austerlitz brethren nor the Nikolsburg church would survive the same persecution, with many of their members also joining the Hutterites. Thus the only Anabaptist group to survive in Moravia was the one so thoroughly and completely reorganized by Hutter. His ideas and his institutions have now survived for four hundred years. But Jakob Hutter himself faced a more horrible fate. In 1535 he daringly rebuked the Moravian authorities for their persecution of the one true Church, fled to Austria, was captured, suffered the rack and brutal whipping without recanting, and joyfully went to the stake on February 25, 1536.[6]

The Hutterites barely endured this serious persecution of 1535. In an age of State Churches and universal membership, the rejection of infant

---

5. Christian Hege, "Austerlitz," *Mennonite Encyclopedia*, I, 192–193; Loserth, "Jakob Hutter," p. 851; Kautsky, *Communism*, p. 194.

6. Loserth, "Jakob Hutter," pp. 852–854; Robert Friedmann, "Hutterian Brethren," *Mennonite Encyclopedia*, II, 855.

baptism struck at the heart of State authority. In 1532, despite the tolerance of local barons, the Moravian *Landtag* had passed an edict banishing all Anabaptists and Jews, but active measures only followed the widespread publicity that followed the extremely radical and compulsory communism at Münster in 1534 and 1535. The Hutterites and the other Anabaptist groups were driven from their dwellings, with many Hutterites hiding in the forests and fields in small groups of six or eight. Many, working as individuals, were able to get positions with sympathetic barons, and within a few years most were able to return to their *Brüderhofs*. Severe persecution began again in 1547 when Charles V began an all-out struggle against the Lutheran Smalkalden League in order to rid his realm of all Protestants. The Moravian nobles were ordered to expel all Hutterites, who by now had over twenty colonies and were quite prosperous. This time the Hutterites found temporary refuge in Slovakia (then part of Hungary), where they had already established one *Brüderhof*. But the Hungarian lords were also forced to expel their valued Hutterite tenants. For years the Hutterites had to live in the woods and caves along the Moravian-Hungarian border, hunted, treated as outlaws and suffering unbelievable hardship and cruelty. Only after the Peace of Augsburg ushered in a new period of relative tolerance were the Hutterites able to return to their Moravian homes.[7]

After 1555 the Hutterites entered their golden age, which lasted until near the end of the century. During these years they established over eighty-five *Brüderhofs*, with an estimated membership of at least fifteen thousand,[8] suffered little persecution, and accumulated a large amount of wealth. They were blessed by a continuous flow of converts from the Germanic areas of Europe, and by excellent leaders. Missionaries were sent on hazardous journeys throughout Europe, not only enlisting converts but providing a growing list of heroic martyrs that were used as examples in song and sermon. It was during the early persecution and these golden years that the great mass of Hutterite manuscript literature was first written. And perhaps most significantly, their doctrinal beliefs were

7. Horsch, *The Hutterian Brethren*, pp. 15–19; Smith, *The Story of the Mennonites*, pp. 346–349.

8. Estimates vary widely on both the number of *Brüderhofs* and the total population. Both Horsch, *The Hutterian Brethren*, and Smith, *The Story of the Mennonites*, estimate only fifty villages. Friedmann estimates over one hundred in his "Hutterian Brethren," *Mennonite Encyclopedia*, II, 855, while at the same time he estimates between twenty and thirty thousand Hutterites. Actually, eighty-five colony locations have been discovered, but no one knows whether they were all occupied at the same time.

further clarified and written even as their social and economic institutions were formalized.

Each of the major Anabaptist groups wanted to restore the primitive or apostolic Church. A few of the more radical German groups became too spiritualistic to found any lasting institution or, as at Münster, madly used the sword to usher in a New Kingdom and thus invited their own destruction. But the Hutterites never followed the alluring wiles of spiritualism, and were able to develop the internal discipline and the external passivity necessary for the survival of any non-State-supported, fully voluntary, and endlessly persecuted sect.

The ideological sources of the Anabaptist restoration movement can scarcely be traced beyond the Bible itself, although one scholar believed that the Renaissance Humanists' exaltation of the primitive, or of a past golden but simple age, might have influenced some of the more educated Anabaptist leaders.[9] The zeal with which the Hutterites searched the New Testament for a model was simply an outgrowth of the intense religious concern generated by the Reformation. Their emphasis upon a community of goods in the early Church was certainly influenced by their lowly social or economic status, although there is evidence that many men of wealth gave up all their property in order to join a *Brüderhof*.[10] In any case, economic explanations cannot account for the long survival of communism among the generally prosperous Hutterites.

The most complete statements of Hutterite beliefs have come from two of the successors of Jakob Hutter—Peter Riedemann and Peter Walpot. Riedemann was bishop from 1542 to 1556, but before that had been one of the most successful Hutterite missionaries. A cobbler who came to the Hutterites from the Gabrielites, he spent much of his early life in prisons, and while in prison in 1540 wrote a book-length confession of faith.[11] His confession is still considered authoritative by Hutterites, even though modern defenses of their religion have been written in recent years.[12]

9. Franklin H. Littell, *The Anabaptist View of the Church* (2nd ed., Boston: Starr King Press, 1958), pp. 48–49.

10. Paul Dedic, "The Social Background of the Austrian Anabaptists," *Mennonite Quarterly Review*, XIII (Jan., 1939), 10–11.

11. Peter Riedemann, *Account of Our Religion, Doctrine and Faith, Given by Peter Riedemann of the Brothers Whom Men Call Hutterians*, trans. Kathleen E. Hasenberg (London: Hodder and Stoughton, 1950).

12. See Paul S. Gross, *Who Are the Hutterites?* (Pincher Creek, Alberta: n.p., 1959), and Peter Hofer, *The Hutterian Brethren and Their Beliefs* (Starbuck, Manitoba: n.p., 1955). Both are small pamphlets. The latter was written by the Senior Elder (Bishop) of the *Schmiedenleut*.

Peter Walpot, bishop after 1565 and Riedemann's successor as intellectual leader and chief polemicist, probably wrote the two other main doctrinal works, a *Great Article Book* in 1577 in defense of five distinct Hutterite doctrines and, almost at the same time, a defense of Anabaptist beliefs and practices against slanderous remarks made at the Lutheran Conference of 1577 at Worms on the Rhine.[13] These doctrinal statements were, in each case, a confession or defense of existing beliefs and practices, and thus were more descriptive than originative. Jakob Hutter in particular, and other Anabaptist leaders in general, were the ones who originated the basic beliefs and institutions.

Basic to the Hutterites, and almost all other Anabaptists, was a wholehearted and literal acceptance of the Bible, and particularly of the New Testament, as the Word of God. Although the Hutterites stressed its role, the Holy Spirit never usurped the complete authority of the written scripture as it did in some of the more spiritualistic sects. The Hutterites, of course, made certain distinctive interpretations of the New Testament, but they never tried to develop an elaborate theology. Except for unrecognized and inherited assumptions current in their day, they had no philosophy, and in their attitude of complete, unquestioning obedience, were quick to rebuke intellectualism.[14] Their leaders were obviously intelligent, completely literate, but simple, unsophisticated, and relatively unlearned in an academic sense. Their attempt to return to an apostolic Church was grounded in what, to them, was an obvious and easily understood account of Christ's life and message, and of the history of the early Church. Every exposition of belief, beginning with Riedemann's, was justified by scriptural quotations. Their greatest strength was in their lack of elaborate rationalizations, their willingness to be consistent and go to absolute extremes however great the difficulties, and in their total refusal to compromise. But these same factors could lead to extreme dogmatism and even arrogance. Unlike some later restoration movements, the Hutterites were not concerned with some of

13. The original *Great Article Book* exists only in manuscript form, but one of the five articles was translated into English and published as: *True Surrender and Christian Community of Goods, From the Great Article Book by Peter Walpot, 1577*, trans. Kathleen E. Hasenberg (Bromdon, Bridgnorth, Shropshire, England: The Plough Publishing House, 1957); Paul S. Gross, trans. and ed., *The Defence Against the Prozess at Worms on the Rhine in the Year 1557* (Lethbridge, Alberta: n.p., n.d.).

14. Robert Friedmann, "Reason and Obedience, An Old Anabaptist Letter of Peter Walpot (1571) and Its Meaning," *Mennonite Quarterly Review*, XIX (Jan., 1945), 29–37.

the more intricate and subtle problems of New Testament theology. They accepted the prevalent view of the Trinity (unlike early Unitarians), and did not reject the prevalent method of baptism (unlike many later Baptists).

The Hutterite concept of the Church logically determined and explained almost all of their other beliefs and institutions. With other Anabaptists, the Hutterites emphatically rejected a State Church and compulsory membership. In keeping with the classic definition of a religious sect in contrast to a Church, they believed in a purely voluntary brotherhood of sincere believers, held together by a close fellowship, dedicated to the highest moral effort, and completely separated from the sinful world. This would always mean a small but select group unless compromises were made, and compromise would destroy the very essence of such a sect.[15]

To the Hutterites the Church of Christ was a separated body of believers, as *pure*, *holy*, and *perfect* as Christ Himself. In fact, this Church remained on earth as the very incarnation of God, as the living embodiment of Christ, or the Word, and thus as a continuous revelation, a permanent beacon of complete truth and righteousness. This Church was not a mystical entity forever transcending the mundane material world, but was actually composed of human beings, of individuals made up in part of flesh and blood. But since the Church was perfect, its members had to be pure and completely sanctified, having been perfected by the Holy Spirit which, given by grace at the time of conversion, destroyed all their sins and sealed them as members of Christ's Kingdom. This idea of Christian perfectionism was alleviated somewhat by a recognition of the reality of temptations and the continued inclination toward sin even on the part of Christians. Also, the Hutterites completely and emphatically rejected the idea of predestination. Christians can, through sin, lose their membership in the Church and their heritage of salvation. Only when tied to a belief in divine election does perfectionism lead to the extremes of antinomianism, or the belief that a Christian cannot sin no matter what he does. Instead of justifying all behavior, the Hutterites used the idea of perfectionism to prescribe and enforce by spiritual sanctions one of the most demanding and elaborate sets of moral standards in human history. To the Hutterites, even today, the standard of a Christian is never less

15. Heimann, "The Hutterite Doctrines of Church and Common Life, A Study of Peter Riedemann's Confession of Faith of 1540, II," *Mennonite Quarterly Review*, XXVI (April, 1952), 154–156.

than full obedience and, despite shortcomings, nothing less is fully acceptable.[16]

Since the Reformation, most Protestant denominations have emphasized justification by faith alone and rejected the Roman Catholic reliance upon the saving efficacy of the sacraments. In the case of the Calvinists, faith itself was an arbitrary gift from God, but remained the determinant element in salvation. The anxiety and uncertainty of inscrutable divine election usually led to the exemplary moral behavior of the Puritans, but the morals had no saving effect. To most Protestant theologians, faith involved a highly individualistic relationship between God and the individual. Faith was usually defined in terms of belief and something more, which could best be described as love. To Calvin, for example, the taint of original sin was always the primal fact of existence; its removal through a mystical, "spiritual" rebirth was the critical moment in an individual's life. Less important and never determinant was participation in an organized church and high ethical behavior. The Catholic religion, with its emphasis upon a continuous outpouring of grace in the sacraments, and thus a continuous Christian experience, necessarily gave more weight to the community, or to the organized Church as custodian of the sacramental system and the earthly arbiter of salvation, and thus somewhat less emphasis upon the lone individual's encounter with God. High ethical conduct was demanded, as among Protestants, but again was not the determinant factor in salvation so long as the Church could alleviate original sin with baptism, and provide access to saving grace in the Eucharist and in Extreme Unction.

The Hutterites, along with most Protestants, rejected the saving efficacy of all sacraments, but, along with the Catholics, always stressed the Church (or community of believers) as indispensably related to salvation. The Hutterites technically accepted justification by faith, but never defined faith exclusively, or even primarily, in terms of belief or some almost mystical love, but in terms of discipleship in Christ's Kingdom. Thus, their emphasis went back beyond Augustine and Paul to Christ Himself, and to His relationship with His disciples. To the Hutterites, disbelief was rarely a problem, while love could only have meaning in obedience. To know about Christ and His Church, and further to believe in the power of His sacrifice, was to stand at the door of salvation. To go the last step was fully to commit oneself to the Church, and to complete and

16. Riedemann, *Account of Our Religion*, pp. 38-40; Horsch, *The Hutterian Brethren*, pp. 123-127; Gross, *The Defence*, pp. 17, 19-20.

perfect discipleship within it. This was not merely a commitment to obey a "spiritual" Lord, but to obey Christ as embodied in the Church, to lose oneself completely in the community. As will be shown later, it was also to submit oneself as completely as any Catholic ever does to the Church as the sole arbiter of salvation. The individual element was completely forsaken; every outlook became social in nature. Since perfect obedience is a human impossibility without divine aid, the Holy Spirit ministered to the Church and to each individual member of it, making perfect obedience possible, and thus making the completely holy Church possible. This emphasis upon a presently existing and perfect church, and complete discipleship within it, nullified the need for sacraments as other than symbols of one's purity. The very idea of a perfect church, with all members completely and thus equally sanctified, removed the possibility of privileged members and gave the keys of salvation to the total body rather than to a custodial hierarchy within it.[17]

The Hutterite emphasis upon a separated, perfect church gave the strongest possible sanction to an impossibly strict and completely selfless morality. Salvation depended upon it. Few have ever dared aspire to so much, or risk so much for so little. To the lofty Puritans, moral superiority was a critical index of God's favor and of one's election, but it was not a condition of election. Even the few groups that have believed, on very convincing scriptural authority, that Christians cannot sin have been forced to appeal to a higher, nonhuman standard in order to explain away conduct that seemed obviously immoral to outsiders. The Hutterites never took such a route of escape, always recognizing the significance of motive but never disregarding the outward act. This emphasis upon discipleship in the Kingdom, and upon the gravity of any lapse from perfect obedience, contrasts with the desperate concern over original sin and irresistible conversion in the Augustinian-Calvinist tradition.

To the Hutterites, Adam's sin introduced both physical and spiritual death. All remain under the indictment of physical death, but Christ fully removed the necessity of spiritual death for all mankind. His atonement was complete; the blight of original sin was removed, although man still shares Adam's nature and is still tempted. But children are saved until responsible for their own disobedience, and infant baptism is thus unnecessary. For responsible adults, a free choice of full obedience

17. Robert Friedmann, "The Doctrine of the Two Worlds," in Guy F. Hershberger, ed., *The Recovery of the Anabaptist Vision* (Scottdale, Pa.: Herald Press, 1958), pp. 105–110; Riedemann, *Account of Our Religion*, pp. 40–43.

to Christ brings complete forgiveness of their own past sins and the gift of the Holy Spirit, which aids them in resisting future temptations. Future sin can lose them their heritage of salvation, which is only for the pure, but, if life lasts, true repentance can lead to forgiveness and a renewed purity. Except for the consistency and rigor with which the idea of obedience was interpreted, this outlook was similar to that of the Mennonites, the Freewill Baptist sects, and other Arminian groups. Unlike the anxious Calvinist, the obedient Hutterite was always completely certain of his salvation at a given moment, but he did not have the Calvinist assurance that his heritage, once secured, was irrevocable. The Hutterite denied that he believed in salvation through good works, for indispensable was Christ's sacrifice and the gift of the Holy Spirit, both of which precede full discipleship. But the Hutterite always insisted that full obedience was necessary; there were no miraculous shortcuts, no sweet and emotional bypasses. The actual rebirth, the moment of commitment, might involve deep inner struggle and even suffering, even as the gift of the Holy Spirit might mean exhilaration and joy, but these experiences could not be separated from the full liberation from sin that followed, and the endless rigors of full obedience.[18]

The Hutterite emphasis upon the existing Kingdom of God tended to lessen their interest in a future kingdom, although Hutter and other early leaders looked forward to an early return of Christ. Of course, to the Hutterites, Christ was already present in His Church. There was no new kingdom to be established, or even to be purified. Yet, there was one limitation. The Kingdom needed to be expanded for it was but a small island in a great sea of worldly evil. In spite of this encirclement, the Hutterites never doubted the final, complete, and miraculous triumph of this Kingdom, and with it a judgment upon the encircling world. Their hopes of ultimate triumph were not tied to a temporal continuity of the true Church, and they never tried to prove historically the continuous existence of the Church in the past. They did feel that their practice of complete brotherhood was important in attracting converts and advancing the Kingdom, even as in times of adversity they could suffer martyrdom without flinching. In their small islands of righteousness, the Hutterites expected, and all too often received, only the worst from the outside world. Thus they tended to exaggerate its evils and overemphasize its hostility. And thus their eschatological longings were expressed in terms

18. Robert Friedmann, "Peter Riedemann on Original Sin and the Way of Redemption," *Mennonite Quarterly Review*, XXVI (July, 1952), 210–215.

of Christ's return and His judgment upon all evil. The details of the end were not too clear. The Hutterites showed only a passing interest in the Book of the Revelation. They looked forward to a resurrection of a perfected body and, perhaps most important from their experience, to the ending of the worldly temptations that always plagued them and the dangerous inner impulses they had always to battle. Unlike Marxian communists, the Hutterites did not use a hostile world as an excuse for incomplete community and brotherhood, but they were always well aware of the hazards and temptations the world presented them. Discipleship, so often a burden or at least a struggle, would become joyous in the full flowering of the Kingdom in some distant future.[19]

The Hutterites observed baptism, the laying on of hands, and the Lord's Supper, but in each case only as signs or symbols. Redemption followed faith and repentance, not baptism. Yet, baptism was required as a covenant of good conscience, or as a bath of rebirth. It followed the real entrance into the Church, but was required as a symbol of the remission of sins. It placed the individual under the discipline of the Church and its power to excommunicate. This stress on baptism was midway between the view of some Protestant groups that baptism was almost an optional accessory to conversion, and the view of Catholics and many Protestants that it was necessary for the remission of sins. After an intense questioning, baptism was performed by an ordained minister before the assembled Hutterite congregation whose prayers were part of the ceremony. It was administered by the laying on of hands and the pouring of water, with an admonition against future sin. For a member reunited after excommunication, the rite was very similar to baptism except that only the laying on of hands was used. The Lord's Supper was considered the best expression of the inner unity of all members of the Church. It was an act of remembrance and a hallowed dedication to the ends of the community. It was restricted, insofar as a Hutterite congregation could judge, to true, and thus sinless, Christians. Unique among Christians, it was as much a lesson in community unity as an act of remembrance. Even as bread was composed of the coming together of many grains in full community, and wine composed of many grapes, even so were Christians of one nature in Christ. The Lord's Supper, having no efficacy in itself, could not create this desired unity. Instead, the unity was a precondition for participation in the ceremony. Only the pure dared approach the table. In line with the Jewish Passover, which the

19. Riedemann, *Account of Our Religion*, pp. 33, 45–46.

Hutterites believed the Lord's Supper replaced, it was observed only once a year, on the day after Easter.[20]

The Hutterites, like other Anabaptists, always detested compulsory religious beliefs, but balanced this belief in religious freedom with the strictest and most exclusive type of spiritual government within the Church. From the view of outsiders, the Hutterite religion was an absolute spiritual autocracy under the preachers, elders, or congregation. To the Hutterites it was a realm of perfect, childlike freedom under the rule of Christ. The absolute Lordship of Christ (an analogue drawn from the medieval setting) was necessarily expressed in the various ordinances and regulations of the community, but to a Christian perfect obedience was not a burden. To one sealed by the Holy Spirit, it should be automatic and unquestioning. The demanding, commanding law of the Old Testament had been superseded by a new human nature in the true Christian, and was no longer needed. But the law, a good schoolmaster for Israel, was still valid, needful especially for children who were training for a spiritual conversion and for the sinful also, who had not the spirit and the willing heart. Each Hutterite *Brüderhof* was a miniature theocracy, with its ordinances adopted by the local congregation or elders, but given ultimate sanction in Christ Himself. This government was purely religious as behooves the Church. No physical punishment was employed.[21]

Closely related to the elaborate set of rules was the community concern for each individual. A Hutterite submitted himself to brotherly scrutiny, admonition, address and punishment, and practiced the same also. No privacy was condoned or allowed. The religious sanctions ran from mild censure to a complete ban, which meant complete social ostracism and loss of community privileges. A decision to ban a member could not be lightly taken, and in practice was rarely used. No man could judge the sincerity of a confession of faith, and thus had to await some further revelation (such as a grievous sin) before passing judgment. A constant, diligent search had to be made of other men's conduct, with warnings before the congregation for minor aberrations. Gross sins, such as theft, violence, adultery, and drunkenness, warranted immediate excommunica-

20. *Ibid.*, pp. 77–87; Heimann, "The Hutterite Doctrines of Church and Common Life," pp. 45–47; Hofer, *The Hutterite Brethren and Their Beliefs*, pp. 26–27; *The Church and the World, Claus Felbinger's Confession of Faith Addressed to the Council of Landshut, 1560*, translated by the Society of Brothers at Primavera, Paraguay (Popular Point Colony, Popular Point, Manitoba: n.p., 1952), p. 15.

21. Riedemann, *Account of Our Religion*, pp. 65–66.

tion unless they could be attributed to some immediate weakness of the flesh, in which case only social ostracism resulted. After true repentance, as proved by behavior or even prescribed penance, a banned member was restored with full love and complete forgiveness. The only difference between the Hutterite ban and the Catholic was its use for many more types of disobedience and its exercise by the whole congregation.[22]

The Hutterite Church has always employed a slightly modified form of congregational government, with each congregation, in theory, being fully autonomous. Actually, throughout most of their history the presiding ministers or bishops (the Hutterites do not like the latter term) have had great influence and advisory powers. Also, some type of meeting or assembly for either ministers or elders has usually existed, again without binding powers but with great influence. As specified by Peter Riedemann, the preachers for the early *Brüderhofs* were chosen by God. The male members of a congregation (women have no part in church government) waited upon God's will in prayer, seeking knowledge of those God considered suitable for the office. If God's counsel (expressed in nominations) indicated more than one suitable candidate, then God had to make the final decision by lot. In addition to preachers, the early Hutterites had their traveling servants of the Word, or missionaries, who, even as the preachers, were ordained by elders and empowered to administer baptism. In addition, each *Brüderhof* democratically elected its own elders and the stewards for secular concerns.[23]

The idea of worldly evil and the complete separation of the Church from the world still determines most Hutterite institutions. The Church, being pure and holy, cannot be polluted by what is sinful and secular. Unlike many theologians, the Hutterites tried never to separate a perfect but purely spiritual church from the visible and necessarily imperfect congregation. Neither did they accept two levels of Christian attainment, one reserved for the masses and the other for monks and nuns. The existing, observable Church was the only Church, and thus had to correspond to the rigid standards of such a perfect body. For a Christian there was no dual membership in a city of God and a city of man; there were no common institutions for the children of light and the children of darkness. The Church had only one Lord, and that was Christ.

22. *Ibid.*, pp. 18–19, 65–66; Hofer, *The Hutterite Brethren and Their Beliefs*, pp. 24–25; Robert Friedmann, "An Anabaptist Ordinance of 1633 on Nonresistance," *Mennonite Quarterly Review*, XXV (Apr., 1951), 117–118.

23. Riedemann, *Account of Our Religion*, pp. 80–81.

Everything pertaining to the Church was holy and sanctified. Nothing secular or worldly was permitted. Any unsanctified object of affection was an idol, whether material possessions, a wife, or a high office. This did not mean asceticism or holy poverty, but that all the secular necessities of life were as nothing to a Christian, to be used only for purely practical needs.[24]

Community of goods, superficially a unique and distinctive added doctrine of the Hutterites, was completely bound up in the foregoing doctrines. The idea of a completely separated people, under the absolute Lordship of Christ, bound in perfect and complete unity and equality, with all secular and worldly affairs sanctified to holy purposes is the idea of a complete community, where anything exclusively individual is divisive and sinful. When this perfect Church of Christ was completely tied and limited to the visible body of believers, and when the community of saints was extended to all the affairs of a perfected people, the acceptance of private possessions was inconsistent and illogical. It violated the purity and sanctity of the Church. It blasphemed the Lord's Supper as a symbol of full unity. It brought the corrupted into the incorruptible. It confused the wordly with the divine. The Church was a complete, organic community with absolutely no exceptions. When the Hutterites, in the past, so far departed from their convictions as to countenance private ownership, they destroyed the very heart of their faith, for then they entered a wedge between the visible congregation and what now became, if there was to be a Holy Church at all, a purely spiritual community. And to all good Hutterites, the purely "spiritual" community was a mockery of Christ's Kingdom, an excuse for proclaiming a faith and, at the same time, refusing the sacrifices necessary to fulfill it. It was, they argued, for other "so-called" Christians to compromise and rationalize in behalf of what was easy, convenient, enjoyable, and selfish.

Apart from its central position in their concept of the Church, the Hutterites had endless arguments in behalf of a community of goods. Always central were the two key descriptions of the first Church at Jerusalem:

All that believed were together and had all things in common. They sold their possessions and goods and shared them according to each man's needs. (Acts 2:44-45)
And the multitude of them that believed were of one heart and one soul;

24. Heimann, "The Hutterite Doctrines of Church and Common Life," pp. 36-39.

none of them said that anything he possessed was his own, for they had all things common.

Neither was there among them any that lacked, for as many as possessed land or houses sold them, and brought the prices of the things that were sold. (Acts 4:32,34).

Peter Riedemann, in his Confession, began the arguments with the Garden of Eden, which surely reflected God's true intentions for creation and in which all things were held in common. Selfish, individual possessiveness resulted from Adam's disobedience, and was unsuitable therefore for God's restored Kingdom. Such was the selfish nature of unredeemed mankind that those blessings of God still enjoyed in common, such as the sun and heavens, would have been usurped also by private individuals if they could have reached and controlled them, for they were of the same nature as the rest of creation. Even the Trinity was testimony to community, for Christians had all things in common "even as the Father hath nothing for himself, but all that he hath he hath with the Son, and again, the Son hath nothing for himself, but all that he hath, he hath with the Father and all who have fellowship with him."[25] Practiced at Jerusalem, ordained for all the Churches that had the opportunity to practice it, and now clearly possible for existing Churches, a lack of community was an unforgivable blight upon Christians, and proof of less than true discipleship. Even as Christians were willing to share their rich spiritual gifts, even more should they be willing to share what is of so little value, the material things necessary for survival. Of course, affirmed Riedemann, community was not for the unregenerate. In fact, without the aid of the Holy Spirit, it would be an impossibility. Thus he never advocated communism for non-Hutterites. It was only for those who were part of the Church.[26]

The most elaborate defense of a community of goods was not written by Riedemann, but by Peter Walpot in his *Great Article Book*. Here he listed 148 arguments for community, beginning with eighteen drawn from the Old Testament. He saw Christ as the One who initiated a permanent period of community to replace the year of release (every seventh) in Jewish law, and viewed the priesthood of believers in the Church as successors of the Levites who were forbidden an earthly inheritance in Israel. The children of Israel in the wilderness shared equally in the manna from Heaven; even so the Church was now in the wilderness of the world and must share equally. He then gave forty-four

25. Riedemann, *Account of Our Religion*, p. 43.
26. *Ibid.*, pp. 88–91.

arguments from the ministry of Christ, who resisted the temptation to a material kingdom, who practiced complete community with his disciples (Judas kept the purse), and who fed the five thousand in a great community repast. Christ blessed the poor, forbade earthly treasures, drove the money changers from the temple, and told all His disciples to seek a heavenly treasure and, as the fowls of the air, trust to God's material care. He taught His disciples to pray by asking God to give *us* our daily bread, and stressed the difficulty, the narrowness, of the life He prescribed, a life forever beyond the rich who could not inherit His kingdom. He told the rich young man to sell all, and asked all His followers to forsake all things in His service. Christ's "Thou shalt love thy neighbor as thyself" comprehended the very essence of community. The great Christian confession of faith referred to a Holy Christian Church and a community of saints, yet too many ignored the word community, thus violating the same principle that led to the death of Ananias and Sapphira in the first Christian *Brüderhof.*[27]

When Walpot turned from Christ's teachings and the Jerusalem Church he had only inferential arguments to prove his thesis that the Gentile churches founded by Paul also practiced communism. He argued that they usually met in a house, and therefore must have lived together, although the evidence was not conclusive. In a rare show of scholarship, he bolstered this argument by references to early church historians and theologians, such as Eusebius, Clement, and Augustine. He even admitted that some members of the early Church did live apart, and thus fell short. Pervading all his arguments were the dual themes of perfect love and complete unity, both of which necessarily prescribe community. Thus, the history of the early Church was not as conclusive as the very nature of the Christian commitment and what must logically follow from it. In a clear slap at the Catholic defense of property, he admitted certain necessary and natural desires—food, drink, sleep—and one natural but unnecessary desire—sex—but argued that property was neither necessary nor natural, as evidenced in the primitive perfection of Eden. One inconsistency in Walpot's argument is still present in Hutterite thought. He condemned private property as an ever-present evil which leads to much of man's unhappiness in war, contention, and strife. But, at the same time, he argued that community is a hard, narrow way, required by Christ as a point of obedience, and that it was therefore not a road to earthly happiness.[28]

27. *True Surrender and Christian Community of Goods*, pp. 8–23.
28. *Ibid.*, pp. 24–45.

The Hutterite belief in a totally separate Church likewise prohibited their taking part in government and warfare. To Riedemann, government was ordained of God, not as an instrument of grace but as an instrument of his anger because of Adam's sin. Civil government, a necessity except in the Garden of Eden and in the Church, was for the discipline and control of secular man. Until the triumph of Christ's Kingdom, it would be a necessity. Since ordained for a purpose, Christians should obey it, but not participate in it. God is pleased with civil obedience, but one should always obey God and conscience first, and thus refuse, at the cost of martyrdom, to obey any law that violates one's religious convictions. Thus, for a Christian, citizenship was always limited by a higher allegiance to a spiritual kingdom. Within the Church, the sword of David was replaced by the love of Christ. No Christian could become a magistrate or even vote. A magistrate might become a Christian, but only by surrendering office, possessions, authority and pride. The way of the Church demanded complete submission.[29] Closely related to this, but with other subtle arguments in each case, a Christian could not swear an oath, sue in the courts, or sit in a jury.[30]

According to the Hutterites and most other Anabaptists, warfare was at an end in the Church. God's Kingdom had to be one of peace. No Christian could resort to violence in any form. Vengeance was left to God. Christ refused to defend Himself, or to let Peter defend Him. He, in word and deed, repealed the Jewish laws of retribution. Thus the Christian should be a complete pacifist, refusing any part in war or any personal defense against the cruelest outrages. He should not contribute to war on the part of others by paying special war taxes, by making munitions, or in any way assisting a military establishment. Even non-combat duty under military control was forbidden. In ordinary circumstances the Hutterites freely paid their taxes, but always rejected special levies for war purposes. When, at one point in their history, a few Hutterites did resist unfair persecution, a Hutterite leader issued an absolute ban against any type of violence. The punishment for disobedience was to be excommunication and no aid in their defense if arrested by secular authorities. Forgiveness would require penance. Along with a violation of the community of property, participation

29. Riedemann, *Account of Our Religion*, pp. 102–106; *The Church and the World*, pp. 4–10; Heimann, "The Hutterite Doctrine of Church and Common Life, II," pp. 150–152.

30. Riedemann, *Account of Our Religion*, pp. 113–114.

in war is still one of the most serious offenses in the Hutterite faith.[31]

Contrary to many "perfectionist" sects, the Hutterites never advocated celibacy, and never condoned any semblance of free love or polygamy. Marriage was recommended for all Hutterites, and procreation was considered to be God's will. To Riedemann, who reflected the prevalent attitude of his day, marriage was a matter of male solicitude and female obedience, as ordained by God. It did not involve any subjective, hedonistic, sentimental, or romantic elements. In the golden period in Moravia, Hutterite marriages excluded all emotion, courtship, and celebration. The choice of marriage partners was ultimately in the hands of the community, or more particularly the elders. In theory, their decision was an expression of God's will, determined through prayer. After the final choice was made for him, the young man, according to Riedemann, was to take his appointed wife "with gratitude as a gift from God, whether young or old, poor or rich, even as God has shown through their council."[32] A visitor to a Moravian *Brüderhof* in 1578 reported that once a year the elders lined up the youth of marriageable age and then suggested to each girl two or three young men from which she could select a husband. This was followed by a mass marriage. A visitor in 1612 reported the same procedure, except that the boys did the selecting and the matching was done twice a year. After marriage, the couples, sometimes almost strangers to each other, were led to an assigned room. Husbands referred to their wives as marital sisters, and, at least outwardly, displayed little sentiment or emotion. More than any other institution, marriage has changed among the Hutterites, until today couples do most of their own matchmaking, although wives still "officially" obey their husbands.[33]

The Hutterites accepted marriage as an eternal union, granting divorces only for adultery. Riedemann argued that marriage occurred on three levels. First, there was the marriage of God with the soul, then the union of soul and body, and only lastly the union of two bodies. Infidelity not only severed the third marriage, but also the other two and thus led directly to excommunication. For the wronged partner to forgive an erring mate, and cohabit with him before he had been received again

31. *Ibid.*, pp. 108–114; Friedmann, "An Anabaptist Ordinance of 1633 on Non-resistance," pp. 120–125.

32. Riedemann, *Account of Our Religion*, p. 100.

33. Robert Friedmann, "Marriage, Hutterite Practice," *Mennonite Encyclopedia*, III, 510–511.

by the whole congregation, was likewise grounds for the ban. In fact, complete marital avoidance was required for any excommunicated member, and there is even record of repeated weddings when an errant one returned to the fold. This only introduced a problem that continuously plagued the Hutterites. What about marriage to unbelievers? Since the Church was the uncorrupted community, an unbeliever had to be banned from the *Brüderhof*. And, on the same token, a believer had to be in a *Brüderhof*. In a time of rapid expansion and many converts, it frequently happened that only one marriage partner was converted. In this case, and particularly if the believer was the wife, the Hutterites sanctioned, or even demanded, a type of divorce. This led to widespread criticism from the rest of Christendom, and was used only as a last resort since it was always preferable to convert both partners if at all possible. Also, this special divorce apparently precluded remarriage, and thus was close to what we today call a legal separation. Later, members with unbelieving mates were sometimes permitted to live near, but not in, a *Brüderhof*.[34]

Since the Church included all aspects of life, Hutterite religious beliefs incorporated both the sublime and the commonplace. Riedemann advocated fasting for the mortification of the flesh, condemned standing drinks and drunkenness (but not alcoholic beverages at the table), and enjoined the clasp of the hand and the embrace as signs of peace and fellowship (the embrace was reserved for members of the same sex). Believing Sunday to be a day of worship only by convention and not by any scriptural authority, Riedemann recommended it as a festival or holy day, dedicated to quiet, prayer, reading of the Bible, singing of hymns (without music), teaching and preachings, and an inner rededication to perfect obedience.[35] Since it is almost impossible for a merchant, trader, or an innkeeper to avoid sin, such occupations were forbidden for all Hutterites. Riedemann specifically condemned all ornamentation and outward magnificence in dress or habits. This prohibition covered fine clothes, jewels, and all decorative effects. The fear of worldly dress led to a ban upon tailoring except for the simple, modest, and standardized clothing of the Hutterites.[36] These rigid requirements for simplicity and austerity were not part of any joyful acceptance of poverty, but were

34. Ernest Correll and Harold S. Bender, "Marriage," *Mennonite Encyclopedia*, III, 502–510; Robert Friedmann, "Divorce from Unbelievers," *Mennonite Encyclopedia*, II, 75–76.
35. Riedemann, *Account of Our Religion*, pp. 125–126.
36. *Ibid.*, pp. 126–130, 133–135.

based upon a desire for unquestioned obedience and a total end to individuality and selfishness. For many Hutterites the simple life was a burden accepted as a duty but without rejoicing. The Hutterite never viewed his *Brüderhof* as a utopia.[37]

In their best periods the Hutterites not only proclaimed an almost impossibly strict standard, but they came as close as any humans ever did to attaining it. Never doubting the truth of their faith, they were fanatics in their adherence to it. Their creed was a total one and demanded total surrender. They were willing to suffer and die for even the smallest peculiarity, and over two thousand Hutterites died a martyr's death. They suffered the rack, were burned, roasted, beheaded, torn with red-hot irons, drowned while bound, burned in their houses, hanged on trees, chopped to pieces, and starved in dungeons. Thus beliefs are only an indispensable preface to the story of the Hutterites, a story that must include their unique institutions and their long historical struggle to preserve their way of life against every possible form of adversity.

37. Littell, *The Anabaptist View of the Church*, pp. 93–96.

II. Three Centuries of Tribulation

The Hutterites have lived through only two periods of greatness—the first in Moravia in the sixteenth century and the second in America in the twentieth century. Between these two successful ages the Hutterites had brief periods of revival, a few scattered years of peace, and even some occasional material prosperity, but in the main they suffered either from external persecution or internal decay. Their very survival was in itself almost miraculous, as their harried remnants fled from country to country in an unending search for isolation and peace. In order to understand this long period of tribulation, one must first view the Hutterites in their days of glory, for without their own remembrance of this golden and inspirational past they would never have survived the long pilgrimage to the present.

In the calm and tolerant years after the Peace of Augsburg, Hutterite life was completely centered on the prosperous *Brüderhofs*. These were mainly located around Austerlitz in Moravia, but a few were across the Little Carpathians in Slovakia. Austerlitz, the site of the first *Brüderhof* under Jacob Wideman, contained the main Hutterite archives and was the home of the senior elder or bishop. Otherwise, the colonies were all quite similar. Each was on rented land under the jurisdiction of local barons. Although a few *Brüderhofs* housed up to two thousand people, the average was probably about five hundred. Unlike today, the colonies were represented in the outside world by missionaries, and by artisans and laborers who were in the employ of neighboring lords. Each *Brüderhof* had at least one preacher, a council of elders, a *Wirt* or steward, and numerous lesser officials.

The buildings at the two oldest Slovakian *Brüderhofs*—Velky-Levary (Levar) and Sabatisch—survived into the twentieth century, providing a detailed picture of early Hutterite architecture. At Levary, forty-seven long dormitory-like buildings surrounded a central courtyard, which contained the schools and some of the shops. The main dormitories were constructed with sunbaked brick and, in typical German fashion, had very steep, thatched roofs covered with clay. The tall roofs enclosed two stories, both divided into sleeping quarters for the married couples. The first floor of each building contained common facilities, such as workshops and meetings rooms. The ground floors were of stamped clay covered with yellow sand, long a distinctive Hutterite construction method. Since all the children beyond the age of two were quartered in special school buildings, each family needed only one private room for sleeping.[1]

The Moravian *Brüderhof* was a beehive of highly organized, very efficient economic activity. By untiring industry, frugality, and exemplary honesty, the Hutterites were always prosperous in those early periods of peace. Their life was extremely simple; their wants few. Each *Brüderhof* was as nearly self-sufficient as possible, with a farm, all types of livestock, and every imaginable type of craftsman. For the few necessary purchases, for taxes and rents, and as a reserve for future needs, the colonies also tried to accumulate surplus capital through the sale of products and the hire of their skilled workmen. The local lords soon learned to prize the Hutterites as managers of farms, vineyards, wineries, and mills. In fact, the degree of toleration achieved in Moravia was won in large part because of the almost indispensable services rendered the barons. The communal economy eliminated much waste and duplication of effort, and permitted what was then an unprecedented integration of activities (from sheep came mutton and wool, which supported spinning, weaving, and tailoring; cows provided milk, meat, and hide for the tannery, shoemaker, and harness maker). Complete organization kept everyone at work, while elaborate guild-like ordinances regulated the high standards of each product.[2] As one of the earlier Hutterite chroniclers admonished, "it is by thorough organization alone that a good work may be established and maintained, especially in the House of God who himself is a God of order and a master-workman."[3] The only economic liability was the precarious political situation, bringing increasingly higher taxes and levies.

Although a few men of wealth, including at least two nobles, joined the Hutterites, a vast majority of converts were either peasants, artisans, or laborers (from Tyrolese mines). The largest group seemed to be the independent artisans. At least they tended to dominate Hutterite life,

1. David E. Harder, "The Hutterian Church" (unpublished M.A. Thesis, Bethel College, 1930), p. 63; Robert Friedmann, "Habaner," *Mennonite Encyclopedia* (Hillsboro, Kan.: Mennonite Brethren Publishing House, 1955–1957), II, 618–619.

2. Robert Friedmann, "Economic Aspects of Early Hutterite Life," *Mennonite Quarterly Review*, XXX (Oct, 1956), 259–266.

3. John Horsch, *The Hutterian Brethren, 1528–1931: A Story of Martyrdom and Loyalty* (Goshen, Ind.: The Mennonite Historical Society, 1931), p. 24.

beginning with Jakob Hutter. Most ministers, elders, and missionaries were skilled craftsmen. In the *Brüderhof*, each young man was required to learn a trade. Hutterite crafts became famous, and were an important part of the Moravian economy. The Hutterites particularly excelled in ceramics, cutlery (never for war), clock and carriage making, textiles, and the manufacture of iron bedsteads. Their products were superior in quality and sold at moderate prices. The various *Brüderhofs* cooperated in acquiring the best techniques, sending delegates as far as Holland, and met in inter-*Brüderhof* conferences to exchange ideas and establish common standards. They were so successful that their enemies accused them of monopoly, while nobles vied for Hutterite craftsmen, sometimes waiting for years because of a limited supply.[4]

Ranking high among the Hutterite craftsmen were the medical personnel. Hutterite nurses and midwives were so often demanded by Catholic neighbors that one priest feared for his people's salvation. Many of the colonies maintained mineral baths both for their own use and as another source of income. The bath attendants acquired a reputation for their cures and were in great demand. Several Hutterite physicians and barber-surgeons acquired fame, one attending the Emperor Rudolph II in 1581, and another serving as personal physician to a Cardinal. Among the many ordinances regulating the crafts, one set applied to these physicians. They indicate that the better physicians, much in demand by non-Hutterites, were least able to adjust to a communal society. Various ordinances warned them against keeping fees for themselves, for forgetting that their service to the *Brüderhof* had to come first, and for arrogance, overbearance, and actual hurt to the peasants they treated.[5]

Although composed mainly of simple artisans and unlearned peasants, the Hutterite *Brüderhofs* initiated one of the most exemplary school systems in all Europe. In an age when only a minority received any formal education, the Hutterites made attendance at schools compulsory and, except for new converts, completely eliminated illiteracy. There were even

4. Robert Friedmann, "Economic History of the Hutterian Brethren," *Mennonite Encyclopedia*, II, 143–145; Harder, "The Hutterian Church," pp. 40–42; Paul Dedic, "The Social Background of the Austrian Anabaptists," *Mennonite Quarterly Review*, XIII (Jan., 1939), 6–19; Johann Loserth, "Crafts of Hutterian Brethren," *Mennonite Encyclopedia*, I, 728–730.

5. Robert Friedmann, "Hutterite Physicians and Barber-Surgeons," *Mennonite Quarterly Review*, XXVII (Apr., 1953), 129; John L. Sommer, "Hutterite Medicine and Physicians in Moravia in the Sixteenth Century and After," *Mennonite Quarterly Review*, XXVII (Apr., 1953), 111–124.

special classes for adults. All *Brüderhofs* had a *kleineschule* (a nursery-kindergarten) for children from weaning age to five or six years, or to an age when they were ready to learn reading and writing. The *kleineschule* was under a school mother and sisters, and mainly taught discipline, prayers, and scripture. At the tender age of two the child had to leave his home and parents to live permanently in the *kleineschule*, and was henceforth a responsibility of the community and not the parents.

After kindergarten the student graduated to the main school, and to the discipline and instruction of the much-revered schoolmaster. Here the children not only received instruction, but continued to live and board together, with sisters still caring for their physical needs. In some cases the Hutterite children were joined by non-Hutterites, whose parents paid for the privilege of a boarding-school education. In the last years of instruction the boys learned trades, and were ready for full-time work by fifteen. They might continue learning as apprentice craftsmen, but received no more formal education. They achieved full adult status only by baptism, usually in their early twenties. Then they could vote in colony meetings and were ready for marriage.[6]

Hutterite education had one primary purpose—the development of pure, completely obedient Christians. By definition, education was religious. Necessarily, it was authoritarian and doctrinaire. The Hutterites, out of fear of worldly wisdom, specifically forbade their members to attend secular schools, and avoided the teaching of secular history in their attempt to escape any knowledge of war. A large part of the educational program was devoted to the elimination of the selfish will and carnal desires of children. This "subduing of the will" probably also, and again by design, eliminated much of the curiosity, the impulsiveness, and the questioning so typical of youth. The unique, the original, the purely individual, were not allowed. Beyond these conditions, the educational practices were surprisingly humane. Play and rest periods were provided in the kindergarten. Peter Walpot, in some revealing instruction to sisters and schoolmasters in 1568, advocated only a brief religious talk each week, with no long preaching and reading beyond the children's comprehension. He also prescribed very humane rules for discipline,

6. Peter Riedemann, *Account of Our Religion, Doctrine and Faith, Given by Peter Riedemann of the Brothers Whom Men Call Hutterians*, trans. Kathleen E. Hasenberg (London: Hodder and Stoughton, 1950), pp. 130–131; Horsch, *The Hutterian Brethren*, pp. 33–34; Paul S. Gross, trans. and ed., *The Defence Against the Prozess at Worms on the Rhine in the Year 1557* (Lethbridge, Alberta: n.p., n.d.), pp. 22–23.

recommending that the rod be used only with discernment and fear of God, particularly for the older youth. To him, kind words, calm reason, and a perfect example were the preferred techniques of training, with the sisters admonished to treat children as if they were their own. Walpot even recognized the need for spontaneity on the part of the very young, and asked for caution about breaking their will too quickly.[7]

The Hutterite school regulations reveal a much greater understanding of hygiene and public health than was generally prevalent in the sixteenth century. Although the girls were up at 5:00 A.M. for their hour of spinning (boys got up at 6:00), they were in bed by 6:00 P.M. in the winter. A nurse remained with the children during the night, and was admonished to be especially considerate and helpful with the bed-wetters among the small tots of two and three. No whipping was administered on bare limbs or to the head. Although full baths were given scarcely more often than once a month, the linens were regularly cleaned, and the children were inspected for lice at least once a week. No food was forced on a child, while sick children were indulged with almost every request. Most surprising for that day, all ill children were quarantined and cared for with separate brushes and combs. The sisters were admonished to wash their hands after any contact with disease, particularly diseases of the mouth.[8]

The Hutterites not only developed their own distinctive schools, but also their own manuscript literature. Few Hutterites ever read beyond the Bible and their own bound manuscripts, which may at one time have numbered a thousand. Their surviving, handwritten codices are, by far, the largest literary legacy of the early Anabaptist movement. Early in their history, the Hutterites developed and encouraged the practice of writing testimonies, chronicles, diaries, epistles, and hymns. These were collected, in most cases recopied, and elaborately bound in manuscript codices, with bookbinding becoming a leading craft and penmanship their most highly developed art. Thus, the present Hutterite hymns and sermons represent survivals of these old manuscripts, with the sermons having been endlessly and skillfully recopied time after time. Their hymns are among the oldest yet in use. Many are full of history, detailing in endless verses the trials of early Hutterite martyrs. Much of this

---

7. Riedemann, *Account of Our Religion*, pp. 30–31; Harold S. Bender, "A Hutterite School Discipline of 1578 and Peter Scherer's Address of 1568 to the Schoolmasters," *Mennonite Quarterly Review*, V (Oct., 1931), 232–240; A. J. F. Zieglschmid, "The Hutterites on the American Continent," *American-German Review*, IV (Feb., 1942), 21.

8. Bender, "A Hutterite School Discipline," pp. 232–240.

early writing was couched in biblical language; all had religious overtones. Today these manuscripts remain as one of the largest extant records of the lives of simple folk in the sixteenth and seventeenth centuries. [9]

In quantity, the largest single type of Hutterite literature was the letters or epistles, written largely during the golden period of the sixteenth century. These included devotional and instructive material written in the pattern of St. Paul. In many cases the letters were written from prisons by missionaries, elders, or plain artisans. Some were letters sent home to loved ones and, more typically, to the whole village. Some were anonymously written, which again was fitting for the nonindividualistic Hutterites. Thirty or forty letters have survived from the same person. The letters were often very long, with one requiring 189 printed pages. The letters even to loved ones were rarely sentimental, followed stereotyped forms of blessings and greetings, were often calculated for their effect upon readers, and gave the Hutterites a continuous flow of good propaganda. Many recorded the exact dialogue of prison encounters with religious protagonists, with the Hutterites always besting their foes with the best arguments. Perhaps disappointing to later scholars, they contained little folklore, almost no passion, and very little slang. Many displayed a disciplined moderation when writing about even the most cruel persecution. From these letters came much of the daily inspiration, many of the sermons, and the main educational texts of the Hutterites. Today, the remnants of this literature are either with the Hutterites in America or in libraries in Czechoslovakia and Eastern Europe. [10]

The greatest single literary legacy of the early Hutterites was their old chronicle or history book, which still exists in well-preserved manuscript form and which has been printed in two different editions. [11] The old chronicle remains the main source of early Hutterite history, and stands only beneath the Bible in importance to modern Hutterites. The chronicle

9. Robert Friedmann, "The Epistles of the Hutterian Brethren: A Study in Anabaptist Literature," *Mennonite Quarterly Review*, XX (July, 1946), 147–149; *Die Lieder der Hutterischen Brüder* (Scottdale, Pa.: Mennonite Publishing House, 1914).

10. Friedmann, "The Epistles of the Hutterian Brethren," pp. 147–175; Robert Friedmann, "Of Hutterite Books," *Mennonite Life*, VII (Apr., 1952), 81–82.

11. The original manuscript of the chronicle is still at the Bon Homme colony in South Dakota. In 1923 the Hutterites had their chronicle published in Vienna as: Rudolf Wolkan, ed., *Geschichtsbuch der Hutterischen Brüder*. Finally, in 1942, A. J. F. Zieglschmid, a German scholar, completed a diplomatic rendering of the manuscript as *Die Älteste Chronik der Hutterischen Brüder* (Philadelphia: The Carl Schurz Memorial Foundation, 1947).

was begun sometime before 1573 by Kaspar Braitmichel, only one of seven scholars who would lavish artistic care in recording Hutterite history through 1665. The chronicle actually begins with the Garden of Eden, briefly tracing the history of the Christian Church up to the time of the Reformation. It gives in rich detail the doctrinal conflicts that led to the Hutterite Church, and then traces the annual history of the Hutterites for almost 140 years. It contains long lists of martyrs (2,175), doctrinal treatises, important letters, and the endless records of external persecution. Its many, almost casual allusions to emperors and kings, lords and generals, and its depiction of local conditions in times of war and peace, make it a valuable sourcebook for European historians. To living Hutterites it is still a very inspirational history of their most revered forebears. Events in it are discussed as freely and fully as events of yesterday. They are part of a history scarcely distorted or rended by time, but perfectly united by not only a common belief, but a common language and similar institutions. In time, four hundred years and endless misfortunes separate the days of Hutter, Riedemann, and Walpot from the modern Hutterites. Culturally, the distance is not nearly so great.[12]

The Hutterite golden age ended in 1593, to be followed by thirty years of mounting disaster in Moravia. In 1593 Turkey and Austria went to war. Soon Austrian soldiers were stationed in Hutterite villages, even as new war levies were assessed and forcibly collected in livestock and possessions. In 1605 the Turks invaded Moravia, destroying 16 colonies, murdering 81 Hutterites, and carrying away 240 captives, many never to be seen again. Then, with hardly a respite, the Thirty Years' War began in 1618, with disastrous consequences for all of central Europe. Moravia early joined with Bohemia and the Protestant cause, only to be invaded by Ferdinand's Hapsburg army in 1619. It destroyed twelve of forty remaining *Brüderhofs*, and murdered many of the brethren. By 1620 the Roman Catholic forces were determined to suppress all other religions in the Hapsburg realm. The soldiers were given free reign as they ravished the Hutterite villages. Torture, robbery, rape, endless sadism of all sorts, and murder by both Austrian and Polish soldiers practically destroyed the Moravian Hutterites, as only the more devout tried to escape to Slovakia (then part of Hungary). After almost all their savings were stolen by open trickery, an irrevocable order for the death or deportation of all Hutterites was given to the Moravian lords in 1622. The last twenty-four *Brüderhofs*

12. Zieglschmid, *Die Alteste Chronik*, pp. xxiii–xxvii; Zieglschmid, "The Hutterian Chronicle," *American-German Review*, VIII (Apr., 1942), 18–24.

were abandoned and lost. Although some local barons extended them temporary protection, all Hutterites had either accepted Catholicism or left Moravia by 1628. Only one thousand Hutterites survived.[13]

In Slovakia the Hutterites began a new epoch that would last until after 1760, but the brotherhood never regained more than a fraction of the fervor, membership, or wealth it had possessed in Moravia. There were never more than fifteen villages, and at one time only four. The first years were bleak ones, with Wallenstein's Imperial army plundering their villages in 1626 and with at least two years of famine before the Thirty Years' War finally ended in 1648. Never again would the Hutterites suffer such brutal persecution. Most of their martyrs had already died. Of inestimable importance to their later survival, one group of fleeing Moravian Hutterites had been persuaded and then almost forced to settle far to the east of Slovakia in Alwintz, Transylvania. Prince Bethlen Gabor of Transylvania had learned of the talents of the brethren and desired a colony for his lands, furnishing them transportation and guaranteeing them religious freedom. Aided by all types of assistance, the brethren quickly constructed the Alwintz *Brüderhof*. It would later become a sanctuary for a few of the persecuted brethren in Slovakia and provided a safe hiding place for valuable manuscripts. More important, the Hutterites would have completely disintegrated in the eighteenth century if it had not been for Alwintz.[14]

In Slovakia the surviving Hutterites tried to reestablish the same rigid discipline and complete obedience they had attained in Moravia, but with only partial success. Under an inspired leader, Andreas Ehrenpreis (1639–1662), the last missionaries were sent out, a few new colonies were established, and strict community regulations enacted to reverse the evident decline in unselfish community spirit. These community ordinances were directed at a deplorable lack of self-discipline, unending evasions of community property, and a total lack of religious zeal. Seemingly, only a minority desired to keep the rigorous rules of Jakob Hutter, for many individuals were keeping money for themselves, owned their own poultry flocks, and were acquiring their own private household possessions. Community work was completed only with promises of wine or money to buy wine. The leading craftsmen were freely expropriating

13. Robert Friedmann, "Adventures of an Anabaptist in Turkey, 1607–1610," *Mennonite Quarterly Review*, XVII (Jan., 1943), 73–86; Horsch, *The Hutterian Brethren*, 51–65; Harder, "The Hutterian Church," pp. 50–55.

14. Horsch, *The Hutterian Brethren*, pp. 55–56.

community property and were not turning all their profits over to the *Brüderhof*, with the result that the craftsmen had full purses and many possessions, but the community could not pay for its grain. The weavers and tailors were even selling their cloth and clothes to other Hutterites or to outsiders, or exchanging them for other village goods, indicating a near private economy within the *Brüderhof*. The true community had become an impoverished secondary part of the *Brüderhof*, made up only of the ministers, a few sincere believers, and all the dependent people. Everyone else was taking care of himself first of all.[15]

These early ordinances also reveal glaring moral lapses in Slovakia. Women were no longer subservient and apart but accompanied their husbands to their work, neglecting their duties and carrying their free food home from the community kitchen. The sleeping quarters had become living quarters, with stoves and other luxuries. Children were being indulged by parents, and were not always sent away to school at the age of two. Unnecessary trips were taken, even on Sunday, and the church services were disgraced by the opening of doors and the calling out of members. There was too much fraternization, too much wining and dining, with outsiders and with apostates. The brethren working away from the *Brüderhof* were no longer contributing to the community purse and were living as they pleased, even though their children lived off the *Brüderhof* while in school. Even sexual morality had declined, as indicated by admonitions against illicit meetings among the young, against young girls attending the bedrooms, and against the householder taking women other than his wife to market. Open flirtation with the cooks and other women was pointedly condemned.[16] Although dating from a period of decline, these ordinances, plus the sermons from the same period, were carefully recorded and preserved. Later they were to provide an excellent guide for a re-institution of full community, and are still used today.

Despite the incipient decline, the Hungarian villages appeared peaceful and prosperous to visitors. The decay was well beneath the surface. A young Catholic who visited in 1668 was overwhelmed with enthusiasm for a way of life "more angelic than human." He found plenty of food, no profanity or complaints, nursing care for mothers and babies, excellent schools, lively industry without constraint, physicians for each sex,

15. A. J. F. Zieglschmid, ed., *Das Klein-Geschichtsbuch der Hutterischen Brüder* (Philadelphia: The Carl Schurz Memorial Foundation, 1947), 519–528.

16. *Ibid.*, pp. 528–535.

excellent health, and no anger, jealousy, pride, passion, or remorse. Except for their heretical beliefs, he would have joined the Hutterites.[17]

Unfortunately for the Hutterites, the actual conditions in 1668 were far from "angelic." Even as the old chronicle was terminated in 1665, the impoverished Hutterites were successfully appealing to the Mennonites of the Netherlands for financial aid. In 1688 one large faction at the Levary colony had so relaxed their religious convictions as to accept infant baptism (with later rebaptism). By 1733, after official pressure and some imprisonment, all the Hutterites were baptizing their infants. Even more indicative of decline, the Levary *Brüderhof* dropped its full community of goods in 1686. The other colonies, even including distant Alwintz, followed within the next ten years. Although justified on the grounds of extreme poverty, and on the vulnerability of large common households to taxation and expropriation, the surrender of such a basic principle clearly indicated a final failure in fervor and discipline, a failure that had been gradually overtaking the Hutterites for years. Not only had individuals cheated in their use of common goods, but others, through indolence, had taken advantage of the community security. Now each family was responsible for its own welfare, although the Hutterites continued to hold their land and their flocks in common. In reality, they turned their communes into complete cooperatives.[18]

With the end of community of goods, the Hutterites entered one of their darkest periods, practically devoid of literature and marked by either stagnation or decline in numbers. Before 1759 there was only occasional persecution, and this was never as cruel as in the past. In fact, the Austrian authorities grew cleverer in their attempts to stamp out heresy, using kind words and eloquent persuasion oftener than the sword. In 1759, Maria Theresa gave the Jesuits full permission to convert the Hutterites to Catholicism. They began by confiscating all the Hutterite literature that was not well hidden, and then tried their persuasion. With great display of force, but little use of it, the individual Hutterites were asked to recant, but none did. Then a Jesuit priest came to preach in their churches, replacing the Hutterite ministers. When no one attended, the churches were closed. The harassment was continued by both officials and clergymen who, if not very successful in making

17. Harder, "The Hutterian Church," pp. 31–32; Horsch, *The Hutterian Brethren*, pp. 65–69.

18. Zieglschmid, *Älteste Chronik*, pp. 880–897; Horsch, *The Hutterian Brethren*, pp. 71–78.

converts, at least consumed much of the food of the brethren by long visits. In 1761 persuasion gave way to force; the ministers and many elders were imprisoned, some in monasteries. A few men fled to Alwintz, but most were captured and imprisoned. Some were beaten or suffered other brutality. A few died, but apparently none were intentionally martyred. Since they were promised freedom for recanting, almost all the men eventually were officially converted to Catholicism and returned to their villages. Within a few years only a few ministers remained openly loyal to the old faith, and they were in prison.[19]

The conversion of the Slovakian Hutterites after 1760 did not mean an immediate end to the old beliefs and institutions. Secretly, the Hutterite faith lived for two or three generations, with a few families escaping in 1781 to join active Hutterite colonies in Russia (for a generation the Slovakian apostates believed that all Hutterites had been converted). The Hutterite Catholics were known as *Habaner*, and were granted certain privileges, such as their own separate churches and schools, exemption from war service, and permission to continue their common shops and fields. By lot they continued to elect a steward to manage their common goods, continued the old Tyrolese dialect in a Slavic area, and preserved a few of their old manuscripts. Some of their fields were not parceled until 1863, and some cooperation continued until World War II. In time they all became very loyal Catholics and almost completely forgot about their old faith. When the Hutterites of America sent an invitation to their old kinsmen, only one man came to the South Dakota *Brüderhofs* in 1892. He soon returned to Slovakia, leaving in America some rare manuscripts. In 1936 two Hutterite preachers went to Slovakia, where they found many similar family names, were warmly received, and were able to arouse faded memories of old stories and traditions. Only the expulsion of German-speaking peoples from Czechoslovakia in 1945 finally ended the *Habaner*.[20]

After the forced conversion in Slovakia, only the solitary *Brüderhof* at Alwintz in Transylvania was left. It became the one tenuous thread to Hutterite survival and later revival, even though the Jesuits began their drive to convert it in 1762. Fortunately, at almost the same time, and under very unusual circumstances, a new *Brüderhof* was being established

19. Zieglschmid, *Klein-Geschichtsbuch*, pp. 231–239; Horsch, *The Hutterian Brethren*, pp. 79–89.

20. Robert Friedmann, "Habaner," *Mennonite Encyclopedia*, II, 618–619; Harder, "The Hutterian Church," p. 63.

at Creutz, about seventy miles from Alwintz. In 1755 a group of Catholics in Carinthia had read the writings of Martin Luther and soon espoused the Lutheran faith. Since Carinthia did not tolerate Lutherans, Maria Theresa had them deported to Transylvania, where they were offered new land and an opportunity to practice their faith in peace. On religious grounds a few of these immigrants refused to take an oath of loyalty to the Queen, repudiated Lutheranism as it was then practiced, and necessarily gave up their rights to free land. As servants and laborers, some met the Hutterites in Alwintz, and found almost complete religious agreement. They read the Hutterite literature, were convinced that a community of goods was necessary for Christians (even though Alwintz did not practice it), and began gathering as a small group in the city of Creutz in 1761. Although landless, by 1762 they had the beginnings of a true *Brüderhof*, with forty-six members, a daily assembly, the use of the ban, a common kitchen, a pooling of all their wealth, and an elected preacher. Five of the present fifteen Hutterite family names came from these Lutheran converts. Only six family names survived from the Slovakian and the Alwintz *Brüderhofs*.[21]

Out of fear, many of the Alwintz congregation accepted Catholicism in 1762. The preacher remained loyal and, before imprisonment, rallied some of the more courageous members, who fled for Creutz to join the new *Brüderhof*. Only one made it, but after imprisonment a loyal group continued to meet secretly in Alwintz. Slowly these members did reach Creutz, only to be sent back by the governor of the province. This happened again and again, as the Alwintz group suffered harsher and harsher persecution and, except for the escapees in Creutz, finally succumbed completely to Catholicism. The Jesuits then began a final campaign at Creutz, but without success. Two exiled members of the Alwintz *Brüderhof* had observed good land in the Turkish provinces of Moldavia and Wallachia (now Romania) and returned to Creutz to lead the brethren across the Carpathians, where they hoped to benefit from Turkish tolerance. In October, 1767, just before the Hutterite children were to be placed in a Catholic orphanage, the small Creutz congregation fled to Krahbach in Wallachia. Only sixty-seven people made the pilgrimage, and only sixteen of these were from the Alwintz congregation. Ultimately carrying their belongings on their backs, they barely struggled

21. Johann Loserth, "The Decline and Revival of the Hutterites," *Mennonite Quarterly Review*, IV (Apr., 1930), 93–98; Robert Friedmann, "Hutterite Family Names," *Mennonite Encyclopedia*, II, 865–866.

across the freezing passes, but were soon joined in Krahbach by several brethren who had been in prison in Transylvania.[22]

The brethren remained in Wallachia only temporarily. In 1769 they moved from Krahbach to nearby Parctschin to escape a low, unhealthy location, but almost immediately were caught up in a Russo-Turkish War. Even as their province was occupied by the Russians, lawless bands of brigands robbed their village. An appeal to the occupying Russian general led to an invitation to settle in Russia, which was seeking German immigrants with advanced farming methods. With free supplies, they traveled to Moldavia to meet the Russian Field Marshal, Count Peter Romanzof, and contracted to settle on his manor at Wischenka, on the Desna River in the extreme northern Ukraine. From the Count they received an escort, loans, a promise of complete religious freedom, military exemption, three tax-free years, hay for their cattle, food until well established, lumber and the services of an engineer for a new *Brüderhof*, and lodging and clothing until established. They were to be free to leave at any time, and agreed to a reasonable money rent after the three years of grace. They were also permitted to practice their trades without charge. These liberal terms were in line with the policies of Catherine the Great toward other German immigrants, particularly the Mennonites, who were soon to settle on Crown lands in various parts of the Ukraine. By 1771 the brethren were able to hold their first religious service in their own church, and by 1778 had a school.[23]

In Wischenka the Hutterites built a model *Brüderhof* and prospered for over a generation. After the liberal Joseph II ascended the Austrian throne, the brethren sent several envoys back to Slovakia. Very few of their former brethren were willing to forsake Catholicism, but at Sabatisch some books, coats, breeches, and shoes were procured, enabling the Hutterites in Russia to revive old customs and modes of dress. An appeal and then a conference with Joseph II failed to yield a return of their confiscated property or to win full toleration for Hutterites in Slovakia. Eventually, fifty-six former Hutterites came from Slovakia and reunited in Russia. With prosperity and growth there was a revival of Hutterite literary activities. Johannes Waldner, who had been a boy of six when the brethren fled to Romania, resumed the chronicle writing. His historical

22. Loserth, "The Decline and Revival of the Hutterites," pp. 99–101; Horsch, *The Hutterian Brethren*, pp. 95–106.

23. Zieglschmid, *Klein-Geschichtsbuch*, pp. 322–327; Loserth, "The Decline and Revival of the Hutterites," pp. 103–105; Harder, "The Hutterian Church," p. 65.

account, now known as the *Klein-Geschichtsbuch*, was written between 1793 and 1802. It summarized, with surprising historical perspective, the period covered by the old chronicle and gave the only surviving detailed account of the later years in Slovakia and Transylvania and of the flight to Romania and Russia.[24]

With the death of Count Romanzof in 1796, the Hutterites lost so many of their privileges under his son that they faced near-serfdom. In 1801, after an appeal to the new Czar, Alexander I, they received the same privileges and exemptions already granted German Mennonites, and were permitted to settle on Crown lands at nearby Reditschwa, also on the Desna River. Here, with a Crown loan of $4,000, they established their new *Brüderhof*, with a total population of only 202. But, in conformity to an ever-recurring cycle, safety and security led only to religious decline. Once again the tradesmen were loath to turn over all their profits to the common treasury. Against the fervid opposition of Johannes Waldner, the chronicler, a large faction under Jacob Walter insisted on individual property, and appealed their case to the Russian government. An agent, investigating the Hutterites at a time of decline and with normal prejudices against communism, reported a cultural backwardness, poor health, and slow growth in comparison to the privately propertied Mennonites. Walter's group withdrew and, when the *Brüderhof* burned in 1819, was followed into a private economy by all the other Hutterites. Although they maintained their close village life and continued their religious services, their land was not sufficient for private operation, the school was permitted to lapse for the first time in Hutterite history, and extreme poverty threatened to destroy their very identity. Without schools, many children grew up illiterate, while many of the valued crafts were either ignored or forgotten.[25]

With the aid of a friendly Mennonite leader and the approval of the Russian government, the Hutterites in 1842 moved south to government lands on the Molotschna River, just north of the Sea of Azov, and adjoining the largest and most prosperous Mennonite settlement in Russia. It was a very fortunate move and, after three centuries, brought the two

24. Zieglschmid, *Klein-Geschichtsbuch*, pp. 355–377; Robert Friedmann, "Hutterian Brethren," *Mennonite Encyclopedia*, II, 857; Horsch, *The Hutterian Brethren*, pp. 108–111; Loserth, "The Decline and Revival of the Hutterites," pp. 108–112.

25. Charles Henry Smith, *The Story of the Mennonites* (3rd ed., Newton, Kansas: Mennonite Publication Office, 1950), pp. 381–383; Norman Thomas, "The Hutterian Brethren," *South Dakota Historical Collections*, XXV (1951), 270; Harder, "The Hutterian Church," p. 68.

main Anabaptist groups together again, although the Hutterites (seventy-eight families) were only a handful in comparison to the flourishing Mennonites. The Molotschna Mennonite settlement (with numerous villages or colonies) was then under the guidance of Johann Cornies, the most dynamic and effective of all Mennonite leaders in Russia. He built his own farm into a widely copied model, introduced and improved breeds of livestock, including horses, sheep, and cattle, developed new techniques of dry farming, and successfully grew trees on the steppes. The Russian government empowered him to supervise the settlement of New Mennonite families and, in 1830, he became the lifetime chairman of the Molotschna Agricultural Union, which exercised almost dictatorial power over Mennonite agriculture. He required an artificial lake for each village, a uniform type of farm buildings, better schoolhouses, and compulsory education. He raised the qualifications of teachers, established several continuation schools, and encouraged industries and crafts by direct subsidization. The Molotschna settlement became a model, visited by people from all parts of Russia and used as a training school for Russian youth. Cornies not only assisted the Hutterites, but also two other small religious sects, the Molokans and the Doukhobors.[26]

The Molotschna settlement had been established in 1803 by Prussian Mennonites who were granted local autonomy, religious freedom, and complete military exemption. Although they had private households and private titles to their land, they shared common pastures and, in some cases, common granaries. Under close supervision from Cornies, the Hutterites had to conform to this village pattern. For the now backward Hutterites, this meant better farming methods, compulsory schools, and a renewed development of crafts. Soon the Hutterites were prosperous once again, and were able to repay all their debts. Through intermarriage they acquired a few new family names and, living outside of their *Brüderhofs*, would undoubtedly have lost their separate identity in a few generations, despite their different dialect and customs. Settlement at Molotschna only increased the long unsettled split between the families that preferred to return to a *Brüderhof* and those that desired private property. But at first there was no alternative, for neither Cornies nor the Russian government would have permitted communal property. The

26. David G. Rempel, "The Mennonite Colonies in New Russia: A Study of Their Settlement and Economic Development from 1789 to 1914" (unpublished Ph.D. Dissertation, Stanford University, 1933), pp. 148–177; Zieglschmid, *Klein-Geschichts-buch*, pp. 436–442.

Hutterites named their first village Huttertal and, with expansion in 1853, named a second village Johannesruh after Cornies, who had died in 1848.[27]

With a growing body of determined Hutterite leaders urging a return to communal living, a small faction completed plans for a *Brüderhof* as early as 1845, but had to wait until 1856 before the government would approve their petition to buy separate land. In 1857 thirty-three families sold their property, pooled the money, and bought a piece of land about seventy-five miles north of Molotschna. Here, in the same year, they founded a *Brüderhof* called Hutterdorf, after having lived thirty-eight years with private possessions. Their first leader was Zorg Waldner, who died almost as soon as the move was completed and was succeeded by Michael Waldner. In 1860 a second *Brüderhof* was founded on the same property by Darius Walter. The spirit of community swept through the old villages of Huttertal and Johannesruh, where families temporarily pooled their possessions and converted private homes into common meeting houses, dining areas, and schools. Although they soon returned to their private possessions, their action indicated an extensive revival, both in religion and in the customs and traditions of the past.[28]

In 1868 one of the two *Brüderhofs* at Hutterdorf (the one led by Michael Waldner) was joined by new converts and moved nearby to a new location. This new *Brüderhof* was named Scheromet. When it migrated to America it became the Bon Homme colony, the oldest in the New World. The Darius Walter group remained at Hutterdorf until they also migrated to America, becoming the Wolf Creek *Brüderhof* in South Dakota. One other *Brüderhof* was founded in Russia in 1866, but did not survive the move to America. These colonies were scarcely well established before many Mennonites and all the Hutterites in Russia were forced to migrate to America rather than compromise their religious beliefs.[29]

By 1870 there was a radical change in the Russian attitude towards their German colonists. Earlier they had been sought as expert farmers for the sparsely settled, unprogressive steppes. Then, no privileges had been denied them. But by 1870 there was no longer a need for settlers, land was

27. Zieglschmid, *Klein-Geschichtsbuch*, pp. 442–443; J. Winfield Fritz, "Brotherhood and the Economic Ethic of the Anabaptists," in Guy F. Hershberger, ed., *The Recovery of the Anabaptist Vision* (Scottdale, Pa.: Herald Press, 1958), pp. 196–197.

28. Zieglschmid, *Klein-Geschichtsbuch*, pp. 443–446.

29. *Ibid.*, p. 447.

becoming scarcer, and, in an age of growing nationalism, the resented Germans remained virtually unassimilated, exceptionally privileged islands, with their own language, schools, local government, and complete military exemption. Thus, even as the first moves were made toward Russification by ending their governmental and educational autonomy, Russia adopted a blanket, universal military training act in 1872. This in effect repealed earlier military exemptions granted by Catherine and renewed by Paul I in 1800. It threatened also a most basic principle of the Hutterites and Mennonites. As a result, early in 1873, a three-man deputation (two Mennonites and one Hutterite) traveled to St. Petersburg to make a direct appeal to Alexander III. Eager to prevent the emigration of valuable citizens, the Czar promised noncombat service for religious objectors. For some Mennonites this was an acceptable alternative, but to the more conservative, and to the rigorous Hutterites, any military service was completely untenable. Thus they looked to America for a new homeland.[30]

The decision to emigrate was made in 1873. It was probably not a hard decision, despite the mildness of the Russian threat in comparison to past persecution. In contrast to earlier hostility, the Hutterite and Mennonite immigrants were now considered most desirable and were eagerly wooed by immigration agencies and railroad officials in the prairie provinces of Canada and in the plains states of the United States. Everyone wanted them, and wanted them badly enough to offer lucrative inducements. In the United States there were already sizable Mennonite settlements in Pennsylvania and the Midwest, where their prosperous farms were excellent advertisements. The best known American Mennonite, at least in Europe, was John F. Funk of Elkhart, Indiana, a religious publisher. He corresponded with the colonists in Russia and advised them to settle in the midwestern United States. Letters to London about Canadian opportunities brought ready promises of complete military exemption there. A Canadian immigration agent even traveled to Russia to plead his case before the Mennonites.[31]

In 1872 four young Mennonites made an unofficial trip to the United States, reporting favorably on their impressions. Then, in the summer of 1873, the Mennonites and Hutterites sent an official committee of

30. Harder, "The Hutterian Church," pp. 72–76; Cornelius Krahn, "From the Steppes to the Prairies," *American-German Review*, XI (Oct. and Dec., 1944), 30–31.

31. Charles Henry Smith, *The Coming of the Russian Mennonites* (Berne, Ind.: Mennonite Book Concern, 1927), pp. 49–50.

twelve (two Hutterites) with a $20,000 expense fund to investigate settlement opportunities in both the United States and Canada. After a welcome by Funk and other American Mennonites at Elkhart, they were greeted, feasted, and wined by effusive railroad and immigration agents. The twelve came in three groups, but joined at Fargo, Dakota Territory, for a steamboat ride down the Red River to Winnipeg. They toured the land around Fargo and Winnipeg, then came back through parts of Minnesota and Iowa and on into Nebraska and Kansas. A newly appointed immigration agent for the Dakota Territory missed the twelve at Sioux City, and thus failed to give them a planned tour of southeastern Dakota, where the Hutterites were to settle the next year. The delegates, sensing the competition for settlers, asked for the following commitments: full religious freedom, complete military exemption, good land in large quantities at low or moderate prices, the right to live in closed communities with their German language, and, if possible, money to cover the transportation. Canada agreed to all of these terms and, even though most of the delegates disliked the Manitoba climate, the most conservative Mennonites decided to settle there because of the greater certainty of complete military exemption.[32]

The majority of the delegates, including the two Hutterites, preferred the land and climate of the United States, particularly the fertile land on the west bank of the Red River in what is now North Dakota. Accordingly, they drew up an agreement with the Northern Pacific Railroad, reserving all its land for fifty miles to the west of the river until March 1, 1874. If plans for settlement were completed, they agreed to buy at least 50 per cent of the reserve at $3 an acre, payable with 10 per cent cash and 10 per cent for the first five years, and then 15 per cent until completed. The railroad promised a 10 per cent freight reduction, reasonable cost for passage, care of all immigrants on arrival, and up to six free passes for the leaders of the group. The only hitch was the attitude of the federal government which, under the terms of the railroad land grants, owned one half (the alternating strips) of the land in the reserve. Without this land, compact settlement would be impossible. Thus, the Mennonites sent a memorial to Congress in December, 1873, asking for a special Mennonite reserve, either under the homestead laws or by purchase. Since such reserves were granted in Manitoba, the United States Mennonites pushed the issue, with a delegation visiting the Commissioner of Public

32. *Ibid.*, 51–65; Herbert S. Schell, "Official Immigration Activities of Dakota Territory," *North Dakota Historical Quarterly*, VII (Oct., 1932), 13.

Lands. The petition was discussed in Congress, and a Minnesota Senator offered it in the form of a bill. A favorable committee report led to an extensive floor debate but to no action in April, 1874. By this time the Mennonites were already on the way. Without federal support, the Northern Pacific reserve could not be utilized.[33]

The two Hutterite members of the committee of twelve were brothers, Paul and Lorenz Tschetter. Paul, a minister, wrote a diary of his travels and impressions on the trip. He was appalled by the worldliness of his fellow ship passengers, was impressed with the friendliness of American Mennonites, and unendingly surprised at frontier mores. He almost daily composed songs and hymns, despite his busy schedule, and accepted several invitations to preach in Mennonite churches. He was dismayed to find so many American Mennonites already forsaking the German language. When he discovered that most American ministers preached extemporaneously, he did a horrible thing for a Hutterite—he preached a sermon without reading it, relying, as he said, on memory of the written texts. It probably did not matter, for only a minority of his congregation could have understood his German dialect. In spite of all his many experiences, Tschetter was most perturbed, and at first most frightened, by a visit to an Evangelical Church in Indiana. The minister, in good frontier revival style, acted "as if he were insane." Tschetter felt like running from the church, feeling that only a mad man could gyrate as he did. His actions, he reported, were those of a general, not a minister. He praised everyone into heaven at one moment, and then damned all into hell. Yet, Tschetter admitted, "a comedy could hardly offer more entertainment." Tschetter, along with the other members of the committee, visited Jay Cooke, who served them excellent wine. They also were surprised to find good beer on the trip, but could hardly enjoy such normal amenities in the presence of so much sin, particularly the almost universal use of tobacco by both men and women. Surprises abounded. For example, the deeply religious Hutterites were greeted early one morning by a good, pacifist Mennonite minister who had just returned from an early morning hunt in the woods, his "awful" rifle still on his shoulders.[34]

33. Smith, *The Coming of the Russian Mennonites*, pp. 77–84; *Congressional Record*, 43rd Cong., 2nd Sess., 1874, p. 570.

34. J. M. Hofer, trans., "The Diary of Paul Tschetter, 1873," *Mennonite Quarterly Review*, V (Apr. and July, 1931), 115–126, 206, 215–217. The original of this diary is in Zieglschmid, *Klein-Geschichtsbuch*, pp. 571–606.

Jay Cooke having given them a letter of introduction, the Tschetter brothers ended their trip with an interview with President Grant. The two brothers had decided in favor of settlement in the United States if they could get favorable terms from the government. They not only wanted a fifty-year military exemption, but were afraid that they might have to swear an oath to get government land, that they might not be permitted to live communally, and that they would not be able to operate their own schools. They had a friendly reception from Grant on July 27, but could not talk much because of the language barrier. Thus, they had to leave a written request for the special privileges and await an answer back in Russia. Written by Hamilton Fish, Grant's Secretary of State, the answer was hardly helpful, since it stressed the federal nature of the government and the jurisdiction of the individual states over the schools. Only Congress could grant an exemption from military duties asked of other citizens, and this seemed very unlikely. But, according to assurances from Grant, there would be no real problem, since the United States would not be in a war in the next fifty years that would require military conscription, and in any case would respect freedom of conscience. In spite of the vagueness of these assurances, the Hutterites decided to come to the United States. All but two families migrated to Dakota between 1874 and 1879.[35]

In the decade of the seventies about ten thousand Russian Mennonites immigrated to the United States. The four hundred Hutterites were practically lost in this mass migration, but they represented a considerable proportion of the "Russian" immigration into Dakota. The largest numbers of Mennonites went to Kansas and Nebraska, where they were aided by two Mennonite immigrant societies and soon had prosperous villages and farms. In 1873 Daniel Unruh led an advance party of Mennonites to the Yankton area of Dakota Territory and probably helped induce the Hutterites to select the same area in 1874.[36]

The two *Brüderhofs* of Hutterdorf and Scheromet, led by their two preachers, Darius Walter and Michael Waldner, sold their land and left for the United States in June, 1874. The Scheromet colony, with 113 people, traveled by train to Hamburg, Germany, where they were joined by the Hutterdorf colony, which was of about equal size. On June 19 all forty families embarked on a steamship and, after calling at Le Havre, arrived at New York on July 5, with the inevitable storm and much

35. Hofer, "Diary of Paul Tschetter," pp. 217–218.
36. Smith, *The Coming of the Russian Mennonites*, pp. 66, 108–110.

seasickness along the way. After the immigration formalities, they left for the Midwest on July 6, and some rather frightening new experiences beyond Chicago.[37]

Both the railroads and the individual states were competing for each shipload of Mennonites after 1873. The Santa Fe Railroad was most successful in luring.immigrants into Kansas, but was challenged by both the Burlington and the Northern Pacific. James S. Foster, the official immigration agent of Dakota Territory, met the first Mennonite contingent at Elkhart, Indiana, in 1873. Either he or unpaid agents, such as merchants and travelers to New York, did all the promotion work for Dakota, almost always fighting a losing battle with the railroads. Even if commitments were secured, it became increasingly difficult to get any immigrants through Chicago. In one case, a Dakota man was arrested in Chicago for acting as an immigration agent without a license.[38]

The Hutterites were entrapped in Chicago by Albert Frank, a smooth, German-speaking brother-in-law to a Burlington Railroad executive. He talked the Hutterites into riding free as far as Burlington, Illinois, in order to look at some promising land. This was only a ruse, for when the train arrived at Burlington he warned of an epidemic and a lack of accommodations. According to the Hutterites, he then promised them a free ride to Lincoln, Nebraska, and, if they were not satisfied with the available railroad land there (the railroad badly wanted to sell it), they were still free to go on to Dakota. The Hutterite women and children stayed in immigrant quarters furnished by the city of Lincoln, with the children suffering through an epidemic of dysentery. While some of the men worked as day laborers, six brethren (three from each colony) surveyed the land around Lincoln. When none seemed suitable, they transferred their search to Yankton on August 1. The whole group followed by train, arriving on August 8. At this point the Burlington reversed its earlier generosity and tried to charge the Hutterites for their fare from Chicago. When they refused to pay, the railroad refused to release their baggage.[39]

At Yankton there was wholehearted support for the Hutterites who

37. Zieglschmid, *Klein-Geschichtsbuch*, pp. 456–457.

38. Schell, "Official Immigration Activities," pp. 8, 15; George W. Kingsbury, *History of Dakota Territory*, I (Chicago: S. J. Clarke Publishing Company, 1915), pp. 710–711.

39. Zieglschmid, *Klein-Geschichtsbuch*, p. 458; *Yankton Press and Dakotaian*, August 13 and 27, 1874.

had braved so much adversity to get to Dakota. A local newspaper stated, in an article subtitled, "Who Stole our Russians?," that the "genius of our Nebraska neighbors runs to stealing emigrants bound for Dakota Territory." The arriving Hutterites were personally aided by Daniel Unruh and other local Mennonites, while an agent was sent from Yankton to straighten things out in Lincoln. His trip was a complete success, with the Hutterite baggage arriving in a few days without any payment to the Burlington. To the native Dakotans, the Hutterites were a strange group, with odd clothing and strange customs. The Hutterites, on their part, came to marvel at the newspaper printing press, bringing with them a large manuscript which they were already hoping to get printed (probably their old chronicle).[40]

The Hutterites faced unusual difficulties in acquiring land for their colonies. They needed large, isolated plots near water and woodland. Their communal living, as well as their antipathy to oaths and to any possible obligation to a government, ruled out homesteading, which required each homesteader to live on his 160 acres. Their religious creed was particularly expensive at this time, for each homesteader in the Dakotas received not only his basic 160 acres, but 160 more for planting forty acres of trees, plus an additional 160 at $1.25 an acre. If each Hutterite family had homesteaded, they could collectively have acquired 12,800 acres of land free, and 6,400 additional acres for $8,000. As it was, on August 24, 1874, the Scheromet group paid a Yankton politician, W.A. Burleigh, an astounding $25,000 for approximately 2,500 acres of land on the banks of the Missouri River, just west of Yankton. This was undoubtedly, in monetary terms, the largest private real estate transaction that had ever occurred in Dakota Territory. The Hutterites, using all their remaining funds, were able to pay $17,000 cash, with the rest to be paid in annual installments.[41]

Since the Burleigh land was in Bon Homme County, the new Hutterite colony simply took this name—a strangely French one for a group of Germans. Still led by Michael Waldner, who was a blacksmith as well as a minister, Bon Homme only included the Scheromet group, or about one half the forty families. The Hutterdorf group, still led by Darius Walter,

40. *Yankton Press and Dakotaian*, August 13, 20, and 27, 1874.

41. The (Yankton) *Dakota Herald*, August 25, 1874; *Yankton Press and Dakotaian*, September 24, 1874; Gertrude S. Young, "The Mennonites in South Dakota," *South Dakota Historical Collections*, X (1920), 491.

temporarily settled on government lands for the severe winter of 1874–
1875, living in temporary sod houses. Since the site was unsuitable, in
1875 they bought a permanent site at Wolf Creek in the valley of the
James River, almost due north of Bon Homme and near Freeman, South
Dakota. At Bon Homme the community buildings were quickly constructed of yellow chalkstone, which, almost miraculously to the Hutterites, lined the banks of the Missouri. At Wolf Creek and other early
Brüderhofs, the native stone was used, always in the sturdy German
manner. The other Hutterites in Russia (about sixty families) disposed
of the remaining property and came to Dakota by 1879. One group of
about thirteen families, led by their ministers, established a third colony
in 1877 at Elm springs (later Old Elm Springs) on the James River and
not far from Wolf Creek. These families, from the Johannesruh village,
had tried communal living for only a brief, temporary period in Russia.
Perhaps in part as a result, they and their later daughter colonies would
always be a bit more liberal than the first two groups. All present-day
ethnic Hutterites trace their ancestry to these three original settlements,
each of which fathered a distinct kinship group (*Leut*) with slightly varying types of dress and some very small peculiarities of organization. Since
Michael Waldner at Bon Homme was a blacksmith, his group was known
as the *Schmiedenleut*. Wolf Creek was the first *Dariusleut*, named after
Darius Walter. Elm Springs, one of whose founders was a high school
teacher, was the mother of the *Lehrerleut*.[42]

Almost half of the Hutterites remained out of *Brüderhofs*, as in Russia,
and in most cases became homesteaders. They all settled near the
colonies and were tied to them by language, religion, and family relationships. In a few cases, these Hutterites later moved into colonies, or their
daughters married young men in the colonies, but in most cases the two
groups grew ever farther apart. For the noncolony people, the term
Hutterite became an ethnic distinction instead of a religious one, as they
joined either the Krimmer or General Conference Mennonites. Today
their churches still have Hutterite names, but this is about their only
distinction. The noncolony Hutterites soon lost many of their religious
sanctions, and thus some later voted and held political offices. Among the

42. Zieglschmid, *Klein-Geschichtsbuch*, p. 461; Harder, "The Hutterian Church,"
pp. 75–76; Eberhard Arnold, *The Hutterian Brothers: Four Centuries of Common Life
and Work* (Ashton Keynes, England: n.p., 1940), p. 28; Zieglschmid, "The Hutterites
on the American Continent," p. 23.

noncolony Hutterites was Paul Tschetter, the diarist. Yet a brother of his later joined a South Dakota *Brüderhof*, bequeathing his name to a still-surviving colony.[43]

In the United States the Hutterites began a new epoch that has rivaled the golden age in Moravia in terms of growth and outward prosperity. The long Hutterite pilgrimage—from Moravia to Slovakia, Transylvania, Romania, and Russia—seemed to have ended in 1874. But in leaving Russia the Hutterites not only moved to a land widely praised for its tolerance of minority groups, but they also, for the first time, moved into the modern world, with its subtle pressures for cultural uniformity. As a near fossilized remnant of the sixteenth-century Reformation, the Hutterites were only curiosities in rural Russia. In the United States they were an anachronism.

43. The noncolony Hutterites were identifiable by their distinctive family names. By 1937 there were Wipfs and Waltners serving in the South Dakota Legislature. John D. Unruh, "The Mennonites in South Dakota," *South Dakota Historical Review*, II (July, 1937), 165.

III. The Hutterites in America

The Hutterites belie almost every well-established concept about sectarian communalism in the United States. They came later, have remained longer, and have grown faster than any other comparative group, even including the Amana villages.[1] They have faced more hostility and open persecution than almost any other group, yet have lost fewer members and have permitted fewer compromises. They, along with the Amana, Oneida, Shaker, and Rappist colonies, have proven the economic strength of religious communism, and have proven it so well that they have been opposed not as impractical or heretical idealists but as dangerous monopolists and unfair competitors. With 142 successful colonies in 1963, and at least twenty more in process of development, they now eclipse in size any other communal movement, sectarian or socialist, and, in numbers and wealth, almost equal all other such movements combined.[2] Yet, in an inverted ratio to their importance, they were long ignored by American historians and by the many students of American communalism.

The early years in South Dakota were difficult ones for the Hutterites. Fortunately, they were also quiet ones, with almost no publicity and near complete isolation. The Hutterites were slack in leaving records of these

1. Technically, this statement can be challenged. The Amana Society practiced a form of religious communism from its arrival in America in 1855 until its conversion to private ownership in 1931, or for only seventy-seven years, but by 1964 it had existed as either a commune or a cooperative for 109 years. A few elderly members of both the Rappites and Shakers lived well into the twentieth century, technically extending each of these communitarian movements to total durations of over one hundred years, although their active period lasted less than eighty years. By 1964 the Hutterites had been in America for ninety years, and were still active and growing.

2. Arthur E. Bestor, Jr., in his definitive work, *Backwoods Utopias: The Sectarian and Owenite Phases of Communitarian Socialism in America: 1663-1829* (Philadelphia: University of Pennsylvania Press, 1950), pp. 235-243, lists only 130 colonies in the whole period between 1663 and 1860. Many of these were of such short duration as to be insignificant. The largest sectarian group, the Shakers, never had over twenty-two communities and approximately five thousand members. Only twenty-eight Fourierist Phalanxes existed, and only one or two of these survived for any appreciable length of time.

early years, although they long remembered the severe winters, the years of drought, and the hordes of locusts. After spending all their money for land, the Bon Homme colony had to seek financial help in its first year. In 1875 two Hutterite ministers delivered personally a request for help to the Harmony Society (Rappites) of Pennsylvania. They wanted a loan of $3,000 to construct a mill on the Missouri River. They acquainted the elderly, completely celibate, but increasingly affluent Rappites with the Hutterian creed and way of life. A Harmonist also visited Bon Homme, finding excellent health, great sincerity, but less than perfect economic prospects. Nevertheless, a loan of $3,000 was granted, and later increased to $6,000 in order to construct a sturdy and lasting mill (it remained in operation until after World War II, when the Gavin's Point dam on the Missouri finally covered it with water).[3]

The Hutterites' first crop season (1875) was one of Dakota's best in years, following serious locust ravages in both 1873 and 1874. The locusts returned in August of 1876, destroying almost all the late grain in the Yankton area. In 1877 the Governor of the Territory requested a day of fasting and prayer in May and, whether for this reason or others, the grasshoppers were rarely a serious menace in subsequent years.[4] In that year (1877) a Yankton editor took a trip to Bon Homme, finding almost no grasshoppers on the way. He did find a near self-sufficient little *Brüderhof* on the high banks of the river. The Hutterite crops were excellent, with forty-two bushels of rye to an acre and every foot of ground fully utilized. The editor predicted that the Hutterites, with their few wants, were "bound to get rich. Struggle against it as they may that fate will sooner or later overtake them." The beauty of it all, to him, was that none would be richer than the others.[5]

Meanwhile, the contacts with the Rappites continued. Except for their one sin of procreation, the Hutterites came very close to meeting the rigid moral requirements of the aging and lofty Rappites. On their part, the Hutterites were impressed by many Harmonist institutions (not by their celibacy). However, they deplored their use of music. Perhaps desiring worthy successors to their own doomed (because of

3. Karl J. Arndt, "The Harmonists and the Hutterites," *American-German Review*, X (Aug., 1944), 24–26.

4. John J. Gering, "The Swiss-Germans of Southeastern South Dakota," *South Dakota Historical Collections*, VI (1912), 358; Harold E. Briggs, "Grasshopper Plagues and Early Dakota Agriculture, 1864–1876," *Agricultural History*, VIII (Apr., 1934), 55–60.

5. *Yankton Daily Press and Dakotaian*, July 23, 1877.

celibacy) movement, the Harmonists worked out a tentative agreement with the Hutterites in 1885, under the terms of which all Hutterites were to move to Harmonist lands in Pennsylvania, where they were promised excellent purchase terms. Even before this offer was tentatively accepted, a daughter colony from Bon Homme (the Tripp Colony) moved to Pennsylvania in 1884. The land they received from the Rappites, being near the Titusville oil fields, was very valuable and had been reserved for some suitable group of Christian believers. The Hutterites were closely supervised in their farming and were given vines, locust trees, and needed goods. The Rappites marketed their wheat, drew up their articles of association, and even considered giving them valuable oil land. But the Hutterites never prospered in Pennsylvania, where the rolling, wooded land was so different from the familiar steppes and plains. Constantly borrowing more Harmonist money and probably homesick for their brethren, they returned to Dakota Territory in 1886 at Harmonist expense. Here they founded the Milltown Colony on the James river. Their descendants in Canada still remember some of the Rappist songs.[6]

In Russia the Hutterite population hardly more than doubled in a century, but in the United States it grew at phenomenal rates, doubling approximately every fifteen years. The Bon Homme Colony early adopted a lasting policy of establishing daughter colonies whenever the mother colony's population grew from 130 to about 150, placing a strain on land and community facilities. This general pattern of expansion has been continued to the present. As the mother colony grows larger, a second minister is elected and trained assistants are developed for each major enterprise. New land is purchased for the daughter colony and may be farmed for several years before the actual moving. During this period, work crews construct the new community buildings. Before the actual division, two balanced lists of families are carefully compiled in order that each will have an equal number of qualified men. By lot, one list is selected for the new colony. Also by lot, the two ministers decide which one will join the new group. At the time of moving the colony assets are divided on the basis of the proportionate populations of the two groups (always nearly equal). Once well established, the new colony is completely on its own.

In 1878, only four years after its founding, Bon Homme found itself

6. Arndt, "The Harmonists and the Hutterites," pp. 25–27; A. J. F. Zieglschmid, ed., *Das Klein-Geschichtsbuch der Hutterischen Brüder* (Philadelphia: The Carl Schurz Memorial Foundation, 1947), pp. 461–463.

already crowded by new arrivals. It sent a daughter group thirty-six miles to the northwest to establish the Tripp Colony, which was naturally referred to most often as Neuhof or Neudorf. It faced immediate diffi-culties and had to borrow money from the Amana Society in Iowa. Then, after only six years, its nineteen families moved to Pennsylvania, as already recounted.[7] The Wolf Creek Colony bought the first land for a second *Dariusleut* colony (Jamesville) in 1884, and established a third colony (Tschetter) in 1890.[8] Elm Springs, the third original colony, pur-chased a mill site six miles north of its own location in 1878. Here, in 1891, it established Rockport, the second *Lehrerleut Brüderhof*.[9]

The years after 1880 were marked by the passing of the great Hutterite leaders who first reinstituted a full community of goods in Russia and then successfully led their colonies to America. Michael Waldner, co-founder of Hutterdorf, head preacher at Bon Homme, and the most revered of all Hutterite leaders, died in 1889. The other co-founder of Hutterdorf, the leader of the *Dariusleut*, and minister at Wolf Creek, Darius Walter, died in 1903, the last of the old leaders. In the same years there was some turnover in membership. About ten families from the noncolony Hutterites joined colonies before 1895, while about seven family groups left the colonies before 1918. One of the defectors was the *Wirt* (manager) at Milltown, who left with his two sons in the vain hope of inheriting money through a rich widow who joined the colony from Danzig in 1893.[10]

With the outbreak of the Spanish-American War in 1898, the *Darius-leut* colonies decided to establish a *Brüderhof* in Canada in order to escape possible compulsory military service. They sent a delegation to Winnipeg, Manitoba, and consulted with Provincial immigration agents, who were still eager to attract settlers. A representative of the Canadian Department of the Interior who visited the seven Hutterite colonies in South Dakota was very much impressed with their farms, estimating their total assets at $750,000. As a result, the full privileges earlier granted to the Men-nonites were extended to the Hutterites by an Order-in-Council in 1899. This gave them complete military exemption, the right of independent, private schools, and permission to live communally.[11] The Canadians had full expectations that all the colonies were planning to move to Manitoba, and they undoubtedly would have if conscription had been

7. Zieglschmid, *Klein-Geschichtsbuch*, pp. 462–463.   8. *Ibid.*, p. 464.
9. *Ibid.*, p. 466.   10. *Ibid.*, pp. 466–467.
11. For the official documents, see *ibid.*, pp. 621–632.

used in the Spanish war. Actually, only one colony was established, and this only a small daughter colony from Wolf Creek and Jamesville. The colony purchased land only ten miles north of the North Dakota boundary, at Dominion City. The colony remained there from 1899 to 1905 only, departing because of poor land, floods, and, even more, because of the great distance from all the other colonies. After Wolf Creek established a new *Dariusleut* colony on the upper reaches of the James River in Spink County in 1904, the Dominion City group sold their Canadian land and purchased a colony site just south of Spink Colony in Beadle County, where they were joined by a few families from Wolf Creek. This *Brüderhof* was known both as the Beadle County Colony and the Lake Byron Colony.[12]

Even before the Spink and Beadle County Colonies were founded, Bon Homme established a second daughter colony (Maxwell) on the James River in Hutchinson County in 1900, and a third (Huron Colony) in Beadle County in 1906, while a granddaughter (Rosedale) from Milltown was established in Hanson County in 1901. A second granddaughter (Buffalo Colony) from Milltown was founded in 1907, but moved again in 1913, becoming James Valley, also in Beadle County. The *Dariusleut* (Wolf Creek, Jamesville, Tschetter, Spink County and Beadle County) added the Richards Colony in Sanborn County in 1906 and, in an unprecedented move, sent a colony of sixty people in a special train of twenty cars from Wolf Creek to far-off Lewistown, Montana, in the spring of 1912. A second *Dariusleut* colony out of Jamesville was established at Warren Range, Montana, in 1913, making a total of eight *Dariusleut* colonies. The *Lehrerleut*, generally desiring slightly larger colonies than either of the other two groups, expanded from Elm Springs and Rockport to two additional colonies along the James—New Elm Springs at the border of Hutchinson and Hanson Counties, and Millford in Beadle County. This made only four *Lehrerleut* colonies, but a total of eighteen Hutterite colonies, an increase of fifteen colonies in only forty years.[13]

12. *Ibid.*, pp. 468–469; A. M. Willms, "The Brethren Known as Hutterites," *Canadian Journal of Economics and Political Science*, XXIV (Aug., 1958), 391–392.

13. This list of colonies came from several sources, including interviews in the South Dakota colonies. The following sources were helpful, although occasionally in conflict and therefore confusing: George J. Zimmer, "Huter's Religious Communism" (unpublished M.A. Thesis, Yankton College, 1912), pp. 10–11; Gertrude S. Young, "The Mennonites in South Dakota," *South Dakota Historical Collections*, X (1920), 491–492; "Schmiedenleut Koloniebaum, 1874–1959," a sheet acquired from the Bon Homme Colony in South Dakota.

Until 1905 the Hutterites purchased and owned property as a religious association, in much the same manner as a religious denomination or church owns property today. But in 1905 all the colonies from all three groups banded together to form a religious corporation under the laws of South Dakota. The articles of incorporation provided for the transaction of all business of the *Hutterische Brüder-Gemeinde* at Bon Homme, and for a thirteen-member board of trustees with complete control over all corporation affairs. The trustees and officers were elected for three-year terms by a majority vote of all male members. The main articles clearly indicated one reason for incorporation. They specifically vested all property rights in the corporation, and denied the individual any right to any private possessions, or any privilege of withdrawing any portion of the corporation's assets upon leaving a *Brüderhof*. They required that all the labor, services, and earnings of all members be given to the corporation. Although formed for the stated purpose of "promoting, engaging in and carrying on the Christian religion," the corporation was to be subject to normal taxation. In effect it simply made the communal system of the Hutterites invulnerable to any legal attack by a dissatisfied member.[14]

The early Hutterite colonies were distinguished by their stone buildings, by their herds of geese and flocks of pigeons, and by their ice houses and tall flour mills. The pigeons were grown for the squab market in Chicago, while the geese were indispensable sources of feathers for bedding and meat and goose grease for the table. A visitor to several of the colonies in 1912 was impressed by the modern equipment in their shops, by the use of gas engines for cream separators and churns, by flowing water piped from artesian wells, by a large gasoline tractor for plowing, and, at Maxwell, by a steam boiler and two water wheels that not only operated the large mill but a dynamo for electric lights and various motors.[15] Most colonies had large herds of sheep under a shepherd's care, and, with European frugality, dried and cut sheep dung for fuel. There was no record of any serious conflict between the Hutterites and their American neighbors before World War I, although Jamesville was forced to substitute a gas engine for water power in their mill after neighboring farmers protested that the dam caused damage to upriver crops. The farmers backed up their protest by tearing out the dam several times and then finally burning the mill.[16] Most of the colonies were virtually isolated, with their main buildings off of the principal roads and hidden

14. The charter is included in Zieglschmid, *Klein-Geschichtsbuch*, pp. 613–618.
15. Zimmer, "Huter's Religious Communism," pp. 12–22.   16. *Ibid.*, p. 12.

in river valleys. Their immediate neighbors were often Mennonites or noncolony Hutterites, particularly in the southern counties.

World War I brought near disaster for the South Dakota Hutterites. By 1917 a fervid, irrational patriotism was sweeping the country, and particularly the states of the Midwest, leaving in its wake the most flagrant violations of civil rights in American history. The Hutterites were perfect, defenseless targets for the "true patriots" of South Dakota, since they were of a German background, still spoke the German language, lived communally, and, worst of all, took no part in the war effort. The Hutterites suffered from governmental policies toward conscientious objectors, from harassment by their neighbors, and from discriminatory state laws and legal maneuvers. This all led to a mass migration to Canada, and then only to more local resentment and harassment there. To the Hutterites it all seemed like a return to the sixteenth century, and strengthened anew their distaste for the world.

With the American entry into war in 1917, representatives of the three Hutterite groups sent a special but almost pathetic appeal to President Wilson. In it they outlined their basic beliefs and their past history, particularly their suffering for conscience sake. They then appealed: "We humbly petition our Honored Chief Executive that we may not be asked to become disobedient to Christ and His Church, being fully resolved, through the help and grace of God, to suffer affliction, or exile, as did our ancestors in the time of religious intolerance, rather than violate our conscience or conviction and be found guilty before our God."[17] The only answer was the forced conscription of Hutterite young men under the Selective Service Act of 1917, which provided for noncombat service for religious objectors under terms to be prescribed by the President.[18] Since as yet there had been no definition of such service by Wilson, in early March, 1918, three Hutterite representatives traveled to Washington to seek further information about conscientious objectors and also to seek permission for their young men to immigrate with the rest of the colonists into Canada. From Mennonite friends they learned of an early clarification about religious objectors and the possibility that their boys would be allowed to come home. On the Canadian question

17. The German version is in Zieglschmid, *Klein-Geschichtsbuch*, p. 479; this English version is from Lee Emerson Deets, *The Hutterites: A Study in Social Cohesion* (Gettysburg, Pa.: n.p., 1939), p. 22.

18. Horace C. Peterson and Gilbert C. Fite, *Opponents of War, 1917–1918* (Madison, Wis.: University of Wisconsin Press, 1957), p. 122.

they received no help, since Secretary of War Newton D. Baker was out of Washington.[19]

Unlike World War II, neither the peace churches nor the United States' government were prepared to deal with the question of conscientious objectors. This was the first completely compulsory conscription in American history, and the problems were all new ones. Most Americans either were totally unaware of sincere conscientious objectors to war, or dismissed all of them as cowards. Although Secretary Baker was quite sympathetic, even he did not always comprehend the subtlety and complexity of such objection, which ranged all the way from those who willingly accepted noncombat service (20,873 in World War I) to the absolutist who resisted any conscription of the individual and who would not obey one single order by military personnel. To the absolutists, even the required civilian public service of World War II was unacceptable, since it involved conscription. The Hutterites were almost never absolutists, but were usually so classified. Believing firmly in civil obedience except when conscience is violated, very few Hutterites could have objected to civilian service not directly related to the war effort. But, probably mainly through lack of understanding, the Selective Service Act did not provide any relief except noncombat service under military control, and for the Hutterites and Mennonites this was no relief at all.[20] The Hutterite young man could not voluntarily don a uniform and do any type of military work without violating his most basic beliefs and without being excommunicated by his church. Death while voluntarily in uniform meant damnation.

Beginning in the fall of 1917, the young Hutterites were drafted and virtually dragged away to Army camps. There they were segregated in special conscientious objector (CO) barracks, reserved for those who rejected noncombat service. On March 20, 1918, President Wilson again gave official recognition to conscientious objectors, both religious and nonreligious, but specified only certain noncombat duties to the extent that they could be performed in good conscience. There was no alternate service as the Hutterites had hoped. On April 27, 1918, Secretary Baker ordered the court martial of insincere or defiant objectors. Then, after many had been convicted, on June 1 a Board of Inquiry was established to pass upon the sincerity of objectors, routinely finding the religious objectors to be sincere. A total of only 3,989 completely rejected

19. Zieglschmid, *Klein-Geschichtsbuch*, pp. 480–481.
20. Peterson and Fite, *Opponents of War*, p. 123.

any noncombat service. After certification by the Board of Inquiry, most of them were furloughed to take part in acute civilian occupations. The Mennonites and Hutterites who had escaped court martial were almost always given farm furloughs.[21]

This bare recital of official action does not begin to reveal the problems faced by all the conscientious objectors, and particularly by the sincere, but somewhat protected and very unsophisticated Hutterites. They faced ridicule because of their beards if married, and always for their strange dress. They were appalled by the coarse language of their associates, and were desperately homesick for their community and friends. Several Hutterite boys, along with approximately five hundred other objectors, were court-martialed and sentenced for refusing to obey military orders before having a chance to appeal before the Board of Inquiry.[22] The court sentences ranged up to life imprisonment and even death, compared with a usual two years in England. The story of four of these Hutterites was one of the most horrible to come out of the war, and was duly exploited by several groups for varying propaganda purposes. It is known by practically every Hutterite, and is excellent testimony to them of the evils of militarism. But though untypical, it certainly was not about isolated events. The large amount of ridicule and actual torture heaped upon the conscientious objectors by near-sadistic army guards has been amply documented.[23]

The four Hutterite boys—Jacob Wipf and three Hofer brothers, Jacob, David, and Michael—were inducted at Fort Lewis, Washington, in late 1917. At camp the other draftees forcibly cut off their beards and forced them into uniforms as the four boys wept from fear and revulsion. At the camp they refused to sign a card promising obedience to all military commands, and likewise refused to march in formation, to give up their unique clothing, or even to do any of the camp work. Thus, they were sent to the guardhouse and, after two months, court-martialed for disobedience. A sentence of thirty-seven years was reduced to twenty

21. Melvin Gingerich, "Discipleship Expressed in Alternative Service," in Guy F. Hershberger, ed., *The Recovery of the Anabaptist Vision* (Scottdale, Pa.: Herald Press, 1958), pp. 265–266; Sanford C. Yoder, *For Conscience Sake: A Study of Mennonite Migrations Resulting from the World War* (Goshen, Ind.: Mennonite Historical Society, 1940), pp. 80–81; Peterson and Fite, *Opponents of War*, pp. 124–131.

22. Guy F. Hershberger, *War, Peace, and Nonresistance* (Scottdale, Pa.: Herald · Press, 1953), p. 121.

23. Peterson and Fite, *Opponents of War*, pp. 126–131; Norman Thomas, "Justice to War's Heretics," *Nation*, CVII (Nov. 9, 1918), 547–549.

by the camp commander, and the boys were sent to Alcatraz to serve their terms, chained together two by two and accompanied by four armed lieutenants. At Alcatraz they again refused a uniform, and went to a solitary dungeon in their underwear. For four days they received no food and only one-half glass of water a day. They slept without blankets. For one and one-half days their hands were crossed above them and manacled to the bars so that their feet barely reached the floor. Beaten once and separated from each other, they yet failed to break. When they came out after five days they were covered with scurvy and their arms were too swollen to go in their shirts. But the hell seemed over. They now ate normally, exercised on Sunday, and lived in close confinement for several months. In November, 1918, they were transferred to Leavenworth, Kansas, again under heavy military guard.

They arrived at Leavenworth at 11:00 P.M. and were driven through the streets with bayonets. Perspiring, they were stripped at the prison and then had to wait outside in the autumn cold for two hours. Then, again, in the morning, they had to wait in the cold for two hours. Joseph and Michael Hofer could not stand the punishment, and had to be rushed to the prison hospital, while the other two boys again entered solitary rather than perform duties under military command. They were manacled to their bars and lived on bread and water for alternate fourteen-day periods. The other two boys died of exposure and pneumonia in the Leavenworth hospital. In answer to a telegram, their wives came by train from the South Dakota colonies, but by mistake went first to Fort Riley. Joseph Hofer died after speaking only a few words to his wife. When she appealed to the Colonel for permission to see his body, she was led to his casket only to find him clothed in an army uniform, whether as a deliberate insult or by accident. Michael died a few days later, after his father had arrived, and by special request was dressed in civilian clothes. David Hofer was released from his cell to be with his dying brother, but spent the next day in his cell, crying, with his hands so manacled to the bars that he could not wipe away his tears. But he was mercifully discharged within a few days. Jacob Wipf remained in prison until April 13, 1919, probably in part because of sickness, for Wilson had already pardoned all the conscientious objectors.[24]

24. This account is in David E. Harder, "The Hutterian Church" (unpublished M.A. Thesis, Bethel College, 1930), pp. 78–85. All or part of the same story is in Jonas S. Hartzler, *Mennonites in the World War* (Scottdale, Pa.: Mennonite Publishing House, 1922), pp. 146–147; Zieglschmid, *Klein-Geschichtsbuch*, pp. 482–485; *Congressional Record*, 65th Cong., 3rd Sess., 1919, p. 2779

All German-speaking Americans in the Midwest were cruelly treated during the war. Mennonites were harassed in Liberty Bond and Red Cross drives, their churches were painted yellow, and their young men were forced to kiss the American flag. In South Dakota the Hutterites were usually called Mennonites, and suffered the same treatment. With the circulation of various rumors about the colonies, practically all trade and communication with the outside world ceased. The most hostile neighbors were in the northern counties of Beadle and Spink. But even at Bon Homme neighbors put glass in the flour mill in order to accuse the Hutterites of sabotage. This led to surveillance by the Federal Bureau of Investigation. The preachers at three colonies were arrested and arraigned on a rather nebulous charge of having bribed army officers at Camp Funston, Kansas, in order to get some of their boys released.[25] Local newspapers condemned the Hutterites for lack of patriotism and for profiting from the high wartime prices.[26]

The battle for loyalty was led in South Dakota by a voluntary but almost dictatorial State Council for Defense, abetted at the local level by county and even township councils. It set as its goal the elimination of all pro-Germanism. Its orders were semi-official, but were enforced throughout the state. In May of 1918 it forbade the use of the "Hun" language anywhere in public, even including church.[27] To the Hutterites this was the equivalent of the Catholic Church having to give up all Latin, and was never obeyed. At Yankton the students were widely praised when they threw all their high school German books into the Missouri River as they sang the Star Spangled Banner.[28] The Hutterites were willing to contribute money for the relief of war suffering, and offered $10,000 for this purpose, but they would not contribute to the Red Cross or buy Liberty Bonds. Nevertheless, in the spring of 1918 the Liberty Bond committee at Mitchell assigned the Hutterites a quota, which they refused to buy. On May 4, 1918, a group of Mitchell patriots visited the Jamesville colony and, without any opposition, drove off one hundred steers and one thousand sheep, taking them to Utica, South Dakota, to ship to market and then to use the money for bonds. Since the packing houses would not touch the tainted cattle, they sold for about half their value, or for $14,000. Even this was refused by the National War Loan Committee, and had to be deposited in a local bank in the name of the Hutterites,

25. The (Sioux Falls, South Dakota) *Argus-Leader*, Apr. 26, 1918.
26. *Ibid.*, May 3, 1918, as reprinted from the (Mitchell, South Dakota) *Gazette*.
27. The (Sioux Falls, South Dakota) *Argus-Leader*, May 25, 1918.
28. *Ibid.*, May 9, 1918.

who refused to accept the money. It was later accepted by a Canadian as part payment on land for a new colony.[29] Even as the war ended, local citizens again raided Jamesville, confiscating the colony's grape wine under the new Prohibition Act, but then drinking it at the county seat.[30]

With the conscription and local hostility the Hutterites decided to migrate to Canada. In correspondence with officials at Ottawa they were assured that the same exemptions granted them by the Order-in-Council of 1899 were still in effect. But their complete military exemption in Canada would not relieve them, as American citizens, of obligations back in the United States. Already the two countries were working out an expatriation agreement for draft dodgers.[31] It was in part to get special concessions for their draft-age men that the unsuccessful Hutterite delegation went to Washington in March, 1918. In spite of this one handicap, in the summer of 1918 the first colonies began to buy new land in Canada and to dispose of their South Dakota holdings, at sacrificial prices if necessary. Although South Dakota was glad to be rid of the Hutterite problem, the Council of Defense requested that 5 per cent of the sale price of their land be invested in war bonds, and $\frac{1}{2}$ per cent be given to the Red Cross. The Hutterites simply lowered their prices this much and had the buyers purchase the bonds. In many cases it was estimated that the Hutterites received only one-half value on their lands in forced sale to speculators.

By the early months of 1920, eleven South Dakota colonies had been sold. One of these, the *Schmiedenleut* colony of Huron or Lake Byron, was sold to a small *Dariusleut* group that came from the Montana colonies via Canada to settle once again in South Dakota in 1920. Counting this small group, only six colonies remained in South Dakota. Many of the old villages were to remain deserted for twenty or thirty years, with broken windows in the almost indestructible stone buildings and with the village streets overgrown with weeds. As a sympathetic neighbor described them, they were ghostly blots on the landscape, an enduring reproach to all South Dakotans who passed them.[32]

Although Canadians did not reach the same depths of patriotic insanity

---

29. *Ibid.*, May 4, 1918; Yoder, *For Conscience Sake*, pp. 94–95.

30. Nanna Goodhope, "Must the Hutterites Flee Again?" *Christian Century*, LVII (Nov. 13, 1940), 1417; Young, "The Mennonites in South Dakota," p. 498.

31. Letter from W. W. Cory, Deputy Minister of the Interior, to Michael Scott, Feb. 7, 1918, in Zieglschmid, *Klein-Geschichtsbuch*, pp. 632–633.

32. Goodhope, "Must the Hutterites Flee Again?" p. 1415.

during World War I as their neighbors to the South, there was a plenitude of nationalistic fervor and intolerance, particularly in the prairie provinces. The entry of the Hutterites, by permission of Ottawa authorities, released a floodgate of protest which was only increased with the return of the veterans in 1919. Reacting to several petitions from Alberta and Manitoba, the Canadian Parliament began placing restrictions on Hutterite immigration. In the fall of 1918 immigration was restricted to one continuous voyage, excluding all Hutterites born in Russia (only a few were still alive). After strong Hutterite protests, a few close relatives were admitted anyway. Then, in April, 1919, Parliament revoked the military exemptions granted the Hutterites in 1899 and prohibited in the future any undesirable immigration due to "peculiar customs, habits, modes of living and methods of holding property and because of their probable inability to become readily assimilated or to assume the duties and responsibilities of Canadian citizenship within a reasonable time."[33] The act specified the Mennonites, Hutterites, and Doukhobors. It left several Hutterites stranded in South Dakota, unable to join the majority of their brethren already in Canada. Fortunately, it was not always strictly enforced, but it did prevent the migration of some of the few remaining South Dakota colonies. In answer to Hutterite queries and accusations of betrayal, the Canadian Minister of Immigration and Colonization, in a very sharp and gruff letter, defended the Canadian position on the basis of strong and hostile feelings on the part of so many Canadian citizens over military exemptions and separate schools, and invited the Hutterites to reverse the prevalent view by becoming Canadian citizens in "the truest and best sense of the term."[34] As feelings lessened, the immigration law was repealed in 1922, allowing several Hutterites to complete their move.

In 1918 and 1919 each of the *Schmiedenleut* colonies except Bon Homme and Milltown completed their move to southern Manitoba, while portions of both Bon Homme and Milltown also moved in full expectation that the other brethren would soon follow. Thus these daughter colonies took the same names. The six Manitoba groups quickly expanded with daughter settlements in 1919 and 1920. In 1922, with the repeal of the Canadian immigration law, the rest of the Milltown Colony moved to Manitoba, forming a new *Brüderhof* on lands evacuated by the Old Order

33. Willms, "The Brethren Known as Hutterites," p. 394.
34. Letter from J. A. Calder to Joseph Kleinsasser, Sept. 15, 1919, in Zieglschmid, *Klein-Geschichtsbuch*, pp. 634-635.

Mennonites, who fled to Mexico to escape the Canadian school laws.[35] Five of the six *Dariusleut* colonies in South Dakota and the two in Montana moved to Alberta. Wolf Creek remained in South Dakota, and was joined there by the small group at Lake Byron. Each of the four large *Lehrerleut* colonies either moved to Alberta, or established daughter colonies. Stopped in their migration by the immigration law, Old Elm Springs remained in South Dakota until 1932, and Rockport until 1934. After this vast rearrangement, there were eleven Hutterite colonies in Alberta, six (nine by 1922) in Manitoba, none in Montana, and only six in South Dakota. In 1917 there had been approximately two thousand Hutterites in South Dakota; in 1919 there were only about five hundred, and even they faced additional troubles.[36]

The South Dakota Council for Defense, in a final move against the fleeing Hutterites, in 1919 persuaded the State Attorney General to use legal action to revoke the articles of incorporation of the *Hutterische Brüder-Gemeinde* and thus, it was hoped, destroy their communal way of life. After all, in 1919, the threat of communism had become greater than that of the defeated "Hun." The State's case was presented in Beadle County before Judge Alva E. Taylor, who rendered his decision in September. In the trial the State (abetted by the Council for Defense) contended that the Hutterite corporation, instead of serving religious purposes as called for in its charter, was really used for economic gain. Arguing that incorporation of the Hutterites was against good public policy, the State claimed that the Hutterites had amassed a vast fortune (over $1,000,000 in assets) and had dedicated none of it to the worship of God according to any religious belief, for they did not even have a church building. Under the guise of religion, the Hutterite leaders had forced obedience to rules which were against the laws of the State and the United States, and even punished members for obeying the laws and contributing to the war effort. Describing the Hutterites as a menace to society, the prosecution pointed to their use of the German language, the deprivation of children's rights to attend fairs and mingle with the outside world, and their prohibitions against outside travel. Behind the stated complaints was a growing feeling that the Hutterites did not do enough of their business locally. The court was asked to revoke the corporate rights, annul the charter, appoint a receiver, sell all Hutterite

35. Peter Hofer, *The Hutterian Brethren and Their Beliefs* (Starbuck, Manitoba: n.p., 1955), p. 7.

36. Young, "The Mennonites in South Dakota," pp. 484–485.

THE HUTTERITES IN AMERICA

property, and use the returns to pay all debts and court costs. Judge Taylor generally ruled in favor of the State, finding that the corporation had abused its articles of incorporation in unauthorized business activities unrelated to religion. He ruled that the corporation within ninety days would have to dispose of all land and secular assets above a maximum value of $50,000, and so amend its bylaws as to exclude all references to secular business. Noncompliance would mean a receivership.[37]

The Hutterites, reluctant to go to court at all, were brilliantly defended by a former Governor and United States Senator, Coe I. Crawford, and they testified in their own behalf. The defense easily showed that the charter had been granted in full knowledge of the character of the Hutterite faith, and that it had been fulfilled within the terms of their religion, which never separated economic concerns from religious belief. Not only were their arguments rejected, but also an appeal for a new trial. The only alternative was an appeal to the State Supreme Court for a reversal. The Stated joined in the appeal, asking for a complete rather than a partial annulment of the Hutterite charter. The Taylor decision seemed, at the moment, a decisive blow to the Hutterites in South Dakota, with the secretary of the Council for Defense boasting that it would exterminate the Hutterites. On the basis of Taylor's decision, the Council invited individual Hutterites to leave their colonies with full assurance that they would get their share of the property. To their surprise, not one Hutterite left.[38]

The case was finally settled in the State Supreme Court in October, 1922. By this time only five Hutterite colonies in South Dakota remained, and at least two of them were already planning to move to Canada. Also, by this time, the passionate feelings of 1919 had almost disappeared. The majority opinion of the Court was against the Hutterites, but at the same time it was very sympathetic toward their beliefs. The court ruled that there could be no prejudice because of conscientious objection, that there had been no substantial profit by the Hutterites, and, through extensive quotations from the Bible and Hutterite literature, that economic undertakings were certainly a legitimate part of their religion. It ruled that the Hutterites could have continued to function as a religious association as before 1905 without violating any laws. But reversing a

37. *Ibid.*, pp. 499–502; Norman Thomas, "The Hutterian Brethren," *South Dakota Historical Collections*, XXV (1951), 278; "South Dakota vs. Hutterische Brueder-Gemeinde," in *South Dakota Reports*, XLVI (Sept. 29, 1922–Nov. 15, 1923), 189–196.

38. Young, "The Mennonites in South Dakota," pp. 502, 506.

prior decision in behalf of the Amana Society in Iowa, it ruled that actions unopposed to public policy in an unincorporated society may be inimical when carried out by a corporation. Since the Hutterites did not constitute primarily a religious corporation, as practically recognized by the State in making their property taxable in the original charter, the stated purposes of the charter were not being fulfilled. Thus, overruling Taylor in favor of the State, the Court annulled the charter.[39] But, most important, it did not request a receiver and liquidation of Hutterite assets. Instead, it remanded the case "with permission to the corporation to transfer all of its property real and personal to trustees of an unincorporated organization."[40] Thus the decision had little effect on the Hutterite colonies.

The twenties were a time of peaceful growth for the Hutterites. In Canada they settled in grain-growing, dry-farming areas that closely resembled their homes in both South Dakota and Russia. Their colonies were usually more modern, and of conventional construction. Unfortunately, their colonies rarely owned as much land as they could have operated in the highly mechanized, extensive type of prairie agriculture. In Alberta, seven of the colonies in the Lethbridge area had a complete crop failure in the first year. Fortunately, three *Dariusleut* colonies had settled about one hundred miles to the north, near Rockyford, and had excellent crops, thus helping the southern colonies with food and fodder. The Manitoba colonies, located on or near the Assiniboine River to the west of Winnipeg, had good crops from the beginning. Both Alberta and Manitoba had strict school laws, which forced each colony to hire a public school teacher at over $100 a month, and to send their children to English schools for up to ten months of the year, leaving almost no time for German instruction. Although English had been required in South Dakota, the colonies had been able to use either their own teachers or sympathetic neighbors. But the requirements were already stiffening in South Dakota, so the Hutterites had little cause for regret on this point.[41]

In the years between 1922 and 1930, the *Schmiedenleut* founded only one new colony (Roseisle in Manitoba), which made ten in Manitoba. Bon Homme remained all alone back in South Dakota. The *Dariusleut* expanded the fastest, founding five new colonies in Alberta. In 1930 the mother colony of Wolf Creek also moved to Alberta, making a total of fourteen *Dariusleut* colonies in Canada, plus Lake Byron still back in

39. "South Dakota vs. Hutterische Brueder-Gemeinde," pp. 201–214.
40. *Ibid.*, p. 214.
41. Zieglschmid, *Klein-Geschichtsbuch*, p. 488.

South Dakota. The *Lehrerleut* as yet had two colonies in South Dakota (but not after 1934), and expanded their Alberta colonies from four to six.

In the depression thirties the Hutterites again became desirable citizens. In parts of the Great Plains they almost alone seemed to be prosperous, although their outward solvency was only a camouflage for much hardship and a severely restricted living standard. South Dakota, alternatingly hostile and friendly, welcomed the Hutterites back from Canada to occupy deserted farm lands, to add to the shrunken tax revenues of local governments, and to give some business to local merchants. Pacifism was a dead issue. In 1934, when the *Lehrerleut* colony of Rockport moved to Alberta (the last major move in that direction), the *Schmiedenleut* colony of Bon Homme (South Dakota) purchased its facilities for a daughter colony. In 1937 the Huron colony in Manitoba migrated to South Dakota, repossessing the old Jamesville colony, which had been used briefly for a subsistence homesteads project in the New Deal. In 1936 another *Schmiedenleut* colony (a daughter out of Maxwell) migrated from Manitoba to reoccupy New Elm Springs. Finally, in 1941, the Barrackman Colony in Manitoba sent a daughter colony to repossess the Tschetter *Brüderhof*. Thus, South Dakota colonies formerly owned by the *Lehrerleut* and *Dariusleut* were all purchased by the *Schmiedenleut*. At almost the same time (in 1937) the *Dariusleut* began moving back into Montana, with the *Lehrerleut* later following. Thus the *Dariusleut* and *Lehrerleut* groups were all in Alberta and in nearby Montana, while the *Schmiedenleut* were all located in southern Manitoba and in South Dakota.[42]

In 1935, in order to attract Hutterites, South Dakota passed a communals act which enabled the Hutterite colonies to incorporate with all the tax privileges granted to cooperatives. This meant exemption from state and federal corporate taxes, but not from local taxes. Under this enabling act, each Hutterite colony acquired a separate but near identical charter, providing for an adult, male membership, annual meetings, an elected board of directors, and for full records of all accounts. Even as the earlier incorporation of 1905, the colonies were protected against the claims of an individual member against corporate property. Eventually, fifteen of these corporations were chartered in South Dakota, and still exist today as the legal agents of their respective colonies.[43] In

42. *Ibid.*, pp. 472–473; Saul M. Katz, "The Security of Co-operative Farming" (unpublished M.A. Thesis, Cornell University, 1943), pp. 24–25.

43. The charter of the Jamesville Colony is in Katz, "The Security of Co-operative Farming," pp. 41–49; the enabling act is in *South Dakota Code of 1939*, I (Pierre: State Pubilishng Company, 1939), 291–294.

Manitoba the first colonies obtained separate corporate charters by special acts of the Provincial Legislature, but had no special enabling legislation.

By 1940 there were approximately fifty-one Hutterite colonies, but only five of these were in South Dakota and only one in Montana. Fortunately, both in the United States and Canada, there was a saner attitude in World War II toward conscientious objectors and very little overt discrimination against German-Americans. One possible effect of this leniency was the voluntary enlistment of twenty-six Hutterite youth in the armed forces of the two countries, much to the sorrow of their parents and the condemnation of their Church.[44]

The United States Selective Service Act of 1940 provided for the assignment of conscientious objectors to work of national importance under civilian direction, or what was called civilian public service. Public service camps were maintained without cost to the Government by various church groups. The Hutterites contributed to the Mennonite camps, paying $3,568.25 during the war under an assessment based on church membership (there were only about two hundred adult Hutterites in the United States colonies).

Most Hutterites were deferred for farm work; the others either defied their Church and entered the armed services or went to the Mennonite camps, serving without pay while performing such tasks as soil conservation, dairy testing, and other agricultural services.[45] In Canada, the alternate service camps under government direction had a greater stigma attached to them than to those in the United States. The camps tended to be completely isolated and without even a minimum of social services. The Canadian colonies were surveyed by Selective Service officials, who determined the number of surplus men available for service. For each youth in alternate service the colony had to contribute $15 a month to the Canadian Red Cross (reduced to $5 at the end of the war). Only about a third of the colonies seriously objected to this solution, and they had to cooperate eventually. Altogether, in both countries, approximately 276 Hutterites performed some type of public service work.[46]

44. Canadian Mental Health Association, Saskatchewan Division, *The Hutterites and Saskatchewan: A Study of Inter-group Relations* (mimeographed, Regina, 1953), p. 18.

45. Melvin Gingerich, *Service for Peace* (Akron: Mennonite Central Committee, 1949), p. 476; Gingerich, "Discipleship Expressed in Alternate Service," pp. 266-267.

46. Gingerich, *Service for Peace*, pp. 415-421; Joseph W. Eaton and Robert J. Weil, *Culture and Mental Disorders: A Comparative Study of the Hutterites and other Populations* (Glencoe, Ill.: The Free Press, 1955), p. 145; A. J. F. Zieglschmid, "Must the Hutterites Leave Canada?" *Christian Century*, LXIV (Oct. 22, 1947), 1270.

Another problem of World War I was solved in World War II. Since both the Hutterites and Mennonites objected to the purchase of war bonds, arrangements were made in the United States with a Philadelphia bank, which purchased large-denomination, civilian-type treasury bonds and then sold shares of them in small denominations to members of the two Churches. By investing in these civilian bonds the Hutterites were able to avoid local resentment and indirectly benefited their country. In Canada the Hutterites purchased special interest-free civilian bonds with special assurance that they would be used for peaceful, constructive purposes. They held about $500,000 of these bonds at the war's end. They also fulfilled their Red Cross quotas.[47]

In the forties the Hutterites expanded at a rapid and, to an increasing number of their neighbors, at a fearful rate. From fifty-one colonies in 1940, they grew to approximately ninety-three colonies by the end of 1950, with an average of four new colonies each year. The most rapid expansion was in the United States, with ten new colonies in Montana and eleven in South Dakota, or an increase from six to twenty-seven colonies for both states. By 1950 there were 8,542 colony Hutterites, an increase of about 3,000 in the decade. There were twenty *Schmiedenleut* colonies in Manitoba, fifteen in South Dakota, and one new but ill-fated colony in North Dakota. *The Dariusleut* had twenty-five colonies in Alberta and four in Montana; the *Lehrerleut* fifteen in Alberta and seven in Montana. In addition, there were five very small, unaffiliated colonies in Alberta. These were made up of liberal Hutterites who remained in colonies but who repudiated the orthodox rules of their kinship groups and were excommunicated.[48]

World War II brought to a head a growing hostility toward the Hutterites in Alberta. This hostility was more economic than political, but fed on the Hutterites' unwillingness to take an active role in defense and their seeming great profits due to wartime prices. With their tremendous growth, Hutterite colonies purchased enough land in certain districts of Alberta to arouse the fear (never the reality) of land monopoly. The Hutterites required large amounts of land for each new colony, and were willing to pay higher prices than individual purchasers, provoking the charge of unfair competition. Although only partly true, it was almost always believed that the Hutterites bought all their supplies at wholesale

47. Zieglschmid, "Must the Hutterites Leave Canada?" p. 1270; Joseph W. Eaton, "Canada's Scapegoats," *Nation*, CLXIX (Sept. 10, 1949), 254.

48. Robert Friedmann, "Hutterite Brethren," *Mennonite Encyclopedia* (Hillsboro, Kansas: Mennonite Brethren Publishing House, 1955–1957), II, 861–862.

prices from the large cities, thus helping to impoverish the local businesses in the declining small towns of Alberta. With these strong preconceptions, it was to no avail to show, statistically, the small proportion of Hutterites to the total population, the relatively small size of their land holdings, the almost universal isolation of their colonies, and the considerable amount of local trade carried on by each colony. Although acknowledged to be honest, to pay all taxes, to be wealthy (not usually true), and to be expert farmers (also not always true), the Hutterites were correctly accused of being aloof nonparticipants, with their parochial-type schools and their total lack of interest in civic affairs and local politics. On this basis they were held to be undesirable citizens. The open opposition of farm groups, the vehement criticism of most local newspapers, and, in some areas, the anger of urban businessmen, was abetted by the vehement hostility of the Canadian Legion, which was mainly concerned with the pacifism and communism of the "un-Canadian" Hutterites.[49]

In 1942 Representative Solon Low introduced a bill in the Alberta Legislature which prohibited all land sales to enemy aliens and Hutterites. He defended his bill as a method of preventing violence against the Hutterite colonies. The bill passed in 1942, and was amended in 1942 to prohibit the leasing of land. Disallowed in 1944 because it dealt with enemy aliens, which came under federal laws, a revised act applying only to the Hutterites was approved. These acts were all temporary, and were due to expire at the end of the war. Thus, the 1944 act was extended, first to one year after the end of hostilities, and then to May 1, 1947. In April, 1947, a new "Communal Property Act" was passed by the Legislature, with the strong backing of the Social Credit Party, the veterans, and farm organizations. This act was the most stringent legal action ever taken against the Hutterites in Canada. It prevented any Hutterite colony, whether incorporated or under trustees, from purchasing or leasing any land beyond the acreage held in 1944. No new colonies could be established within forty miles of any other colony, and no new colony could contain more than 6,400 acres. No person could sell land for a new colony without first offering it for sale for sixty days under the Veterans' Land Act of 1942, which provided provincial assistance to

49. Canadian Mental Health Association, *The Hutterites and Saskatchewan*, pp. 21–25; Victor J. Peters, "All Things Common: The Hutterians of Manitoba" (unpublished M.A. Thesis, University of Manitoba, 1958), p. 62; *Votes and Proceedings of the Legislative Assembly, Province of Alberta*, 14th Legislature, 4th Sess., Mar. 28, 1962, p. 2.

veterans entering farming. The act was sustained by the courts and was rigidly enforced.[50]

The Alberta act involved a virtually new area of civil rights—the right to purchase land. The purpose was not so much a matter of vehement persecution as a protective measure against what was believed to be an expanding evil. Its ultimate effect, it was hoped, was to be the assimilation of the Hutterites into the dominant culture. Pervading the modern opposition to the Hutterites has been the idea that they are basically good but misdirected people who must somehow be forced to become good Canadians. Their greatest sin is their refusal to participate fully in our wonderful society. Of course, the Alberta law did not have its intended effect. The Hutterites even considered mass migration, and began establishing their colonies farther to the north in Alberta until they exhausted the available farm land under the forty-mile limitation. They began a rapid expansion in Montana and, after 1952, in Saskatchewan. They even established one colony in the State of Washington, and contemplated British Columbia as an area of possible expansion. When, in 1957, they obtained a special Order-in-Council to enable them to purchase 28,000 acres in southeastern Alberta, the local protest was so vehement that the Cabinet had to withdraw the permission. In 1962 the Alberta Legislative Assembly, in an amendment to the Communal Property Act, established a board to negotiate expansion agreements between the Hutterites and the municipalities, thus abolishing the forty-mile restriction and inviting more flexibility and more local control.[51]

Although they would resent the very use of the word, the Hutterites have had poor public relations. Their strange customs and beliefs, their unfamiliar language, and their own desire to be separate from the world has fostered false rumors, strange distortions, and a complete lack of sympathetic understanding on both sides. When the Hutterites began their expansion into Saskatchewan in 1952, the Provincial Legislature authorized an intensive study of intergroup relations between Hutterites and their neighbors. Carried out by the Saskatchewan Division of the

50. Zieglschmid, *Klein-Geschichtsbuch*, pp. 639–640, 650–653; Eaton, "Canada's Scapegoats," p. 253; "Homes for Hutterites," *Time*, XLIX (Feb. 10, 1947), 40; Dorothy Giffen, "The Hutterites and Civil Liberties," *Canadian Forum*, XXVII (June, 1947), 55–56.

51. The (New York) *Times*, May 15, 1955, I, 47; "The Promised Land," *Time*, LXVIII (Aug. 13, 1956), 24–25; (Toronto) *Financial Post*, June 16, 1956; George A. Yackulic, "The Hutterites' Problem," *Saturday Night*, LXVII (Sept. 6, 1952), 11.

Canadian Mental Health Association, it revealed the stereotyped and misinformed attitudes of the people in the area of new colonies. More important, the Mental Health Association published accurate, informational articles in local newspapers in an attempt to alleviate some of the conflicts so typical in Alberta. The effect of this work cannot be gauged, but Saskatchewan has not yet passed any restrictive legislation, despite eleven Hutterite Colonies as of 1963.[52]

In the post-war years hostility toward the Hutterites was almost as intense in Manitoba as in Alberta, but it never resulted in restrictions on land purchase. In Manitoba the early colonies all formed individual corporations, but beginning in 1946 the Manitoba Legislature refused to grant any more charters, forcing all new colonies to hold land under trustees. In March, 1947, two local protest meetings against the Hutterites in two small towns west of Winnipeg were attended by several provincial legislators. For the next two years there were repeated requests for land restriction laws. The hostile forces were led by farmers, local businessmen, and the veterans. Unlike in Alberta, a Manitoba Civil Liberties Association, several church groups, and the two Winnipeg newspapers all came to the defense of the Hutterites. In 1947 a legislative committee which investigated the Hutterite problem recommended better education and a special committee to investigate legislation that would provide departing or expelled colonists with an equitable share of the community property, but urged that no restrictions be placed on the "fundamental right" to purchase land. The special committee was appointed, held hearings, and recommended positive legislation, but its recommendations were rejected on the floor of the Legislature in 1948. Meanwhile, the Hutterite schools were placed under the direction of a single trustee appointed by the Manitoba Department of Education.[53]

Largely as a defensive move, all the Hutterite colonies of Canada united in a formal church organization in 1950, and received a charter from the Canadian Parliament in 1951. Through annual meetings and more centralized direction, they hoped to be able to predict and deal with local hostility, and also to be able to maintain common standards and a united front against cultural assimilation. The charter established a republican or Presbyterian type of church government. Each *Leut* is

52. Canadian Mental Health Association, *The Hutterites and Saskatchewan*.

53. *Ibid.*, pp. 26–29; Giffen, "The Hutterites and Civil Liberties," p. 57; Peters, "All Things Common," pp. 56–70.

now organized as a church conference, with a board of directors made up of two members from each colony. Each conference board, at every third annual meeting, elects three members of a nine-member Board of Directors for the whole Hutterite Church. The elected chairman of this central board is the head, or Senior Elder, of all Canadian Hutterites. The central board meets annually, or by special call, in Alberta. The charter clearly sets forth the main doctrines and practices of the Hutterites, recognizes Riedemann's Confession as a doctrinal guide, and very specifically vests all property rights in the individual communities.[54]

In Manitoba the Hutterite problem remained dormant from 1948 to 1954, when the Union of Manitoba Municipalities asked for restrictions on both the acreage and location of Hutterite colonies. This new agitation did not lead to legislation, but rather to a voluntary settlement. In 1957 the *Schmiedenleut* approved a gentlemen's agreement with the municipalities. In it they promised to limit expansion to a maximum of two colonies in large municipalities (over six townships) and one colony in small ones, to limit each future colony to a maximum of 5,120 acres, and to keep all colonies at least ten miles apart. This has prevented any further legal maneuvers in Manitoba, and has ushered in a period of comparative peace for the colonies.[55]

The threat of restrictive legislation in Manitoba during and after World War II hastened the migration of Hutterite daughter colonies back to South Dakota. In 1944 the old Huron Colony in Beadle County was reoccupied, followed in 1945 by a reactivation of the Spink County Colony and of Rosedale in Hanson County. In 1948, a new colony was established at Gracedale in Lake County. Then, in 1949, six new colonies were established, a record for any one year. Two of these were at entirely new locations in Hand and Charles Mix Counties. One, Maxwell, was on the James River at the old site near Scotland. But three—Glendale, Riverside, and Pearl Creek—were in Beadle and Spink Counties, the area traditionally most hostile to the Hutterites. This explosion of colonies was followed by single new ones in 1952 and 1955, and by extensive publicity about the high birthrate among the Hutterites.[56] The net result was a successful six-year drive for restrictive legislation against the Hutterites in South Dakota.

54. The charter is printed in Peters, "All Things Common," pp. 290–299.
55. The (Toronto) *Financial Post*, May 18, 1957.
56. Joseph W. Eaton and Albert J. Mayer, *Man's Capacity to Reproduce* (Glencoe, Ill.: The Free Press, 1954). This is a detailed demographic study of the Hutterites.

Organized groups in South Dakota opposed the Hutterites for virtually the same reasons as the Canadians, but they never dared attempt such an openly discriminatory law as in Alberta. The first bitter opposition was in Spink County, where in 1949 Representative J. W. Dawson referred to the Hutterites as Russians who lived an un-American existence, with huge profits but nothing for the defense of their country. He argued that the colonies destroyed family-type farms and forced other people to move out. On the basis of only two new colonies, he predicted that the prolific Hutterites would eventually take over the whole county. For protection, he organized seventy-five farmers in Redfield to resist their further expansion.[57] Other opponents argued that new colonies disrupted whole townships, destroyed local business by wholesale purchasing, and that the colonies exercised an authoritarian discipline over children. There was one rumor about a Hutterite mother who was persecuted for the sole reason that her son defected and left the colony. This type of agitation certainly reflected the insecurity and near-hysterical fear of the period after 1949, a period of seeming international disasters, of domestic conflict and suspicion, and, in South Dakota, of declining farm prices. The Hutterites were excellent local scapegoats.[58]

Beginning in 1949, every South Dakota legislative session was presented with bills either to abolish the existing corporate charters of the Hutterites or at least to repeal their enabling act and prevent any future incorporation and expansion. On March 4, 1955, the South Dakota Legislature finally passed one of these bills. Despite the popular press description of the bill as a restriction on all future Hutterite expansion, it actually only annulled the corporate privileges granted to the Hutterites in 1935 when they were being lured back from Canada. The fifteen existing incorporated colonies were to retain their privileges (corporate tax exemptions and legal immunity against defectors), but were prohibited from any future expansion by either purchase or lease. Since the enabling legislation was repealed, there could be no more such corporations. The legislative debate over this act was a long, protracted one, with the bill passing in the House by a narrow 40-32 margin. Those opposed to Hutterite expansion endlessly disclaimed any religious bias, and correctly argued that they were repealing rights granted by only one other state (of course, only one other state—Montana—had any Hutterites). The issue was so controversial that a House Judiciary Committee reported it without

57. The (Minneapolis) *Morning Tribune*, Dec. 3 and 9, 1949.
58. The (Sioux Falls, South Dakota) *Argus-Leader*, Feb. 25 and Mar. 2, 1955.

any recommendation. The committee hearings were attended by over fifty Hutterite opponents from Spink County, but by no Hutterites. A representative from Spink County led the floor fight for the bill, but was opposed by a representative from Hanson County, the very heart of the Hutterite country. The law was well reported throughout the United States, giving South Dakota some very unfavorable publicity and the "poor" Hutterites some unexpected condolences.[59]

The South Dakota law of 1955 did not prohibit Hutterite expansion. It only prevented expansion by means of state incorporation. Under trustees, Hutterites were as free to buy land collectively as they were before 1935. Thus, the law was not nearly as unbearable as the one in Alberta. Between 1955 and 1963 three new Hutterite colonies were established in South Dakota, and one each in neighboring Minnesota and North Dakota. In 1963 two other new colonies were being developed in South Dakota. The law against expansion by old colonies was tested in June of 1956, when the Spink Colony purchased eighty acres of formerly leased land. The State entered a suit to vacate the colony's charter, but in an appeal to the State Supreme Court lost in this case because the land had already been used by the Hutterites and thus hardly constituted expansion. On the other hand, the Court, unlike a local Circuit Court, indicated that it would uphold the act in any future attempt at expansion by an incorporated colony. The Hutterites have simply decided to live with the law.[60]

The land-purchase restrictions on the Hutterite colonies of Alberta speeded their expansion into neighboring areas of Montana after the end of World War II. There was only one Hutterite colony in Montana in 1945, but by 1963 the *Darius* and *Lehrerleut* together had sixteen colonies in north central and central Montana, with several others under development. The rapid growth aroused public opposition, based once again upon the same fears and myths as in Alberta and South Dakota. As a result of widespread citizen opposition to Hutterite expansion, three Republican representatives from central Montana introduced a communal expansion bill (HB406) in the 1961 Legislature. An elaborate bill apparently

59. *Ibid.*, Feb. 25, Mar. 2, and Mar. 5, 1955; *Proceedings of The Senate, State of South Dakota*, 34th Sess., Jan. 4 to Mar. 4, 1955, pp. 351, 524–525, 585; *Proceedings of the House of Representatives, State of South Dakota*, 34th Sess., Jan. 4 to Mar. 4, 1955, pp. 859, 1001.

60. "All Things Common," *Time*, LXVII (June 4, 1956), 74; "Expansion for Hutterites," *Time*, LXVIII (July 23, 1956), 51; the (New York) *Times*, Dec. 4, 1955, I, 138.

modeled in part on the Alberta legislation, it provided for a three-member communal property control board to supervise the Hutterite colonies. The board was to divide the state into zones according to agricultural uniformities, and then set an acreage limitation (never to exceed 6,400 acres) for each Hutterite colony in each zone. Without approval from the board, the existing colonies could not expand their acreage, and in no case could they exceed the zone limitation. Most crucial, the act stipulated that new colonies had to be established at a minimum of forty miles from any existing colony. Hearings on the bill were held in both the House and Senate Judiciary Committees, and in both cases the report was against passage. Nonetheless, the bill was called to the floor of the House and passed by a vote of 50 to 43. In the Senate the committee report was at first upheld, but after House passage the bill was recalled and tabled by a one-vote majority.[61]

The legislative debate in Montana attracted attention to the isolated Hutterites, and also led to widespread support, from newspapers, churches, and even one farm organization, the Farmers Union. Also, more forcibly than ever before, the Hutterites fought back. They used legal counsel and appealed directly to public opinion. In a pamphlet prepared for the legislative committees and for the public, they defended their religion and way of life, pointing not only to the Bible but to the American tradition, to the Constitution, and even to the United Nations Declaration of Human Rights.[62] Because of active support for the Hutterites, the restrictive legislation will probably never pass in Montana, although a similar bill (HB362) was introduced and then tabled in the 1963 Legislature.[63]

By 1963 the Hutterites, except possibly in Montana, probably faced less external hostility than at any time since World War II. In some areas they were becoming accepted fixtures, and were themselves helping to create more friendliness on the part of their neighbors. In February, 1963, approximately 14,000 Hutterites were living in 142 colonies, with six or eight new colonies being founded every year. The fully developed colonies were distributed as follows: fifty-six in Alberta (thirty-five

61. State of Montana, *House Journal*, 37th Legislative Assembly, Jan. 2 to Mar. 2, 1961, pp. 206–207, 377, 430, 444, 545, 563, 594; State of Montana, *Senate Journal*, 37th Legislative Assembly, Jan. 2 to Mar. 2, 1961, pp. 358–359, 470, 493, 501, 523.

62. *The Hutterian Brethren of Montana* (Augusta, Mont., 1961), pp. 32–41; letter to author from the Rev. Joseph J. Waldner, Jan. 26, 1963.

63. "House Bill No. 362, Introduced by Schye, Bashor, Laas, Asbjornson, Hemstad," a mimeographed copy; the (Missoula, Mont.), *Missoulian*, Jan. 28, 1963.

Dariusleut, twenty-one *Lehrerleut*), with some colonies north of Edmunston, but a majority south of Calgary; eleven in southwestern Saskatchewan (eight *Dariusleut*, three *Lehrerleut*); thirty-five *Schmiedenleut* colonies in Southern Manitoba; twenty-one *Schmiedenleut* in South Dakota; one *Schmiedenleut* each in North Dakota and Minnesota; sixteen colonies in Montana (eleven *Lehrerleut* stretching south from the Alberta border at Sweetgrass to Martinsdale, and five *Dariusleut* in the Lewistown area); and one *Dariusleut* colony at Espanola, just west of Spokane, Washington.[64]

But in spite of seeming prosperity and accelerating growth, the Hutterites are today in greater peril than ever in the recent past, for their greatest threat has never been of a hostile, external nature. They have usually strengthened their unity in times of adversity. The greatest present danger is a pervasive, friendly, and outwardly appealing culture that leeches away, slowly but surely, at their unique customs and their most fundamental beliefs. The Hutterites have always feared the encircling world, and should fear it most of all when it is more curious than shocked, more helpful than hostile, more alluring than repelling. The siren is more deadly than the soldier.

64. Robert Friedmann, "Hutterite Brethren," *Mennonite Encyclopedia*, II, 861–862; "Schmiedenleut Koloniebaum, 1877–1959," and "Lehrerleut Koloniebaum, 1877–1961," both available from the Hutterite colonies; letters to author from the Rev. David Decker, Jan. 18, 1963; the Rev. Joseph J. Waldner, Jan. 26, 1963; and the Rev. Paul S. Gross, Feb. 1, 1963.

IV. The Community Way—1963

Regional or national peculiarities are disappearing so rapidly in the United States and Canada that the Hutterites, like the Amish, are increasingly rare curiosities. They are sociological antiques, with great tourist value if exploited by state and provincial governments and if such exploitation is permitted by the Hutterites. Some of their customs are merely traditional; most involve deeply held religious convictions. In both cases they are part of a deliberate attempt to be separate, apart, and totally different. They consciously desire to be a "peculiar" people, for they believe that to be the demand of Christianity. Yet, in so many ways, even the Hutterites share the changes of the world around them and, despite their elaborate defenses, absorb much of the hated and despised spirit of this world. Thus, what follows will inevitably be an overly static picture of their life.

With over 140 colonies today, there is no stereotyped Hutterite architecture nor any invariant design for their villages. There are only common features. All are rural and almost all are in secluded areas. The average colony has a population of about one hundred. All have at least four or five apartment buildings for family living quarters, although some families live in individual dwellings. Each family has from two to five rooms, depending upon the number of children. One room is used as a sitting room as well as for sleeping. The others are all bedrooms. There are no kitchens or bathrooms (only community outhouses and, in some colonies, community showers). The earlier use of low, long stone buildings has given way to frame construction. Many new colonies simply move and use the buildings already on the land they purchase.

Every village has a large, central dining hall and kitchen, with baking, refrigeration, and storage areas. The dining hall in the more prosperous colonies has two areas, one for adults and one for children. The tables are always unadorned, but the bare wood is bright and polished. Everything in the kitchen and dining area will be clean, but not necessarily spotless or in perfect order. Also in the heart of the community are the combination school and church, with its bare classroom benches, and the small kindergarten building. The village streets are unpaved, and thus are often either dusty or muddy. Only recently have their yards been dignified by tended grass or flowers and, in only a very few colonies, by sidewalks. Surrounding the village proper are the barns and shops. They are usually equipped with the best of machinery, but are not as scrupulously neat nor as well painted as those of the Amish or Mennonites. The community fields and pastures surround the village, with large orchards and gardens close to the homes.

In organization the colonies have changed little in over four hundred years. Each *Brüderhof* still has one and usually two preachers, from five to seven elders, and a *Wirt* (or business manager). In the time-honored manner, the new minister is selected by the cooperation of God and the adult males. After the colony members select two or three qualified candidates, all adult males in the colony, plus invited delegates from other colonies, vote for one of the candidates. The names of all candidates with over five votes are then placed in a hat and one is drawn. The ministers and all other officials are chosen for life on their good behavior. The board of elders always includes the preacher, the *Wirt*, and the farm manager. All officials except the minister are elected by a democratic vote. Almost all the adult males occupy some position, if only as the head of one of the economic departments. Although there is no rule, the elder minister is usually the beekeeper. The junior minister may become the head minister of a daughter colony, or succeed the existing elder minister. In any case he has to serve a long probationary period (up to eight years) before his ordination. Absolutely no special privileges are supposed to go with any of the offices. By long tradition, the ministers eat in the home of the elder minister and not in the dining room. Against their own wishes and regulations, they sometimes receive special foods prepared for the sick, but they are called by their Christian names and work as hard as anyone else. If the colony is incorporated, the legal board of directors and officers represent a second but rather perfunctory governing body.[1]

All important decisions in a colony are made by a democratic majority of the baptized men, called together in a business meeting by the minister. Day-by-day decisions are made by the elders or by the *Wirt*. The women are completely in the background, but probably exert a conservative influence on their husbands. The actual operation of the colony government is quite simple and informal, with most issues settled with near

1. Lee Emerson Deets, *The Hutterites: A Study in Social Cohesion* (Gettysburg, Pa.: n.p., 1939), pp. 31-33.

unanimity and without a formal vote. The colonies more closely approach the mythical "common will" than perhaps any other existing society. By training and doctrine the arbitrary and the individual are subjected to the traditional and to the community. The Hutterites all share a well-defined and completely common creed and, in most cases, an identical set of values. With their social order validated by God, and with their complete security of conviction, the right way is usually quite clear. In this case complete democracy is possible without serious factions or near anarchy, and without any of the physical coercion that has typified large, nationwide, one-party "democracies" such as the Soviet Union. The Hutterites have a truly monolithic and classless society. Issues that provoke a serious division of opinion are usually minor ones, at least in the view of outsiders. On major issues a little "talking up" will produce a common consensus. Once a decision is made the minority submits without complaint. The whole Hutterite emphasis is upon surrendering the individual will and impulse and accepting the decision of the group. Perhaps democratic government is practical only in societies with large majorities sharing roughly similar basic beliefs and values, or in societies without strong ideological commitments or interest and without strongly held values. The Hutterites are an extreme example of the former.[2]

Although fully autonomous, each Hutterite *Brüderhof* is closely related to other colonies in the same *Leut*. Intercolony visits, correspondence, and trade maintain these contacts. Each *Leut* has its much revered Senior Elder or presiding minister. The *Schmiedenleut* hold an annual ministers' council in one of the Canadian colonies each year, and here recommend common ordinances or rules to the individual *Brüderhofs*. Since these are always accepted at the local level, there is a continuing uniformity in creed and conduct. Although no central body represents all the colonies in both the United States and Canada, the Canadian colonies now have their church organization. In addition, there is much intercolonial correspondence about common problems. Despite the contacts and the uniformity of creed, distinct variations between individual colonies exist even in the same *Leut*. This variation is usually based upon the strictness of the ministers and elders. As a result certain colonies are known as "conservative" or "progressive."

Today the Hutterite colonies are all dependent upon agriculture. Their religion condemns commercial pursuits and, at the same time, glorifies a

2. *Ibid.*, pp. 17–20.

simple rural life. The Hutterite identifies the large city with everything worldly and evil. In the past this agrarianism was joined with a great emphasis upon village crafts, but in America the Hutterites had no market for their craft industries and either lost the required skills or used them solely for their own consumption. Their flour mills were important sources of income in the early years in South Dakota, but because of commercial competition soon were used only for their own grinding and have now completely disappeared. Their expert carpenters, mechanics, and blacksmiths still do some custom work, and certainly are indispensable to the colonies. In the past the South Dakota colonies made and sold brooms, but that has also ended. The women may still learn spinning, but the colonies actually buy all of their cloth. A few Hutterites still bind books, but have no outside business. Even the colony shoemaker is destined to disappear soon, since almost all shoes are now purchased.

Hutterite agriculture is highly diversified. Because of their location in arid, marginal, dry-farming areas, the colonies grow truck crops and orchards for their own use only. They also eschew row crops, growing instead small grain and hay. In the past they had large herds of horses and sheep, but both are now gone. They still raise beef and dairy cattle, hogs, and poultry. With an average of about 3,500 acres for each colony, the land is rarely ample enough for the commercial production of money crops, such as wheat. In fact, some colonies have to buy additional grain for feeding purposes. In recent years almost all the colonies have specialized in the raising of some type of fowl, whether turkeys, chickens, or geese. These use the available labor, require small acreages, and are most profitable in the large-scale operations so well suited to the colonies. The colonies buy the best eggs or chicks, poults, or goslings, have excellent hatcheries, brooders, and barns, and grind their own feed. In some cases they have facilities for processing the meat for marketing. In various colonies there are specialized crops, such as canary seed in Manitoba. Also, many colonies market their honey commercially.[3]

Although they are not nearly as self-sufficient as in the past, the very diversification of Hutterite agriculture insures that a large proportion of their foodstuff is still grown at home. In addition to fruit and vegetables, they have their own pork and beef, their milk supply, and do their own baking. They now buy all staples, including flour, but have the advantages of bulk purchases. As late as the twenties the average colony spent as

3. Victor J. Peters, "All Things Common: The Hutterians of Manitoba" (unpublished M.A. Thesis, University of Manitoba, 1958), pp. 142-156.

little as $10,000 a year for outside purchases.[4] This has completely changed, despite the home foodstuffs. Now almost any colony will have yearly purchases of over $100,000. These are for feed, fertilizer, oil and gas, machinery, medical expenses, cloth and shoes, and groceries. Thus, the Hutterites are very much a part of the over-all commercial economy, and are ever more dependent upon outside factors, such as prices, governmental policies, and national prosperity. A depression would affect them a great deal more than it did in the thirties.

The Hutterites are enlightened in their farming methods. Despite their basic conservatism and strong religious concern, they have gradually adopted the most modern machinery. Considering the investment, this may not insure them greater profits, but does make the work much lighter than in the past. They have tractors and combines, electric milkers and coolers, large feed mills, and endless other types of equipment. New colonies sometimes have to delay the purchase of new machinery or the use of electricity, but they soon catch up with the others. The Hutterites take great pride in their machinery. For the young men it is a needed outlet. The colonies have always cooperated with governmental control programs, use fertilizer and cover crops, consult with county agents, do experimental work, and subscribe to the better farm journals. Through an almost complete division of labor, the manager of an enterprise becomes a true specialist. Young men of fifteen or older rotate from job to job and, according to abilities and inclinations, soon become virtual apprentices to the manager of one enterprise.

The Hutterites are usually adjudged to be very hard workers and to be quite wealthy. Neither judgment is necessarily true. They rise by 5:30 on a summer morning, complete their chores, and then eat a communal breakfast. They then work until a 11:30 lunch, resting until 1:00. They then work until about six, with an afternoon break. The older men have pride in their work, but some of the young people are as anxious to escape the more difficult tasks as anyone on the outside. Although they affirm the value of work, the Hutterites do not consider it a joy and go about most tasks in a leisurely manner. They deny themselves almost every luxury except labor-saving machinery. In spite of all the local ideas about Hutterite wealth, the parent colonies, in an age of high land prices and low agricultural profits, are barely able to save enough for necessary expansion. The Hutterites are not always shrewd businessmen, occasion-

4. Bertha W. Clark, "The Hutterian Communities," *Journal of Political Economy*, XXXII (June and Aug., 1924), 371.

ally paying too much for land or making wrong decisions. Some young colonies have suffered from poor management; a few have failed economically. Their standard of living is actually very low when the austerity and lack of luxuries are considered. Hutterites can live on less than their neighbors and still appear to be wealthy. The average colony supports a population that is made up of over 50 per cent children, which means a very low ratio of able workers to the total population.

The visitor to a colony is usually confused by the seeming complexity of the economic organization. The village bell is constantly ringing, with its code-like orders to the women to take part in some colony task, or its call to everyone to come to a meal. The general manager or *Wirt* is directly responsible for the total economic welfare of his colony. He handles the money and the checkbook, approves all purchases, and makes the over-all decisions concerning the use of labor. Under him are the various departmental foremen, headed by the farm manager. Specialized farm tasks are assigned to permanent foremen. There are separate bosses over the dairy, the hogs, the garden, orchard, bees, and poultry. Some men fill two of the smaller positions. The heavy field work is done by work crews under the farm manager, with the young, unmarried men representing the largest body of mobile laborers. In harvest or other busy periods almost all the colonists will assist in the fields. Directly under the *Wirt* are the artisans, who rarely work outside their shops. A woman supervises the kitchen work, while other women have fixed responsibilities in the garden or in the kindergarten. Ironically, they are elected to their position by the men. The more odious kitchen work (such as dishwashing) is either rotated or performed collectively (such as the peeling of potatoes and fruit). By long habit, the organization is almost perfect. Everyone knows his job and does it with a minimum of confusion.[5]

In the early Moravian *Brüderhofs* the Hutterites almost completely replaced the family by the community. Today the family unit is becoming more important, although it is still secondary. Children, once completely cared for by sisters in the schools and kindergartens, are now primarily a parental responsibility. The trend is even away from the kindergarten, which has been discontinued by a few colonies and operates only during the summer in others. The community table (a separate one for children over five), the lack of family privacy, and the cooperative nature of all

5. Deets, *The Hutterites*, pp. 33–34. For an economic study of Hutterite colonies, see Saul M. Katz, "The Security of Co-operative Farming" (unpublished M.A. Thesis, Cornell University, 1943).

work still tend to obscure family differences. Children roam in groups, and often identify more with their own age group than with either parents or siblings. There are few joint family activities. Even at church the children are segregated apart from adults and according to age groups. They do have their own rooms in family apartments, and receive love and discipline from their own parents, but even here the family is not all important. The living areas are open to any other colonist; there are no locked doors or polite knocking. The children may be disciplined by a preacher or any adult. The colony is the large family in which everyone is a brother.

The Hutterite child is usually born at home under the care of a colony midwife. The husband is present during the delivery. If there are complications, the wife goes to a nearby hospital. Birth control is absolutely prohibited as a form of murder, and pregnancy is honored. The expectant mother is relieved of almost all duties and has at least a month of rest after each delivery. Most babies are breast fed, but some are supplemented by a bottle. Until they enter the kindergarten at two and one-half, children are fed in the home. The young baby is swaddled for a four-week period, is clothed in loose dresses, and is rocked in old-fashioned cradles. A distinctive Hutterite vehicle is the small, iron-rimmed, two-wheeled, long-handled cart used for baby carriages. Children are taught obedience, submission, and conformity at very young ages. Toilet training begins by six or eight months, or as soon as a baby can be propped on a "potty chair." By one year children are able to hold their hands in a prayer position. A thick leather strap is kept in full view in each family apartment, and is used whenever needed. Corporal punishment and an authoritarian attitude do not preclude real, open affection for children. Neither do they produce model children. Hutterite parents are quite tolerant of some disobedience and aggressive tendencies, permitting their children to play freely in their early years. They roam about the colony in groups, seemingly having a very good time. They assume certain tasks when young, but only become full-time workers at 15. Older girls are responsible for much of the child care. To many visitors, the most distinctive feature will be the large number of children (six to twelve in most families) and, consequently, the lack of personal attention for the individual child. There is no time for pampering and no desire to be permissive.[6]

6. Bert Kaplan and Thomas F. A. Plaut, *Personality in a Communal Society: An Analysis of the Mental Health of the Hutterites* (Lawrence, Kan.: University of Kansas, 1956), pp. 14–16; Joseph W. Eaton, Robert J. Weil, and Bert Kaplan, "The Hutterite Mental Health Study," *Mennonite Quarterly Review*, XXV (Jan. 1951), 53.

With hardly an exception, Hutterites marry and have children. Once a community function controlled by the elders, marriage is now based upon free choice. The young Hutterites are limited to baptized members of their own faith, for marriage with an unbeliever is still prohibited. In practice, they are also limited to individuals from their own *Leut*, since personal contacts between the three groups are rare. Marriages are usually happy and always permanent. Only one divorce and four separations are known to have occurred between 1874 and 1950.[7] Because of the many complex family relations, a genealogical chart is kept by the minister of each colony, and is used to discourage marriages between close relatives, although first cousins sometimes marry. Young men of marriageable age often travel to other colonies to work and woo, while young people travel in groups for Sunday visits to neighboring colonies where they meet eligible marriage partners. Technically, parents still have to approve a marriage and the elders and ministers can certainly help guide and direct romances. There is no open courtship until the engagement is announced in church. The wedding usually follows very quickly. Sexual morality is very high among Hutterite youths, who not only have strong moral sanctions but are rarely alone with members of the opposite sex. No major sex crime has ever been recorded among the Hutterites, and not more than ten illegitimate babies have been born.

The Hutterite wedding is held after a Sunday church service and always at the groom's colony. The ceremony is quite conventional, with the couple being bound by a prayer. The groom has to promise that he will not entice his wife to follow if he leaves the colony. The groom wears his best Sunday suit, while the bride has a special, colorful wedding dress and apron. In anticipation of the marriage the bride has kept and treasured her own hope chest and has been the center of attentions as she prepared for the wedding. The actual ceremony is only a prelude to a whole day of gaiety and festivities. The bride's colony and the last daughter colony from the groom's *Brüderhof* have invitations to attend. Always special, the Sunday dinner now becomes a virtual feast, with many courses of food and an abundance of wine and soft drinks. The colonists visit, sing songs, and celebrate into the evening. In the past the celebration often lasted for two days. The bride and groom exchange simple gifts (no rings) and receive from the colony a Bible and a copy of the old chronicle. They have no honeymoon, but are temporarily excused from

7. Joseph W. Eaton and Robert J. Weil, *Culture and Mental Disorders: A Comparative Study of the Hutterites and Other Populations* (Glencoe, Ill.: The Free Press, 1955), p. 143.

work and move into a two-bedroom apartment in the groom's colony. At the age of fifteen each youth receives from his parents a chest for personal belongings. These are now moved to the apartment, where the couple will live until the forthcoming babies necessitate more room. By then, new honeymooners will be ready to take over their first home.[8]

Since all of Hutterite life is necessarily a reflection of religious belief, the conventional religious functions often seem perfunctory and merely habitual. An almost ritualistic prayer, led by an elderly member, precedes and follows each meal. Each evening there is a short, thirty-minute church service, with singing, prayer, and a very brief sermon. On Sunday the long morning service is followed again in the evening by a second service. Religious meetings are announced by a child who goes from house to house. In the church the elders sit on a bench with the ministers, while the men and women sit on separate sides of the church, with the children toward the front. Prayers and sermons are either read or recited in the old German that has been handed down for generations. The Hutterites have up to four hundred sermons, preserved for centuries and still copied by hand by newly ordained ministers. The sermons are both expository and hortatory, with many fitted to special occasions. One of the few differences between the three groups (*Leut*) is a slight variation in the sermon repertoires and in the number of special religious observations. For the normal one and one-half hour Sunday morning service, the minister wears a frock coat and conducts a very formal service. The audience stands for the Scripture, which is almost chanted and is probably not understood by most in the congregation. Although the 385 surviving Hutterite hymns were first collected and printed in 1914, many were written by the earliest Anabaptist and Hutterite leaders. Some include one hundred stanzas, and all are lined out by the minister and then, without accompaniment, shrilly and loudly sung by the congregation. Even the sermons, endlessly repeated in a literary instead of the colloquial Hutterite German, are more ritualistic than directly instructive. In worship as elsewhere, tradition is more important than relevance. Besides, obedience in daily life is really the most important aspect of Hutterite worship.[9]

8. The most vivid description of a Hutterite wedding is in a novel based on author Marcus Bach's actual residence in a Hutterite colony: see Marcus Bach, *The Dream Gate* (Indianapolis: Bobbs-Merrill Co., 1949), pp. 225–231. Also see Peters, "All Things Common," pp. 112–118.

9. Deets, *The Hutterites*, pp. 23–24; H. Goerz, "A Day with the Hutterites," *Mennonite Life*, VIII (Jan., 1953), 14–16; George J. Zimmer, "Huter's Religious Communism" (unpublished M.A. Thesis, Yankton College, 1912), p. 27.

A total creed requires careful and patient indoctrination. To neglect this is to lose the total commitment of the youth. The early Hutterites recognized this and established their excellent system of compulsory education. In South Dakota the Hutterites were able to maintain their own schools and meet rather nebulous state requirements until after 1900. This meant a kindergarten and a German elementary school under a colony schoolmaster. In 1912 the regular school lasted four hours a day, six days a week, ten months of the year. But even by 1912 some instruction in English was required, with some of the Hutterite teachers acquiring state certificates. In other cases, beginning in 1909, outside teachers were requested from the local school superintendents. In 1921, when a South Dakota law required all-English instruction, no Hutterites were able to qualify as teachers. As a result all the colonies had to hire certified public school teachers. Since then only a few Hutterites have completed correspondence high school work and attended colleges in order to qualify as teachers (there were only two such teachers in South Dakota in 1960). Some Hutterites who did attend a South Dakota college either deserted their religion or failed to finish.[10]

Today the major survival of the old school system is the kindergarten, which is still continued in almost all the colonies. It is under the direction of a school mother, who is elected to her position for life. She has an alternate and several part-time assistants. In the warm months, all children between two and one-half and five spend the whole day (8:00 to 5:00) at the kindergarten. The small building has an area for their afternoon naps, and here also they have their meals, which are carried from the neighboring kitchen. They have a fenced yard and playground equipment. In addition to games, they hear Bible stories, learn hymns and prayers, and indirectly acquire some knowledge of classical German.

Since the children have to attend an English school by the age of five or six, the Hutterites try to counteract its worldly influence by continuing a rather pathetic remnant of their old German schools. For about one-half hour before and after the regular school, all Hutterite children are required to attend classes under an elected colony schoolmaster. He is untrained for his task, but is still honored as a man of stature. He not only teaches the German classes but supervises the children in their separate dining room. His classes are used for indoctrination and for rather elementary instruction in the German language. The children read in a German primer and in the Bible, learn some Hutterite history,

10. Deets, *The Hutterites*, pp. 39–43; Zimmer, "Huter's Religious Communism," pp. 23–24.

and memorize a catechism and numerous hymns and prayers, reciting them in unison. The German teacher is supposed to be a rigid disciplinarian, using corporal punishment whenever it is needed. The children often find the German school hard or boring, but appreciate its brevity.[11]

All colonies have "public" schools. In most cases a Hutterite colony is formed into a rural school district, although the Hutterites are unwilling to be elected to school boards or to hold any offices. But as school districts they receive state or provincial aid for their small, one-room schools and, in effect, hire and pay for their own school teachers. In an increasing number of cases, Hutterite colonies are part of larger school districts and, rather than place an unwanted burden on the existing schools and in order to have more control over their own children, provide their own schoolhouses and hire their own certified teachers without governmental assistance, at the same time paying their local school taxes. Technically, these schools are private and parochial, but in practice the Hutterites do not try to control the curriculum or to influence the teacher. Only in a few new colonies have Hutterite children temporarily attended outside schools, although a few Hutterite schools have a few outside students. In Manitoba a state-appointed trustee supervises all Hutterite schools, whether public or private. Since the colonies are usually in sparsely populated areas, their one-teacher (or occasional two-teacher) schools have, in the past, been comparable to most other schools in the area. But today, with a trend toward consolidation, their small schools are already becoming isolated survivals of a past educational era.[12]

The English schools and the outside teachers are a perennial source of unwanted ideas, habits, and desires among Hutterite children. They are a subversive influence right in the heart of the colonies. The outside teacher, whether male or female, inevitably introduces some popular culture, tempts children with better clothes and talk of forbidden luxuries, stimulates the more intelligent to think critically and to desire more "worldly" knowledge, teaches patriotism and a love of war, and lines children up in military array for physical education. The children develop an interest in politics, learn to want a higher living standard, and acquire forbidden magazines and comic books. Yet, the outside teacher is always treated with the greatest of courtesy and respect in the colonies. Most quickly learn to admire the Hutterites and to conform to their

11. Deets, *The Hutterites*, pp. 41–43; the (Minneapolis) *Morning Tribune*, Dec. 8, 1949; Peters, "All Things Common," pp. 162–167.

12. Peters, "All Things Common," pp. 230–237.

customs as much as possible. Fortunately, many of the teachers are of a German background. Some women teachers wear few cosmetics out of respect; a male teacher may give up smoking while in the colony. At Christmas the teacher is showered with gifts, and usually forms lasting friendships with parents. The German teacher takes care of the janitorial duties and often provides liaison between the outside teacher and the rest of the colony. Isolated Canadian colonies provide teacherages at a very moderate cost, and even then practically board their teachers.[13]

The colony schools are plain frame buildings that also serve as churches. Many have only outdoor toilets and are heated by solitary stoves. The colonies usually provide an adequate supply of books and playground supplies, but still reject all audio-visual aids. The parents may frown upon plays and skits, upon too much frivolity, and upon field trips away from the colony. The new teacher may give children forbidden articles as gifts. A few teachers have deliberately tried to disillusion children about "old fashioned" Hutterite beliefs or customs, only to meet an insurmountable wall of silence and passive resistance. Although the public schools are supposed to be instruments of cultural assimilation, they make slow progress in the colonies. Most children retain a complete loyalty to colony ways, and rarely aspire to any other position than that held by their parents. Teachers report favorably on Hutterite intelligence, but find the children amazingly lacking in aggression, ambition, and competitive spirit. Many are equally happy in any grade. Hutterite children end their formal education at fifteen and after the eighth grade. Because of early language difficulties, these usually coincide. The colonies now reject the idea of any higher education because of its worldly influence upon impressionable adolescents, and not out of any basic antagonism to learning. They have great respect for the teacher and scholar, but expect them to be orthodox. At present several colonies have students taking correspondence high school courses as a first step toward teacher certification. Although opposed to compulsory secondary school education, the Hutterites would undoubtedly accept it if required by law.[14]

The Hutterites have lost their past medical leadership, although each colony has a trained midwife. There are also a few untrained but proficient dentists and chiropractors in the Canadian colonies. One chiropractor has regular office hours in a neighboring town. But, with the present educational requirements, they have none of their own physicians.

13. *Ibid.*, pp. 234–235; Deets, *The Hutterites*, pp 41–43.
14. Peters, "All Things Common," pp.239–248.

Yet, when the need is great, they seek the best possible medical care, with many of the South Dakota colonists going to the Mayo clinic. They are endlessly concerned about good health, which is a very popular subject of conversation. The prevalent opinion among local physicians is that the Hutterites have better physical health than their non-Hutterite neighbors. This is balanced by a higher than average incidence of obesity and arterial hypertension, both possibly resulting from an unusually high fat diet. Until quite recently the infant and child mortality was well above average, but was in part due to the large number of children in each family. In 1950 the average medical cost to the colonies was approximately $24 for each individual. Longevity is not a marked trait in the Hutterites, with very few people living beyond eighty. Because of a limited number of marriage partners, there has been much inbreeding in the past. Yet, there is only an average number of congenital defections, physical and mental. Hutterite health and intelligence seem to be close to the average in the United States and Canada.[15]

The Hutterites enjoy food and drink. The enforced austerity of their life does not preclude good but simple food and occasional allotments of beer, homemade wine, and even whisky. Gluttony and drunkenness are strictly forbidden, but both do occur. The Hutterites eat in their large dining hall, with women and men on opposite sides. Until the last two decades, four people ate from common dishes in the center of the table. Meals are eaten quickly, and in near silence. A visitor in 1912 found the plainest of food, with an excess of pork, goose grease, breads, sweet syrups, and a special type of Hutterite coffee. The noon meal included liberal allotments of grape wine, enjoyed even by children as a stimulant to the appetite. A snack or small meal was then served in the afternoon. Practically the same food habits prevailed in the twenties, but since then the Hutterites have adopted regular plates and silverware, and have increased the variety of their foods. Pork and fowl are the principal meats, with the starchy vegetables much in evidence. Coffee and snacks are no longer served communally, but in the family apartments. The Hutterite kitchens are becoming ever more modern and efficient. The old wood stoves and large kettles have been replaced by gas ranges and large gas cookers. The long wooden troughs are being replaced by electric dish washers. Either as a separate part of the dining hall building or in a

15. Eaton and Weil, *Culture and Mental Disorders*, pp. 235–237; Joseph W. Eaton and Albert J. Mayer, *Man's Capacity to Reproduce* (Glencoe, Ill.: The Free Press, 1954), p. 342.

separate building, each colony has a communal laundry in which the wives are allotted time for their weekly washing.[16]

The main visible symbol of Hutterite separation from the sinful world is clothing and idiosyncrasies of personal appearance. The largest number of village rules and ordinances deal with banned dress, for here the world is always pressing its temptations. Yet, the Hutterites are not as plain, as rigid, or as inflexible as the Amish and some conservative Mennonites. They allow some variety in individual dress and permit some color and simple decorations. The male attire is not too unconventional. In the past the *Schmiedenleut* and *Dariusleut* used only hooks and eyes, but today they have buttons (of the same color as the material) except for suit coats. The men wear dark trousers, suspenders, normal work shirts (or white dress shirts on Sunday), and a dark hat, usually of the large, round, Quaker-like variety. All married men are required to grow beards and all men cut their hair much longer than is now the custom on the outside. The young men dress as their fathers, but shave and occasionally "hep up" their appearance by creased trousers and bright socks.

Hutterite women use no cosmetics of any kind, wear only the plainest types of glasses, and have a standard type of dress. They all wear very wide, dark (but not black or solid), ankle-length skirts gathered at the waist. A dark-colored, fitted bodice is worn over a light-colored, long-sleeved, tight-necked blouse. They generally wear aprons with plaid patterns and, particularly for festive occasions, with bright colors. Small decorative effects are not forbidden. The one invariant, from woman to woman and colony to colony, is a blue scarf with white polka dots, under which the hair is braided and bound. After years of agitation the women were given permission to wear bonnets in the hot sun. All children are dressed as small adults, making it very hard for a visitor to distinguish their ages. The women's clothing is made at home from large bolts of purchased cloth. Most men's clothing is bought ready-made.[17]

The beards and odd dress make the Hutterites objects of curiosity and suspicion when they visit nearby towns. They also make some Hutterites

16. Zimmer, "Huter's Religious Communism," pp. 14, 18–20; Clark, "The Hutterian Communities," p. 362.

17. Although the Hutterites discourage pictures of individuals as a form of idolatry, many have appeared in books and articles. By far the best detailed pictures of Hutterite dress are by Margaret Bourke-White, and appear in: Erskine Caldwell and Margaret Bourke-White, *Say, Is This USA?* (New York: Duell, Sloan and Pearce, 1941), pp. 41, 43, 45, 47.

feel self-conscious or embarrassed. A few colonies are on or near main highways, and thus have constant contact with the outside world. Increasingly, even girls make frequent trips to nearby towns. Salesmen, the public school teacher, Department of Agriculture personnel, the daily mailman, and a small trickle of tourists all visit the Hutterite colonies, displaying not only luxuries but contemporary fashions. Finally, colonists often take, or have access to, local newspapers, Mennonite religious publications, and farm and home magazines. These influences exert a constant pressure for change in dress and customs. Since 1900 there has been a steady liberalization in dress, with buttons, store-bought shoes, and tailored suits all being approved after years of opposition. The same changes are taking place in the houses, where bright calendars, beautiful china, an occasional picture, elaborate embroidery, and decorative woodwork are alleviating the earlier austerity. The traditional feather ticks have all been replaced by purchased mattresses.[18]

The Hutterite population, in 1950, was the most youthful and the most prolific ever recorded. An elaborate demographic survey showed an average of 10.6 live births for each woman between the ages of 43 and 54. For the few who married as young as 18, the average was 12.3 live births. Children under 15 accounted for 50.6 per cent of the total Hutterite population of 8,542; an astounding 61 per cent were under 19. Only 10 per cent were over 45. These figures may represent near the maximum possible reproductive rate for women who marry at the average age of 22, and is nearly four times the United States average. Between 1940 and 1950 the Hutterite population increased by 52.1 per cent; at the same rate of growth there will be 19,200 Hutterites in 1970, and nearly 65,000 in 2000. The Hutterite birth rate has increased slightly but steadily since 1900, along with better living standards and better technology, which is in direct contrast with almost all other societies. This extraordinary birth rate reflects the complete economic security of a communal society, the religious sanctions against birth control, the complete absence of divorce, the amazingly low incidence of sterility among Hutterites, and the near absence of spinsters in a society that encourages marriage if at all possible. Only 3.4 per cent of Hutterite couples are childless; only 10 per cent have three or less children. The high fertility probably accounts for one reversal in the normal life expect-

18. Eaton and Weil, *Culture and Mental Disorders*, pp. 196–197; Katz, "The Security of Co-operative Farming," pp. 67–68; Elma Waltner, "South Dakota's Hutterite Colonies," *Travel*, CV (May, 1956), 28–29.

ancy of modern society; above forty there are more Hutterite men than women and, on the average, they live longer.[19]

The Hutterites have no organized recreation, no formal entertainment, and no social organizations beyond their church. Culturally, they read very little except in religious or practical subjects, permit no music, and, except for their needlework and crafts, have no art. Apart from eating and church-going, their main form of diversion is visiting and conversing with each other. They are delightful conversationalists, although somewhat limited as to topics. They delight in Sunday trips to neighboring colonies, or even in prolonged vacations to more distant colonies. The children have their own organized games; the young people delight in group singing. Radios, television sets, movies, and musical instruments are forbidden temptations to the youth. Some colonies have exhibited in local fairs and permitted colonists to attend. There is always the thrill of a trip to town. In the past the Hutterites were often woefully ignorant of events in the outside world, but that is scarcely true today. They have not only the influence of the public school, but each colony takes local newspapers and, in some cases, news magazines. The preacher and *Wirt* are usually well informed about current events. Although they have no publications of their own, at least one Mennonite periodical in Canada has a Hutterite news column. Hutterites with creative abilities may or may not find an outlet in their work. Those with musical ability are completely frustrated; those of an intellectual bent have little mental stimulation outside of theological discourse. The Kingdom of God has no room for frivolity, for intellectual arrogance and pride, or for any purely sensual pleasure.

Colony old people are virtually free from cares and seem to be happy and content. Relief from binding duties comes very early (as low as forty-five for women), but few Hutterites really retire. They continue to work as they can and have an elevated status in what remains a very patriarchal society. They have complete economic security and, if alone, often have a single room in the apartment of one of their children. Perhaps most important to them, they are never separated from their familiar surroundings and from their children and grandchildren. At death, a Hutterite is buried in a homemade, wooden coffin without excessive grief. Their feeling of complete security extends to the next life. They have a funeral service in the church before interment in the nearby "garden of the dead." This cemetery is in the corner of some field, and is cared for voluntarily by the colony women. Headstones are simple

19. Eaton and Mayer, *Man's Capacity to Reproduce*, pp. 206–253.

and homemade, varying according to the desires and tastes of surviving loved ones.[20]

Are the Hutterites happy? They insist that they are, pointing to their economic security, their peaceful, harmonious life, and, most of all, to their feeling of satisfaction in obeying Christ to the fullest. Yet, at other times they rejoice in their suffering and point to the extreme difficulty of the Christian life when viewed from a human perspective. They are rightly proud of some of the results of their way of life. Open aggression is almost unknown in adults. There has never been any major crime among Hutterites, although a few boys have been arrested for minor thefts. No Hutterite child or old person has ever been known to suffer any serious neglect. No Hutterite has ever been on relief while in a colony. Only 258 Hutterite men and eleven women voluntarily left Hutterite colonies between 1880 and 1950, and more than half of them returned. Although many young men are tempted to leave the colony (about one in twenty does), only 106 were listed as permanent deserters in 1950. The young prodigal is gladly readmitted, and may even become a colony leader. Contacts are maintained with apostates, who are welcome to visit relatives still in the colony. Most deserters have been successful on the outside, although almost none have attained any important status.[21]

The Hutterites, in their near complete separation from the rest of the world, provide an ideal laboratory for social scientists. Thus, in the early fifties, an extensive study was made of Hutterite personality and mental health problems, giving some very suggestive answers to the problem of Hutterite happiness and well-being. Most casual visitors to Hutterite colonies had been impressed by the seeming lack of tension and stress that lead usually to anxiety, neurosis, or even psychosis. There seemed to be a perfect adjustment between Hutterite society and Hutterite personality types. Some were led to view their communal society as a near-utopia, contrasting its peace and security with the tension and strain exhibited by the surrounding world. Perhaps, it was thought, the Hutterites alone had found the social institutions best suited to man's nature or, conversely, perhaps they alone had perfectly adapted themselves to their institutions.

But a closer study quickly destroyed the illusions of visitors. The

20. Peters, "All Things Common," pp. 125, 134–135.
21. Eaton and Weil, *Culture and Mental Disorders*, pp. 145–146; Kaplan and Plaut, *Personality in a Communal Society*, pp. 18–19.

Hutterites suffer a normal amount of anxieties and tension, and are far from being free from personality problems and poor mental health. While the Hutterite society generates at least an average amount of tension, it allows fewer acceptable means of expressing it. Although all forms of aggression are prohibited, Hutterite responses to personality tests indicated an excessive number of concealed aggressive tendencies, even to the point of criminal urges. Yet the colonies have almost always been completely successful in curbing these impulses. In fact, even when aggressive desires were obvious, the Hutterites almost unbelievably denied their existence. The Hutterite women, in particular, had strong feelings of inadequacy and strong needs for more approval and commendation. They worried excessively about other people's opinions about them and all had strong guilt feelings. The tests showed almost no competitive feelings, no sibling rivalry, and very little jealousy. As befits their society, most Hutterites, and particularly the men, were excessively dependent and passive, with only a minority striving for full personal autonomy. The normal acquisitive urges of Hutterites found outlet in hope chests for girls, in children for women, and in assigned machinery for boys and men, but most Hutterites secretly yearned for more possessions. It is probable that all humans have approximately the same desires and needs, but that the type of society causes a variation in their distribution and intensity. Each society finds methods of dealing with and controlling what it defines as antisocial behavior. From a purely social standpoint, the Hutterites have been amazingly successful in this control, but possibly at a cost to the individual.[22]

One of the most intensive mental health surveys ever conducted thoroughly disproved the popular picture of happy, peaceful, contented Hutterites. Serious psychiatric problems develop as frequently among Hutterites as in other comparable societies. At the most serious level of mental illness—psychoses—the Hutterites revealed a lifetime rate of 6.2 patients per 1,000 of population. In 1950 there were 20 psychotic persons in the 93 colonies; from 29 to 33 others had recovered from earlier illnesses. The one unusual feature was the abnormally large proportion of manic-depressives, which accounted for 39 of the 53 diagnosed cases of psychosis. There were only nine cases of schizophrenia, and five cases of brain disorders. Yet, in American hospitals, schizophrenia accounts for a majority of all the mentally ill. It seems that communal life, with its established and clearly understood values, and its complete suppression

22. Kaplan and Plaut, *Personality in a Communal Society*, pp. 1–105.

of the individual, eliminates the stresses and strains of an open, highly complex society that produce the large numbers of schizophrenics in our hospitals. But, at the same time, communal life drives more individuals into deep states of depression, with loss of self-esteem and an obsession with sin and personal omissions. The depressive Hutterite patients rarely have to be institutionalized, and rarely reach states of manic excitement. Most eventually recover, some to lead completely normal lives. Only two have ever committed suicide (a mortal sin since forgiveness is impossible), and one of these only after leaving the colony. Hutterites accept depression as a trial by God, attach no concept of shame or guilt to it, and are exceptionally considerate and patient with their mentally ill, providing the best possible environment for full recovery. If able, the depressed patient continues to work as much as possible, and to care for their children if they are women. Most visit physicians, but relatively few receive psychiatric help. Most of the few schizophrenic patients had been under psychiatric treatment; some were able to work but others were completely withdrawn. But even for them antisocial acts were rare and social functioning was abnormally high. A few of the patients had spent time in mental hospitals.[23]

The same mental health survey also showed a relatively high proportion of neurotic Hutterites—8.1 per 1,000. In most of the 69 observed cases in 1950, some psychosomatic ailment was present or believed to be present. Thus, neurotic patients usually went to regular physicians instead of psychiatrists, in some cases piling up large medical bills and undergoing needless operations. As in psychoses, neurotic reactions tended toward depression rather than to anxiety or paranoid tendencies. There was almost no compulsory or obsessive behavior, although some were fanatical in their orthodoxy. Over four-fifths of the neurotics were women. The amount of neurosis was very high, but the symptoms were usually mild and most individuals functioned normally in the community. Although no Hutterite children were found to be seriously neurotic, their public school teachers believed that large numbers were poorly adjusted, with over two-thirds indicating a tendency toward depression. The children agreed that they had many emotional problems. On the other hand, there were few serious behavior problems and no real juvenile delinquency, which again illustrates the effectiveness of the Hutterites in handling, if not in preventing, serious emotional problems.[24]

23. Eaton and Weil, *Culture and Mental Disorders*, pp. 98–114.
24. *Ibid.*, pp. 115–136.

Except for business contacts, the Hutterites have few personal relationships with even their immediate neighbors. They take no part in neighbor-
hood events except in times of emergency, such as river floods. Most of
their charity is reserved for their own people. Although they may attend
the funeral of a respected neighbor, they rarely visit in neighboring
homes, perhaps fearing such worldly dangers as radios and television sets.
On the other hand, they welcome visits by friends and are hospitable
hosts, although a stranger may be taken aback by their complete frankness
and directness. It is revealing that most bitter opposition to Hutterites
has come from more distant neighbors and from people who know very
little about them from firsthand contacts. The Hutterites receive casual
visitors and tourists, give them a short tour of their colony, but can scarcely
welcome too many of them. As a religious principle, they will not charge
for any services, meals, or even lodging. Neither will they turn away a
visitor or guest.

Even as the Hutterites want to be left alone, so they leave others alone.
For example, they never try to force their religious views on another,
although they will argue religion all day with an interested visitor. Even
without missionaries and open proselytizing they have attracted an
occasional convert, but never enough to challenge their traditional customs.
Between 1930 and 1950 thirty converts joined the colonies, and by 1950
they had thirty-four descendants. In 1958 there were five converted
families in the Manitoba colonies. Such conversion requires a complete
surrender of all private property and a difficult adjustment to an entirely
new way of life. The Hutterites require at least a year's trial at colony
life and in doctrinal study before baptism. During this time the prospective
convert has no vote, keeps his possessions, but works in the colony. In
addition to complete converts, there are frequent prolonged visits to
colonies by idealistic individuals who either consider joining the Hutterites or who want to share their way of life for a period.[25] More important
than these integrated converts, and ultimately more disturbing to the
Hutterites, have been two affiliated communal movements. The largest
of these began in Germany.

Eberhard Arnold, a leading theologian and Secretary of the German
Christian Student Union, became very interested in Anabaptist songs
and history while still a student. In 1920, as a result of his own deepening
religious conviction, he joined with several other Christian families in
communal living and devoted the rest of his life to a brotherhood (or

25. *Ibid.*, p. 33; Peters, "All Things Common," pp. 251–252.

Brüderhof) movement which was purposefully modeled on the Hutterites. In 1926 his communal group moved to the Fulda area and took the name of *Rhoenbrüderhof*. It had special tax exemptions before Hitler came to power, expanded into new colonies in Germany and in England, operated a school and a children's home, and marketed books and woodcraft products. In the name of his *Brüderhof*, Arnold came to Canada in 1930 to unite with the ethnic Hutterites. He was also ordained a Hutterite minister by the elders at Stand Off Colony, Macleod, Alberta. They were most impressed by his zeal, and undoubtedly flattered at his conversion.[26]

In 1937, at the time that two Hutterite ministers came from Canada on a visit, the *Rhoenbrüderhof* was confiscated by the German authorities. Because of earlier threats from the Gestapo, a temporary colony had already been established in Liechtenstein and many of their young men of military age had fled to Holland. As a result of earlier contacts with English Quakers and Mennonites, the German and Liechtenstein colonists all moved to England, where the Cotswold *Brüderhof* had already been established. Here they remained until the European War of 1939, when they were refused permission to come to Canada and, instead, moved to Paraguay to escape war service. Here, with almost unbelievable early hardships, they eventually established four colonies, with hospitals, libraries, and very progressive schools. A few members who remained in England to settle the business affairs attracted so many converts that they eventually purchased a farm and formed the Wheathill *Brüderhof*. Arnold died in 1939, but his movement (called the Society of Brothers) remained one of the largest communal movements of the twentieth century. His colonies continued to attract highly idealistic and cultured members, with several from the professional classes. The members adopted at least part of the Hutterite dress and many of their customs, but their religious beliefs were often more nebulous and more humanistic and their community rules were less rigid. But, alas, they could not maintain unity and internal harmony. Because of disagreements, the movement lost half of its members and had to sell the Wheathill *Brüderhof* and all the South American colonies between 1960 and 1962. The surviving members

26. E. C. H. Arnold, "Eberhard Arnold, 1883-1939," *Mennonite Quarterly Review*, XXV (July, 1951), 219-220; Eberhard Arnold, *The Hutterian Brothers: Four Centuries of Common Life and Work* (Ashton Keynes, England, 1940), p. 38; "Third Bruderhof Letter," a pamphlet (Ashton Keynes, England, Aug., 1937), pp. 3-5.

joined either a new *Brüderhof* in England or three small colonies in the United States.[27]

The American Hutterites gave Arnold's movement their wholehearted support in its early years. But as they received rumors of such worldly pursuits as folk dancing and smoking in the Paraguayan colonies they became more skeptical. In 1949 two delegates from Paraguay came to the American colonies to allay their fears and to seek aid. They amazed the Canadians by their flawless Oxford accent and were so persuasive that the Hutterites gave them over $60,000 in money and needed supplies. The *Schmiedenleut* colonies then sent two visitors to Paraguay, finding their worst fears to be all too true. They made their complaints, and were in turn challenged by the Paraguay colonists for their lack of missionary zeal. In effect, this visit and a later rebuke from the American colonies terminated the close tie between the two groups, although there was still some correspondence. Also, the Paraguayans continued to publish many of the old Hutterite manuscripts.[28]

There is one interesting sequel to this story. The Society of Brothers in Paraguay asked permission to send some of their brethren to American colonies in order to act as Hutterite missionaries. In concert, the colonies rejected the offer, perhaps fearing that the aggressive and educated brothers would either corrupt or take over their colonies. But one new colony at Forest Lake, North Dakota, voted to receive some of the missionaries, led by Eberhard Arnold, Jr. A minority group, led by the elder minister, immediately withdrew back to the mother colony in Canada. The Paraguayans proved to be able educators and missionaries, establishing a complex educational system and opening the colony to all interested visitors. But they were poor farmers. Besides, North Dakota was too cold and isolated for effective proselytizing. Since a small group from Paraguay had already established a *Brüderhof* and a toy factory at Rifton, New York, most of the Forest Lake Colony moved to Farmington, Pennsylvania, where they bought a luxury hotel for dormitories and began manufacturing toys, with some economic success. Only four

27. A. J. F. Zieglschmid, ed., *Das Klein-Geschichtsbuch der Hutterischen Brüder* (Philadelphia: The Carl Schurz Memorial Foundation, 1947), pp. 658–662; *Work and Life at the Bruderhoefe in Paraguay* (Wheathill Bruderhof, England, 1943), pp. 1–24; Henrik F. Infield, *Utopia and Experiment* (New York: F. A. Praeger, 1955), pp. 48, 52–53; C. Frank Steele, "Canada's Hutterite Settlement," *Canadian Geographical Journal*, XXII (June, 1941), 310; letter to author from Francis Hall, former member of a colony in Paraguay, Feb. 7, 1963.

28. Peters, "All Things Common," pp. 265–268.

disgraced and bewildered Hutterite families were left in the North Dakota colony, which was now not even recognized by the other colonies.[29]

In a less important, but similarly disillusioning experience, Julius Kubassek, a Hungarian immigrant from British Columbia, came to the Alberta colonies and lived for a year. Impressed by the communal system, but not by Alberta agriculture, he established a new colony at Bright, Ontario, in 1940. Not only did he have Hutterite support, but actually took some Hutterite families to the new *Brüderhof*, where they established a thriving goose farm. But soon there was factionalism and Kubassek, a dictatorial leader, expelled two members who came back to the Alberta colonies. Rebuking Kubassek for his methods, the Hutterites discontinued their support. Most of the ethnic Hutterites came back to Alberta, but the colony attracted new converts and continued to thrive.[30]

Almost every visitor to the Hutterites since 1912 has predicted their eventual complete assimilation into American society and an end to their peculiar beliefs and customs. Even some Hutterite leaders of today, sadly watching the slow changes and gauging the pressure for more change, regretfully predict that, as in the past, their way of life may soon completely succumb to the secular ways of the world. Confronted with constant demands for innovations, the Hutterite leaders have wisely accepted some in order to reject others. Thus they have so far retained the loyalty of most youth and preserved their more basic institutions. One sociologist has called this "controlled acculturation," and sees in it a method of postponing or even preventing complete assimilation. But it is also a method of slowly erasing the differences between the Hutterites and the dominant culture surrounding them.[31]

In the technological realm, the Hutterites have already joined the twentieth century, always carefully trying to distinguish between the purely practical tools, which they accept as means, from the luxury items, which they reject as ends. Thus they have trucks but no automobiles; modern electrical appliances in the kitchen but only bare light bulbs (or no electricity at all) in their living quarters; farm magazines but no fiction. They have compromised on clothing details, but never on their desire for separation. They necessarily see more of the world, but

29. *Ibid.*, pp. 268–270.

30. *Ibid.*, pp. 259–260.

31. Joseph W. Eaton, "Controlled Acculturation: A Survival Technique of the Hutterites," *American Sociological Review*, XVII (June, 1952), 331–340.

do not condone its ways. They permit public education, but try to overcome its harmful effects.

The point of greatest stress in Hutterite life is probably the desire for luxuries, entertainment, or a better standard of living. This, in turn, threatens the community of property, for individuals try to get extra things for themselves. For years the colonies have recognized the desire for some spending money, and have provided small family or individual allowances. In the *Schmiedenleut* colonies, each individual gets 30¢ a month as pin money. In addition, some colonies have distributed candy and toys for children. One Canadian colony even permitted ten private geese for each family. There have been many cases of petty theft by young boys, who either trapped and sold fur or took articles from the colony and sold them for money. In other cases young men refuse to work any harder than anyone else, rejecting jobs that were once gladly performed. In frequent trips to town, young people slip away to see movies or a rodeo, or feel cheated when they cannot go. Girls secretly wear lipstick, decorate their rooms, or wear forbidden clothing. Minor luxuries are now found in most colonies. These include mirrors, ornaments, hairbrushes, rocking chairs, lace curtains, pictures, and fancy needlework. Boys slip in radios, pose for photographs, read comic books, and secretly smoke. The colonies near large cities, such as Winnipeg, have faced the greatest decline in discipline and organization, while the more isolated ones have more easily remained conservative and strict. Some ministers have been more tolerant of slight deviation than others.[32]

The very size of the Hutterite religion presents new dangers to their continued orthodoxy. If their present growth rate continues, they will have increasing difficulty in acquiring large tracts of land, in keeping uniform customs, and in maintaining even their present degree of seclusion and separation. For over four hundred years the Hutterites have sought under-populated, frontier areas for their settlement. Now there are few available frontiers, although the Hutterites have in the past considered a mass migration to Paraguay. But it is very unlikely that they will ever again move to a new area and there experience a new revival, partly because there will not be enough persecution to motivate such a move. Thus, all present and future decline in their distinctive institutions will most likely be permanent. There will be no going back, and no starting over again. But, at the same time, future change will be slow and, at

32. Deets, *The Hutterites*, pp. 9–10; Katz, "The Security of Co-operative Farming," p. 84.

times, hardly perceptible. Their name, their separate religious identity, their more distinctive customs and rituals—in fact the whole empty shell of their ideology and faith—will remain for endless generations. Total creeds rarely die, although they may be destroyed or slowly lose their meaning. Whether, or how rapidly, the Hutterite religion will lose its essential meaning is beyond prediction.

Part Two

LLANO DEL RIO

V. The Last Cooperative Commonwealth

The Llano colony was the last and by far the largest of the colonies inspired by the dream of a cooperative commonwealth. Established in 1914 by Job Harriman, a socialist lawyer from Los Angeles, Llano represented a somewhat belated attempt at implementing an idea that had flourished in the last decade of the nineteenth century. The earlier, completely utopian socialism of Owen and Fourier, which led to a veritable explosion of communitarian colonies in the United States, was slowly replaced after the Civil War by the harsh, "scientific" socialism of Karl Marx. Yet, as Marxism spread in the United States, it was almost always tempered and softened into a mild, moralistic idealism. This revised Marxism led most directly to the cooperative commonwealth movement and to a dramatic but brief rebirth of communitarianism. Later, when thoroughly chastened by the failure of practical experiments in colonization, it led to the mild political protest of the American Socialist Party.

In its purer and more militant forms Marxism, which flourished mainly among German immigrant groups in the United States, inspired early communist clubs and, in 1877, the formation of the Socialist Labor Party. Few Americans were influenced by these "radical" movements. In 1884 a Danish immigrant, Laurence Gronlund, published *The Co-operative Commonwealth*, a popular analysis of Marxism written in English. In it he indicted competition as immoral, predicted the eventual collapse of capitalism, and proclaimed the coming of a pure and glorious socialist state, which he called a cooperative commonwealth. Rejecting the harsh doctrines of class conflict and revolution, he expected the "Kingdom of Heaven on Earth" to be ushered in by "God's will" and as a result of "deeply religious leadership."[1] His somewhat stodgy appeal

1. Laurence Gronlund, *The Co-operative Commonwealth* (revised ed., Boston: Lee and Shepherd, 1890), p. ix; also see Howard H. Quint, *The Forging of American Socialism: Origins of the Modern Movement* (Columbia, S.C.: University of South Carolina Press, 1953), pp. 28-30: Seymour Bassett, "The Secular Utopian Socialists," in *Socialism and American Life*, eds. Donald Drew Egbert and Stow Persons (Princeton, N.J.: Princeton University Press, 1952), I, 155-211.

made a deep impression on another idealist, Edward Bellamy, who in 1888 incorporated many of Gronlund's ideas into his more popular and subtle appeal for socialism, *Looking Backward*. Within two years at least 158 Nationalist clubs had been formed in the United States to work for the achievement of Bellamy's utopia. As many other young Americans, Job Harriman joined a Nationalist club, imbibing its heady idealism but finding in it few concrete political or economic programs and little practical accomplishment.[2]

By 1890 utopianism was again respectable. Eschewing forcible political methods, many optimistic American socialists desired an immediate practical demonstration of the cooperative commonwealth. A few Christian ministers extended their social gospel to include socialism and communitarian experiments. Growing out of a small Christian Socialist colony in North Carolina, a major attempt at Christian communism was launched in south Georgia in 1896. Called the Christian Commonwealth, it survived for four years and attracted intense interest not only in the United States but in Europe.[3] Even earlier, and more important to the later Llano, a liberal Unitarian minister in California formed an Altruria Movement in 1894. Drawing his inspiration from William Dean Howells' utopian novel, *A Traveller from Altruria*, the minister and approximately eighteen associates founded a small but ambitious colony in the Sonoma Valley, near Santa Rosa, California. They pooled their property, paid a small fee, practiced complete democracy, dreamed of a coming prosperity through the mining of coal, the sale of a special cleaning polish, and a booming tourist trade, and always enjoyed a gay social life. In a few months they had small houses, tents for weekend visitors, a community kitchen, a small school, an excellent eight-page weekly newspaper, and regular festivals and dances. Altruria clubs were formed throughout the state, spreading the hope of a new order to countless converts who awaited their opportunity to move to a colony. Unfortunately for their hopes, the colony failed after only seven months because of economic difficulties. But it disbanded without bitterness. Job Harriman never lived at the colony but, as president of Altruria Subcouncil Number Five, was probably a constant weekend guest. In many respects, his Llano was to be modeled on Altruria.[4]

2. Quint, *The Forging of American Socialism*, pp. 72–83.

3. James Dombrowski, *The Early Days of Christian Socialism in America* (New York: Columbia University Press, 1936), pp. 132–170.

4. Robert V. Hine, *California's Utopian Colonies* (San Marino, Calif.: Huntington Library, 1953), pp. 101-113.

The first major attempt to create a secular cooperative commonwealth was made in 1894 by Julius A. Wayland, an affluent, middle-aged Indiana businessman who was converted to socialism after reading Gronlund. Wayland initiated a very popular socialist magazine, *Coming Nation*, and personally financed the boom-and-bust, dissension-racked colony of Ruskin, near Tennessee City, Tennessee. Early membership in Ruskin could be acquired by selling a large number of subscriptions to *Coming Nation*, the publication of which was to provide the only income for the new colony. Poor land, primitive conditions, and splits in the membership all contributed to the early failure of Ruskin. Wayland turned his beloved *Coming Nation* over to the colony, but left in anger within the first year, only to begin a second and even more popular socialist journal, *Appeal to Reason*. The remaining Ruskin colonists first moved about six miles to better land, and then dissolved the colony in 1899, although some members made a new but unsuccessful attempt at Duke, Georgia.[5]

Earlier, in 1896, the beleaguered Ruskin colonists had joined forces with another struggling socialist movement, the Brotherhood of the Co-operative Commonwealth. Only a year old, limited to a few chapters in Maine, and much too weak to carry out its plan of establishing numerous colonies, the Brotherhood was now able to use the declining *Coming Nation* to attract national support. By 1897 it had over two thousand members, including Eugene Debs, and ambitiously planned to colonize the whole State of Washington. Actually, it established its first and only colony at Equality on the Puget-Sound in 1897. By 1902 Equality contained 105 people, living on a very plain diet in two apartment houses, four log cabins, and fourteen frame houses, earning a bare subsistence by the sale of lumber and grain.[6]

In 1897 the Brotherhood of the Co-operative Commonwealth joined with Eugene Debs' American Railroad Union to become the Social Democracy of America, which was still dominated by a group more dedicated to colonization and economic action than to politics. It appointed a colonization commission to explore sites, optioned a colony site on the Cumberland Plateau in Tennessee, and actually purchased some

5. Quint, *The Forging of American Socialism*, pp. 175–209; Frederick A. Bushee, "Communistic Societies in the United States," *Political Science Quarterly*, XX (Dec., 1905), 632–633; Lincoln Phifer, "The Story of American Socialism," *The Internationalist*, VI (June, 1918), 8.

6. *The Co-operator*, Apr. 19, 1902; Bushee, "Communistic Societies in the United States," pp. 635-636.

land in Colorado. In the first annual convention of the Social Democracy in 1898, Victor Berger of Milwaukee, the leader of a growing faction desiring political action, led a bitter fight against colonization. When his group lost in a showdown vote, it withdrew to form the Social Democratic Party of America, which was soon to be the nucleus of the American Socialist Party. This split in the Social Democracy in reality marked the shift of American socialists away from colonization. Yet the majority within the Social Democracy reorganized as the Co-operative Brotherhood Movement and established a Brotherhood Colony at Burley, Washington, in the fall of 1898. The colony lasted for over a decade, but never contained over 150 colonists. The Co-operative Brotherhood Movement had only 550 scattered members in 1902, all of whom, at least theoretically, had retirement rights in the declining Burley colony.[7] Many members of both the Equality and Burley colonies later came to Llano, which, in many ways, was only a latter-day continuation of these two earlier attempts at successful cooperation.

Job Harriman, the founder of Llano, grew up on an Indiana farm in the years after the Civil War. Although trained for the ministry at what is now Butler University, he soon rejected religious orthodoxy, studied law in Colorado, and established his practice in California in 1886. Converted to socialism by 1890, he was active in a Nationalist club and, by 1892, had formed a local unit of the Socialist Labor Party, running for its candidate for governor of California in 1898. Undogmatic in his socialism, he divided his support between the colonizers and the political activists. In 1899 he joined a New York socialist, Morris Hillquit, in a violent revolt within the Socialist Labor Party against the high-handed leadership of party head, Daniel DeLeon. The Hillquit faction, or, as they were called, the "Kangaroos," set up an independent Socialist Labor Party in Rochester, New York, and nominated Job Harriman for the presidency in 1900. Then the Hillquit group proposed a joint socialist ticket with the Social Democratic Party, now headed by Berger and Eugene Debs. Although only asking for the right to name the vice-presidential candidate, the Hillquit group used clever campaigning to enlist a majority of the Social Democratic convention delegates for Harriman as president. Eugene Debs, who had formerly rejected the idea of personal candidacy, saved the day for the Social Democrats by reluctantly agreeing to be the presidential candidate on a joint ticket; Harriman automatically became the vice-

7. The detailed history of the Burley colony is contained in its weekly (later monthly) journal, *The Co-operator*, which began publication in December, 1898.

presidential candidate. Despite the common ticket, a violent struggle between the two factions was ended only with the formation of a unified American Socialist Party in 1901.[8]

After the campaign of 1900, Harriman returned to his profitable law practice, only to re-enter politics again in 1911 as a socialist candidate for mayor of Los Angeles. Since he was supported by the labor unions, he was given an even chance for victory. The big issue in the campaign was the guilt or innocence of the McNamara brothers, who had been accused of the tragic bombing of the *Los Angeles Times* building in 1910. Socialists and labor leaders had flocked to the support of the two brothers, who were members of the American Federation of Labor. Five days before the election the two brothers confessed the crime and practically destroyed Harriman's campaign. Completely frustrated in politics, Harriman turned once again to the idea of practical economic activity, which had long since been repudiated by a vast majority of American socialists. Desiring to demonstrate the superiority of a fully cooperative society, Harriman proposed a new colony based on equality in ownership, wages, and social opportunities.[9]

Harriman was able to enlist support for his colony from several interested friends in California, including bankers and businessmen. After a long search for a suitable site, they optioned approximately nine thousand acres in the Antelope Valley, about forty-five air miles north of Los Angeles. The site had been partially developed by an earlier colony made up of temperance advocates, who had completed a three-mile-long irrigation tunnel and who had sold $150,000 in bonds in order to finance an irrigation district. For a small sum, Harriman and his friends purchased the almost worthless bonds, reorganized the company—the Mescal Water and Land Company—selected a nine-member board of directors, and began selling stock in the fall of 1913. The proposed colony was publicized in the labor and socialist press and, after its establishment, intensively promoted and glowingly described in the *Western Comrade*, a monthly socialist journal which Harriman purchased in 1914. Its one editorial theme was the desirability of cooperation as the main emphasis

8. Quint, *The Forging of American Socialism*, pp. 338–349; Daniel Bell, "Marxian Socialism in the United States," *Socialism and American Life*, I, 257–258; Roy Ginger, *The Bending Cross: A Biography of Eugene Victor Debs* (New Brunswick, N.J.: Rutgers University Press, 1949), pp. 208–213.

9. Job Harriman, "Introduction" to Ernest S. Wooster, *Communities of the Past and Present* (Newllano, La.: *Llano Colonist*, 1924), p. iii. For an intimate account of the McNamara affair, see Lincoln Steffens, *The Auto-biography of Lincoln Steffens* (New York: Harcourt, Brace and Co., 1931), p. 666.

of American socialism. The prospectus for the colony, *The Gateway to Freedom*, which was first published in *Western Comrade* and later as a small book, was optimistic enough to attract many a dedicated socialist or struggling laborer.[10]

As described in the *Western Comrade*, the site in the Antelope Valley was a veritable Eden, just waiting for the new heaven which was to be the gateway to freedom for the economic slaves of capitalism. The desert land was at an altitude of approximately 3,500 feet, of decomposed granite, fertile, but lacking in organic matter. It was in an area of even and pleasant temperatures and, most important, near seemingly abundant supplies of water for irrigation. The valley was in view of the Tehachapi Mountains far to the north, and was bounded by the San Bernardino range to the east, both of which provided beautiful vistas all through the year. The main valley land of the colony contained sites for orchards of apples and, particularly, pears, fields for alfalfa and small grains, and suitable areas for vegetable gardens. The colony also owned land in the foothills of the mountains, providing sites for recreation or possible tourist development. The land was watered by two creeks, which not only promised to irrigate up to ten thousand acres of land but also contained power sites. One of the creeks, the Big Rock or, as it was still sometimes called, Rio del Llano (River of the Plain), when reversed to Llano del Rio, lent its musical Spanish name to the colony.[11]

The Mescal Water and Land Company was soon reorganized as the Llano del Rio Company of California, which was eventually capitalized at $2,000,000, issuing 2,000,000 shares at $1 each. Membership in the colony required the purchase of 2,000 shares of stock, although the first settlers only had to pay cash for 500 shares (this was soon raised to 750 and then to 1,000, while a few early settlers did not have to pay any cash). Each settler was promised a daily wage of $4, but had to allot $1 of this to the purchase of his remaining 1,000 shares of stock. The exact terms and conditions of employment were incorporated into the work contract, which was not an automatic result of stock ownership. The company

10. Archie Roy Clifton, "A Study of Llano del Rio Community in the Light of Earlier Experiments in Practical Socialism" (unpublished M.A. Thesis, University of Southern California, 1918), pp. 27–29; Ernest Wooster, "They Shared Equally," *Sunset Magazine*, LIII (July, 1924), 21–22; Job Harriman, "The Gateway to Freedom," *Western Comrade*, II (June, 1914), 13.

11. Frank E. Wolfe, "Llano del Rio, Land of Achievement," *Western Comrade*, II (June, 1914), 16–17; W. A. Engle, "Co-operative Colony Plan in Action," *Western Comrade*, II (June, 1914), 13.

agreed to provide all supplies at cost to the colonists, and estimated that the remaining $3 wages would more than cover all living costs. Any surplus wages were to be held by the company, with only a certain percentage to be paid in cash to the colonist each year, and only then if the colony had a surplus (it never had one). In addition to this somewhat illusionary wage, the colonist was promised a yearly vacation of two weeks, and was permitted to retain purely personal property, including automobiles.[12]

The Llano Colony was officially opened on May 1, 1914. The first members included only five people, a team of horses, a cow, and five pigs. In subsequent May Day ceremonies in California these first citizens paraded before hundreds of cheering colonists. The early growth was quite rapid. By January, 1915, over 150 people were in the colony. The one cow had grown to over a hundred, the five hogs to 110. Life in the early colony centered on a club house, which was used for assemblies and dances. Single men lived in an attached dormitory, while many married couples lived in tents. A post office, a new dairy building, and a laundry had been added. The colony was formed as a separate water and school district, with all elective offices being filled with socialists. The early colonists were mainly from the West Coast, with more farmers or businessmen than wage laborers in what had been characterized as a Marxist colony. On the negative side, there were personal clashes and violent disagreements from the very beginning, resulting in a constant turnover of members.[13]

Llano in California reached its maximum growth in the summer of 1917, with over 1,100 people living in the colony for one brief period. By this time the colony had developed an impressive number of industries, and a large, though somewhat temporary, physical plant. Slowly many of the canvas homes were replaced by adobe homes, while a large dining room, industrial buildings and warehouses, a hotel, and one of the largest rabbitries in the United States were constructed. The state provided an elementary school, while the colony developed an industrial school. Approximately two thousand acres of land was irrigated, with most of it in alfalfa and in new orchards. In 1916 the *Western Comrade* was moved to the colony, where a new printing press was also used for a weekly newspaper and for the job printing of other socialist literature.

12. Harriman, "Gateway to Freedom," pp. 7–8.

13. "Seven Months' Progress at Llano del Rio," *Western Comrade*, II (Jan.–Feb., 1915), 25–27; Clifton, "A Study of Llano del Rio Community," pp. 44–46, 49–55, 64.

The farm contained steam tractors, a large apiary, up to a hundred horses, over two hundred cows, and large numbers of rabbits, chickens, turkeys, goats and hogs. The following industries were in operation at one time or another, although some of them were very small: shoeshop, laundry, cannery, garage, machine shop, blacksmith shop, rug works, planing mill, paint shop, lime kiln, sawmill, dairy, cabinet shop, brickyard, flour mill, bakery, fish hatchery, barber shop, commissary, and print shop.[14]

Life in the California colony was full of privation and excitement. The temporary adobe houses melted whenever the roofs leaked. The food was monotonous and poorly cooked, with carrots the only vegetable for one long period. Even the minimum food was obtained only by harvesting neighbors' crops on shares. There were always grandiose schemes for sudden wealth, but none ever worked. One colonist built a low-priced, low-powered airplane, hoping for a large family market for his model T of the air, but was so scared when it came to fly it that he set it on fire and watched it go up in smoke. A prospector arrived with a secret method of producing gold, and led several colonists on hopeless digging expeditions to a nearby butte. Another colonist promised to solve the water problem, using a willow wand to indicate the perfect spot for a gushing well. The dry hole was abandoned only after much wasted digging. A turnip enthusiast from Slovakia somehow never got his land ready for planting, while an arduous IWW member named Gibbons was always suffering from undiagnosed aches and pains despite his ambitious plans. All subsequent slackers were called Gibbonites in memory of his uselessness.[15]

Harriman and other leaders in the colony dreamed of a beautiful new Llano in the future that would replace the rather makeshift reality. Nothing was more talked about among the hopeful colonists, and nothing inspired more hope in the midst of adversity. The first map of the future Llano was drawn in 1915, and contained a community center surrounded by six large residential blocks accommodating up to ten thousand colonists. By 1917 this was replaced by an even more elaborate plan, which was constructed in miniature and exhibited in a dormitory. It provided for row houses facing inward to a central park and playground. Each colonist

14. "Industries, Institutions, Recreations," *Western Comrade*, IV (June–July, 1916), 22; Fred Hanover, "Llano Cooperative Colony: An American Rural Community Experiment" (unpublished M.A. Thesis, Tulane University, 1936), pp. 55–56; Wooster, *Communities of the Past and Present*, pp. 122–123; Clifton, "A Study of Llano del Rio Community," pp. 32–34.

15. Wooster, "They Shared Equally," p. 80; Ernest Wooster, "Bread and Hyacinths," *Sunset Magazine*, LIII (Aug., 1924), 22–23.

was to have a large living room, a dining room, two large bedrooms, a bath, and an attic bunk room for up to eight children. This was certainly a nice contrast to the tents and two-room adobe shacks that always typified the colony.[16]

The first great crisis in the colony came in 1915, when the California Commissioner of Corporations investigated and condemned the Llano del Rio Company for violation of the state "Blue Sky" law. The investigation purported to find waste in the distribution of water and discriminatory prices and open profiteering at the cooperative store. Since this was perfect ammunition for those who opposed Harriman's leadership, a minor revolution broke out in the colony. In a harried and memorable ordeal, Harriman defended his policies to the colonists in an eight-hour assembly meeting and then rushed to Carson City, Nevada, to carry out a neat legal trick. The Llano del Rio Company had already purchased some land in Nevada in hope of establishing a second unit of the colony. Harriman chartered a new corporation, Llano del Rio of Nevada, and used its stock to purchase all the property of the old California corporation.[17] The trick worked and Llano remained a Nevada corporation until its liquidation in 1938.

In addition to the trouble with the State of California, the Llano colony was widely criticized by many socialists, who pointed to the corporate organization, the wage system, and the definite middle-class orientation of its founders and board of directors. Other socialists desired political action as the sole road to a new society. Harriman admitted that the colony was not fully socialist and, under the circumstances, could not be, since the new order had to be developed within the legal framework of the old. But, on the other hand, he argued that cooperative ventures like Llano should be the first goal of socialists, and attributed the weakness of the Socialist Party of California to a lack of economic endeavors. In Marxian style, Harriman insisted that capitalism would not die until the "industries from which it draws its subsistence should have first been transformed into cooperative enterprises."[18] An industrial system cannot

16. "Map of the City of Llano," *Western Comrade*, II (Mar., 1915), 19; also see the map in *Western Comrade*, IV (Apr., 1917), 16–17.

17. A. James McDonald, *The Llano Co-operative Colony and What it Taught* (Leesville, La.: n.p., 1950), pp. 20–21.

18. Job Harriman, "Co-operation a Necessity," *Western Comrade*, II (Aug., 1914), 10; see also Harriman, "Co-operation vs. Theory," *Western Comrade*, II (July, 1914), 5; and editorials by Harriman in practically every issue of *Western Comrade* in 1916 and 1917.

be voted out of existence. Practical steps must precede political reorganization. But unlike orthodox Marxists, Harriman believed the cooperative society could be achieved by peaceful means, and viewed Llano as the first demonstration of a successful method. He believed that socialism would wither and die if individual socialists had to turn to capitalists for employment. The capitalists were not planning to surrender to socialism, but if socialism could demonstrate a greater economic efficiency, capitalism would lose its supporters. Political parties and labor unions could not make this demonstration. Direct economic action could. Finally, in 1917, the Socialist Party of California adopted an economic platform that had been prepared at Llano.[19]

As a middle-class lawyer, Harriman always rejected a rigid, doctrinaire form of Marxism. He believed socialism should be a working hypothesis and not a dogmatic religion. If it were a true philosophy, it should be put to work. He saw plenty of need for it. His hatred of capitalism was complete, although not excessively bitter: "Out of the Universal Conflict of interests waging in the outside world, a condition has arisen in which the physically strong and the intellectually cunning survive. The heart plays no part in our affairs. The powerful and crafty succeed; the good and humane too frequently go down before them. It is a survival of the unfit. . . ."[20] He hoped that Llano would provide a peaceful, cooperative oasis within the capitalist system. Located in the very midst of "the thorns and thickets and swamps of capitalism," the Llano community was to create a "new order of things," a "new social spirit," and a "pathway to a higher social life." This hope was founded on his faith that humanity was "neither depraved nor wicked; but rather that the hearts and minds of men would be as sweet and gentle and loving as in babyhood, if the stream of life were not polluted by the vicious methods produced by the universal conflict of interests."[21]

In spite of all Harriman's optimistic predictions, Llano in California was an economic failure. In 1917 the population of Llano climbed to over one thousand, but conditions in the colony did not improve. In the annual May Day celebration the usual optimism about Llano's future was strained. There.was talk of worsening housing problems, of poor food, and, most significant, of a water shortage. The constant influx of paying members had kept Llano growing and had kept it solvent. Yet,

19. Harriman, "Co-operation a Necessity," p. 11; Harriman, "Llano—Community of Ideals," *Western Comrade*, IV (Mar., 1917), 8.
20. Harriman, "Llano—Community of Ideals," p. 8.   21. *Ibid.*, pp. 8–9.

the hopes of a thriving agriculture, a necessity for such a colony, never materialized. The promise of sufficient water for irrigation was illusory, for in dry years, such as 1917, an earthquake fault took most of the water. Unknown to either the colonists or the public, Harriman began looking for a better site for the colony as early as 1916. In the summer of 1917 he learned of a possible bargain in Louisiana, and personally investigated it. The Gulf Lumber Company was willing to sell approximately twenty thousand acres of cut-over land and a small lumber town for $125,000, payable over a period of several years. The offer was accepted by the board of directors, presented to the colonists for approval in August, and finally announced to the world in September.[22]

Very conscious of the implications of announced failure in California, the contemplated move of Llano was publicized in terms of a long-awaited expansion, which was now imperative because the California site would not support a large population. Although most of the "venturesome" colonists were expected to take advantage of the new opportunity, Llano in California was to be retained for those who liked the climate. It was to become a fruit farm, necessitating only a few colonists to carry on the needed work. The advantages of the Louisiana site were extolled in language strangely reminiscent of the early announcements about Llano in California. In addition to the attractiveness of the site, great success for the new colony was predicted on the basis of new members that would join. An investigating committee from California had contacted socialists in Texas, and had enlisted about thirty new colonists; up to a hundred were expected by December, 1917. These new members, at $1,000 per family, were expected to pay most of the cost of the new site.[23]

The move to Louisiana began in October, 1917. It was the hegira of the Llano faithful, for most of the California colonists never made the trip. Harriman and a few assistants came first in order to prepare the facilities. The equipment and supplies came by train, arriving over a period of several months. Most of the industries were moved from California, including the valuable printing equipment. A courageous group of about thirty moved in a cavalcade of five automobiles, an adventure that was fully exploited for its romantic value in the columns of the *Western Comrade*. Finally, the mass of colonists (but only 130) came in a chartered train of six coaches. These groups, plus about

22. Hanover, "Llano Cooperative Colony," p. 66; "Llano's Louisiana Purchase," *Western Comrade*, V (Oct., 1917), 6–8.
23. "Llano's Louisiana Purchase," pp. 6–8.

twenty-five Texas families, a few local additions, and some few straggling arrivals from California, gave the colony a population of about three hundred by January, 1918.[24]

The destination of the great move was a small, abandoned lumber town named Stables, located only a few miles south of Leesville in Vernon Parish, approximately halfway between Shreveport and Lake Charles on the main line of the Kansas City Southern Railroad. The departing lumber company had left a few large homes and approximately one hundred smaller, unpainted shacks, some of which were already inhabited by goats. In addition the village contained an eighteen-room hotel, a store, an office, a school, a sawmill, some warehouses, endless tramways, and, perhaps most valuable, several concrete drying sheds. Although drab in appearance, the site was complete enough for the colony to move in with very little construction. Stables was quickly renamed Newllano (the colony was still called Llano), foremen were appointed, and work began. Unfortunately, only about twenty-five Texas families arrived, and few of them were able to pay their membership fees. Also, many of the California colonists were so disappointed with the new site that they soon departed.[25]

The first three years in Louisiana were marked by poverty, bitter quarrels, a slow erosion of members, and a faltering attempt to start farming and manufacturing industries. By the spring of 1918 the last published numbers of *Western Comrade* were full of pleas for support for the colony. News of the California colony was dropped, while pioneering conditions were described in Louisiana. By April, colony land was offered for sale in order to raise funds for meeting the payments to the Gulf Lumber Company. Harriman was usually back in California trying to salvage what he could from the old colony. Through the unfortunate and self-motivated policies of one of the original trustees, the California colony was foreclosed and liquidated, leaving a slight debt for the Louisiana colony. Without some heroic legal maneuvers by Harriman, the loss would have been greater. In Harriman's absence, the Louisiana colony was led by Ernest Wooster, a journalist who had managed the colony newspaper in California, by Robert K. "Doc" Williams, a popular osteopath, and increasingly by George T. Pickett, who had directed the industrial school in California.

24. *Ibid.*; "Llano in Louisiana," *Western Comrade*, V (Jan.–Feb., 1918), 6–7; *Llano Colonist*, Feb. 25, 1933; Robert K. Williams, "Louisiana-ing Un-de Luxe," *Western Comrade*, V (Jan.–Feb. 1918), 6–8, 37.
25. "Llano's Louisiana Purchase," pp. 6, 8.

Within the first year a bitter power struggle was waged between the Texas and California colonists. Most of the Texans were poorly educated, simple farmers who little understood cooperation. Their leader, in opposition to the Californians, wanted to use colony land for oil speculation. To the expansive, breezy Westerners, the mules and plows of the Texans were utterly primitive, although actually better suited for farming around pine stumps. Frustrated in their desires, angered by the superior air of the Californians, and dismayed at the near poverty, the Texans rebelled, refused to farm, and eventually were forced to leave the colony. But even after agreeing to leave, they fought over the division of property. Actual physical combat in the streets of Leesville led to the arrest of Wooster and Williams, and gave the colony a bad name among the Louisiana neighbors. Meanwhile, the 1918 crop was severely hurt by a drought, most of the industries had to close down, and, by winter, only twelve able-bodied men remained in the colony. The only source of income was the sale of cord wood.[26]

In 1918 the Gulf Lumber Company, recognizing the hardship of the colonists, granted a new and very liberal contract. At a base price of $6 an acre, the colonists agreed to buy 1,000 acres by 1919, another 1,000 in 1920, 2,000 in 1921, and the remainder of approximately 15,000 acres in 1923. The colony had to pay all taxes on the land from the beginning. In these early years in Louisiana the main source of income was gifts from interested friends. An ambitious venture into the broiler business failed when a carload of poor-quality chicks all died. The 1919 crop was destroyed by weeds and wet weather. In addition to the sale of stovewood in Beaumont, some of the small cabins were sold out of sheer necessity. Until the baker left the colony, pastry products were marketed locally, while the livestock was mortgaged to buy needed food. The only certain income was provided by the shoemaker who moved his shop into Leesville. In the midst of poverty and sickness the school remained open only a few hours a day, the women had to do all laundry in open wash tubs, and most colonists who could moved back to California. When a Mexican recruit brought four mules, a freight car of pinto beans and one of broom corn, the colonists ate beans three times daily and made brooms for sale.

26. "Editorial," *Western Comrade*, V (Mar.–Apr., 1918), 5; "As Others See Us," *Western Comrade*, V (Mar.–Apr., 1918), 6–7; "Colony Development," *The Internationalist*, VI (June, 1918), 10; Hanover, "Llano Cooperative Colony," pp. 69–72, 81–82; Wooster, *Communities of the Past and Present*, pp. 128–129; Ernest S. Wooster, "The Colonists Win Through," *Sunset Magazine*, LIII (Sept., 1924), 30–32.

The shelves of the colony store contained only chile con carne and toilet paper. By the fall of 1919 only fifteen families remained. In February, 1920, General Manager Wooster could report only one bright spot—some land had been plowed for crops.[27]

In 1920 the Llano colony was reorganized. By April, Ernest Wooster, the general manager and vice-president, was willing to give up and liquidate the colony. Meanwhile, George T. Pickett had returned from a "begging" trip to the North in November, 1919, with a most valuable recruit, Theodore Cuno, an elderly but affluent socialist publisher. Cuno's membership for himself and his wife, plus a loan, met the $6,000 payment to the Gulf Lumber Company. Pickett soon assumed the position of general manager. Always a dynamic leader, Pickett, on April 20, 1920, rallied a few of the old members, particularly Ole Synoground, a large, strong Swede who would remain a rock of Gibraltar to the colony, and, in an impassioned speech, urged the people to stay and support the colony. In a showdown of strength with Wooster, Pickett was elected vice-president and virtually took over the complete management of colony affairs. Harriman, who was usually away from the colony, remained president of the corporation.[28]

Pickett centralized the power under himself and a board of directors, directed a concerted campaign for contributions, and began an industrial expansion program. In 1920 a brick kiln and a sawmill opened, both providing needed building materials. By 1921 a dairy was in operation, with the colonists doing without milk in order to sell it in Leesville for needed cash. In 1921 an able socialist editor, Carl "Dad" Gleeser, arrived with full membership fees, ready to begin a weekly newspaper, the *Llano Colonist*, which had been forced to suspend publication soon after the move from California. The printing press was also used for job work, and for the publication of a local parish weekly, which soon was the leading newspaper in Vernon Parish and which won many local friends for the colony. The newspapers and other publications spread the news of Llano to socialists and radicals around the world, and provided an effective means of soliciting needed contributions. To add to the new

27. Hanover, "Llano Cooperative Colony," pp. 81–83; Letter, I. E. Shafer to Robert Synder, Oct. 24, 1919, and letter, Ernest Wooster to Robert Synder, Feb. 20, 1920, in the personal papers of George T. Pickett, Newllano, Louisiana; Wooster, "The Colonists Win Through," pp. 32–33.

28. Wooster, *Communities of the Past and Present*, p. 130; *Llano Colonist*, Mar. 4, 1933; McDonald, *The Llano Co-operative Colony*, p. 25; George T. Pickett to Robert Synder, Apr. 20, 1920, Pickett papers.

growth, the depression of 1921 influenced many unemployed workers to seek a membership at Llano. By the winter of 1921 there were approximately 165 colonists. In 1922 a new colonist provided a loan to construct an electrical plant, while the State of Louisiana pushed a new highway through the colony. By then the school was active, the farm had expanded to 250 acres, and, as always, social life was booming. The colony was prosperous enough to take an option on a rice ranch about seventy-five miles to the south of Leesville, and began there a second unit that was always an asset to the colony. It seemed that the vale of tears had been replaced by the nearest approximation of a boom in the colony's history.[29]

In the history of Llano major crises seemed to develop about every three years. The peaceful period following Pickett's surge to power in 1920 was broken by a new and very involved struggle for power in 1923. Perhaps the foundation of this struggle was the return of ailing President Harriman from a long stay in Brazil. This meant a temporary loss of complete power for Pickett and invited political jealousy. Also, in February, two of the leading socialist journalists in the United States, Kate Richards and Frank O'Hare, picked Llano as a new site for the publication of the *American Vanguard* (formerly the *American Rip Saw*). They were to retain ownership of the magazine for one year, retire its debts, and then turn it over to the colony in exchange for membership. Since it had a circulation of over 20,000 (all possible benefactors of Llano), this seemed a fortunate bargain. Yet, before the year was up, the O'Hares were accused by the Pickett faction of not living up to the bargain.

In December, 1923, William E. Zeuch, an economist from the University of Illinois, selected Llano as a site for a special cooperative college that he had long advocated. Thus, an agreement was reached with the colony, and Commonwealth College began operations in 1924, with prospects for about seventy-five students. The college was granted forty acres of land, and one building was constructed. The students were to contribute twenty-four hours a week to the colony and were to receive free room and board.

Pickett, displeased with the new magazine, left the colony in the fall of 1923 to take a badly needed rest and to receive treatment for a back injury from "Doc" Williams, who had moved to New Jersey. There he raised money for a kindergarten, or "Kid Kolony," and returned in March, 1924, prepared for a showdown fight with not only Harriman and the

29. *Llano Colonist*, Mar. 11, 18, 1933; Hanover, "Llano Cooperative Colony," pp. 91, 96.

O'Hares, but also with Zeuch, who, to Pickett, seemed to be using the college to control the colony. In a sixty to forty assembly vote in June, 1924, Pickett won over his opponents and, according to a prior agreement, the losers left the colony. Commonwealth College moved to Mena, Arkansas, where it was to survive a turbulent career in the thirties. The Harriman supporters also took their share of the colony assets to Arkansas, where they established a new colony which soon failed. Harriman, now very ill with tuberculosis and completely disillusioned with Llano, died back in California in 1925.[30]

Harriman's years of personal leadership at Llano, years of endless bitterness and strife, of duplicity and betrayal, had changed many of his ideas about people, cooperation, and Marxism. He had found many colonists who were good on cooperative theory, but almost all of them had been poor on practice. Most of the colonists had been selfish, arrogant, egotistical, and lazy, beginning work late, quitting early, talking much, and criticizing always. Almost everyone wanted the best house and the most furniture. Neither the class nor the philosophy of a colonist seemed to affect their ability to cooperate. Economic determinism could not separate the sheep from the goats, for many of the poor colonists were the most selfish and some of the best colonists came from a wealthy background. Harriman decided that his own materialistic philosophy had not proved sufficient to the facts. Possibly reverting to some of the ideas of his youth, when he trained for the ministry, he decided that ethical behavior was based on an inner "spiritual nature," and not on intellect or on economic institutions.[31]

Harriman had discovered the complexity of cooperative colonies. He found that prospective members should be carefully selected, with moral and ethical tests, and a probationary period. Children within the colony should be trained for the high ethical concern necessitated by close cooperation. Although a cooperative society permits more leisure time, it also invites irresponsibility on the part of many, and selfish glory seeking on the part of a few ambitious and active men. In such close human relationships, strife is difficult to avoid even with the best colonists. But Harriman never doubted that for those who can meet the demands of such a society, the rewards are more than worth the effort. At Llano were found the finest

30. Hanover, "Llano Cooperative Colony," p. 98; McDonald, *The Llano Co-operative Colony*, pp. 31–38; *Llano Colonist*, Mar. 25, 1933.

31. Wooster, *Communities of the Past and Present*, pp. 126–127; Job Harriman, "Introduction" to Wooster, *Communities of the Past and Present*, pp. iv–vii.

friendships and the most delightful relationships of life. To him, the intimate relationships of communal living more closely corresponded to the gregarious nature of man than those in a free enterprise system. Community living removes the economic shackles on feelings and emotions and requires the discipline of self-control, the essence of character building. Harriman had discovered that the greatest danger to such a community as Llano was a dogmatic attitude instead of kindly feelings toward others. "The moment an idea becomes more important than the welfare of the humblest being, that moment the individual who entertains the idea enters upon the dogmatic highway."[32]

After Pickett obtained control in Louisiana, Llano became even more communal. The wage or work credit system used in California was abolished and an experiment with aluminum script was soon terminated. Each colonist had to work forty-eight hours a week at some task suited to his abilities, and received the necessities of life plus any luxuries that the colony could afford (these were few). All means of production were owned by the colony, but members were permitted to keep personal possessions and, if married, were granted the free use of a house or, more nearly in many cases, a shack. A few even grew vegetable gardens in their small yards, although all such work had to be on their own time. Most of the single men either lived in newly-constructed barracks or in the centrally located hotel, which contained the large dining room and kitchen. Everyone was supposed to eat the same food, but families could carry the food from the communal kitchen to their homes. The colony assumed complete responsibility for members, from education to postage stamps, from health services to final interment in the communal cemetery. In theory, a person could spend a lifetime in Llano and never need a penny of money. Of course, the colony itself continued to use money in all its dealings with the outside and, in practice, many members retained some money beyond their membership fee or received some income from outside sources. This they freely spent in Leesville or even in the colony store. A few members retained real estate and bank accounts outside the colony, even though Pickett usually tried to borrow these assets for the colony.

Under Pickett the ideals behind Llano became even more general and vague, while the membership became more and more heterogeneous. In California practically every colonist had been a socialist. The first May Days were celebrated to the playing of "The Red Flag" and the flying

32. *Ibid.*, p. x; see also pp. vii–ix.

of more red flags than in any other United States community, the number
being limited only by the lack of crimson material. At one election every
colonist turned out to vote, and to a man voted socialist.[33] Pickett was a
proclaimed socialist, but he never defined socialism in other than cooperative terms, was never an important leader in the American Socialist
Party, and was scarcely interested in the fate of socialism as a political
movement. His campaigns for Llano were directed as much at gentle,
pacifist Christian ministers as at tough-minded Marxists. His clever
propaganda utilized the motif of the Golden Rule rather than the revolutionary threats of the Communist Manifesto. But his dedication to Llano
was never in doubt. Along with the more enthusiastic colonists, he saw
Llano as just the beginning of a world movement, as only the first unit
in a coming cooperative commonwealth that would encompass all mankind. This ultimate faith, though often blind to fact, was a solace in the
many periods of adversity. As one colonist expressed it: "Ours is the new
era. The real civilization! We are bonded together, the few elect, who will
lead the grand parade of freedmen and freedwomen, who shall no longer
suffer from the imbecilities of overlords and their 'spiritual,' military,
'legal,' and economic tools of oppression. This is now our mode of self-
expression, and by our example we will teach the inert multitude of the
unenlightened to join actual freedom's procession."[34] The ideals of
Llano were best summarized in the Declaration of Principles, which
remained as an abbreviated constitution:

> The rights of the community shall be paramount over those of any individual.
> Liberty of action is permissible only when it does not restrict the liberty of
> another.
> Things used productively must be owned collectively.
> Law is a restriction of liberty and is just only when operating for the benefit
> of the community at large.
> Values created by the community shall be vested in the community alone.
> The individual is not justly entitled to more land than is sufficient to satisfy
> a reasonable desire for peace and rest. Productive land held for profit shall not
> be held by private ownership.
> Talent and intelligence are benefits which should rightly be used in the service
> of others. The development of these by education is the gift of the community
> to the individual, and the exercise of greater ability entitles none to the false
> reward of greater possessions, but only to the joy of greater service to others.

33. "Colony Celebrates Anniversary," *Western Comrade*, III (May, 1915), 15; "Cooperative Colony Shows Rapid Growth," *Western Comrade*, II (Dec., 1914), 16–17.
34. *Llano Colonist*, Dec. 3, 1927.

Only by identifying his interests and pleasures with those of others can man find real happiness.

The duty of the individual to the community is to develop ability to the greatest degree possible by availing himself of all educational facilities and to devote the whole extent of that ability to the service of all.

The duty of the community to the individual is to administer justice, to eliminate greed and selfishness, to educate all, and to aid in time of age or misfortune.[35]

Llano never required any ideological test for membership, although members were asked to subscribe to the Declaration of Principles and to express a belief in "integral" cooperation. Throughout the twenties a majority of converts were at least mild socialists. Some were also strong agragarians, seeing in Llano an example of the back-to-the-land movement. Many who came were as much enthused about pacifism as about economic injustices. A conscientious objectors' union organized in 1928 contained up to 115 members, or most adults in the colony.[36] The Llano press was a center for the publication of pacifist literature. Politically, the colonists who expressed an opinion remained overwhelmingly socialist until the depression. For the election of 1928, a straw vote showed only one colonist each backing Hoover and Smith, while twenty-four supported Norman Thomas and four backed William Z. Foster, the Communist Party candidate. After the depression of 1929, many new members flocked to Llano for purely economic reasons, and slowly modified the political radicalism. In 1932 Roosevelt received thirteen straw votes, Hoover three, and Norman Thomas fifty-five. By 1935 Roosevelt led Norman Thomas in a popularity vote by seventy-nine to twenty-eight; Foster had only two votes, and Huey Long a surprising thirty-eight.[37] Before the depression, Pickett disclaimed any interest in the "political game" and discouraged colonists from participating in either of the major parties. Party loyalty was listed with religious sentiments as a useless carry over from the teaching of youth. Major party candidates were equally denounced as tools of the capitalist class.[38]

The Llano colony moved to Louisiana at the same time as the Soviet

35. Bob (Robert Carlton) Brown, *Can We Co-operate?* (New York: Roving Eye Press, 1940), p. 171. Also published often in the *Llano Colonist* and in colony pamphlet literature.

36. *Llano Colonist*, Jan. 12, 1929, Dec. 15, 1928.

37. *Ibid.*, Nov. 10, 1928, Sept. 16, 1933; Hanover, "Llano Cooperative Colony," p. 185.

38. *Llano Colonist*, May 19, 1928.

Revolution occurred in Russia. Critics of Llano could always point to certain similarities between the huge national experiment in the Soviet Union and the miniature commune in the pine forests of Louisiana. At Llano the prevalent attitude toward the Soviet Union was one of intense interest and unashamed sympathy. The *Colonist* carried glowing, full-page articles on the "New Russia," while the colony always contained a few Communist Party members. As late as 1933 a Worker's Study Club was formed by the Marxist element and was able to attract a large number of colonists to discussions of Marxist philosophy and the Soviet experiment, "the crowning achievement of scientific government."[39] Marxist literature was frequently published and the accepted title of address within the colony was always "comrade." Yet the more radical Marxists and Communist Party members were an embarrassment to Pickett, and were often disliked by the more orthodox colonists. According to one visitor, some members asked the Worker's Study Club to apologize to the Leesville American Legion for tacking up a red flag in honor of the Soviet Union.[40] In any case, radicals hurt the reputation of the colony and were resented by Pickett, who tried to maintain excellent public relations. Pickett personally backed Upton Sinclair and helped form a Sinclair Club in the colony. Without doubt, it was much closer to the prevalent opinion than the Marxist groups.[41]

In addition to an interest in the Soviet Union, the Llano colonists identified themselves with the world-wide cooperative movement and with democratic socialist and labor parties in other countries. The *Colonist* carried a complete cooperative news section each week. Yet, Llano was endlessly condemned by the more conservative Co-operative League of America, and had few connections with the consumer co-operative movement. In the twenties a journalist of the British Labor Party supplied the *Colonist* with a weekly, full-page report on British politics, while an Australian laborite supplied similar reports for a briefer time. Llano had active supporters in most countries of the world. A Llano discussion group met regularly in England, published a bulletin, planned colonies, and contributed a few members to Llano. Subscriptions to the *Colonist* were received from every major country, with extensive interest being manifested in India. There was a tendency for foreigners to be more enthused about the colony than Americans, and

39. *Ibid.*, Nov. 25, 1933.
40. Brown, *Can We Co-operate?* p. 167.
41. *Llano Colonist*, June 9, 1934.

it was undoubtedly better known in England than in the United States.[42]

In one way or another Llano was related to practically every communal colony or adventure in the twentieth century, with the Hutterites almost alone excepted. The pacifistic Doukhobors of British Columbia sent regular letters to the *Colonist*, and received sympathetic support. A son of one colonist attended the organic school in the single-tax colony at Fairhope, Alabama. Gerald Geraldson, of the Brotherhood House in New York City, supplied Llano with badly needed shipments of old clothes. Several English garden city exponents inquired about Llano, and one leading colonist left Sir Ebenezer Howard's Welwyn Garden City to join what he hoped would be the true heaven on earth.[43] Some of the older colonists had been at Ruskin or at the early cooperative commonwealths in the State of Washington. Long articles described the Amana Colony in Iowa, while Sherwood Eddy contributed detailed articles on his Delta Co-operative Plantation in Mississippi.[44] The depression-motivated but unsuccessful Jewish colony at Sunrise, Michigan, rendered periodical reports to Llano, which it adopted as a model. The many communities of the New Deal were not only described by the *Colonist*, but Pickett spent years trying to get government aid for Llano. Ernest Wooster, the former manager of Llano, wrote one of the most comprehensive descriptions of utopian communities in his *Communities of the Past and Present*, which was published at Llano.[45] Thus, Llano was never blind to the experiences of other similar experiments, but seemingly failed to learn from them a few obvious and necessary lessons.

The Llano schism of 1924 was followed by two relatively calm years of slow growth. A Kid Kolony building was completed in partial fulfilment of Pickett's dream of a large nursery-kindergarten. The most successful of all Llano's many industries, a modern ice plant, was completed in 1925. The colony purchased and methodically salvaged a nearby lumber village (Cravens, Louisiana), using the lumber and brick for construction in the colony. A new industrial building, which included a store, garage, and machine shop, was completed in 1925, only to be

42. See almost any copy of the *Llano Colonist* in the late twenties. Also see the following articles in *Co-operation*, the official organ of the Co-operative League of America: G. D. Coleman, "Truth About the Llano Co-operative Colony of Louisiana," IX (Aug., 1923), 132–133; "The Llano Colony Again," XIII (Mar. 1927), 49–50.

43. *Llano Colonist*, Jan. 12, 1929, June 16, 1928, Oct. 13, 1928, Jan. 17, 1931.

44. *Ibid.*, Oct. 29, 1927, Nov. 12, 1927, June 6, 1936.

45. Wooster, *Communities of the Past and Present*.

destroyed by a disastrous, $100,000 fire that may have been set by some
dissident colonist.[46] By 1926 there were over 250 people in the colony,
but not all happy people. In July Pickett left for a three-months vacation
and business trip. While he was gone a rebellion was organized against his
leadership, leading to a civil war, a receivership for the colony, and a long
but successful court fight by Pickett's forces.

After the court fight ended in 1928, Llano remained outwardly calm
in spite of a cauldron of underlying discontent which broke out in new
rebellions in 1932 and 1935. The population of about two hundred remained stable until 1930, when the depression forced scores to seek the
security that Llano seemed to offer. Up to a dozen new colonists arrived
each day during one period.[47] Many of the new converts to cooperation
brought needed skills, but a majority scarcely understood the meaning of
complete cooperation, only adding to the housing and food problems and
creating new reasons for dissatisfaction and discontent. By Christmas,
1930, there were over five hundred colonists, a number that would
fluctuate often and slowly decline by 1937. To meet the expanded population, new school buildings, a few new homes, and a new hotel were
constructed. The electrical and water systems were expanded beyond
capacity, and another very destructive fire ravaged the colony in March,
1931.[48]

As fully developed, Llano was impressive in its size but depressing in
its lack of beauty. The completed colony lay on both sides of the parallel
road and railroad that led northward to Leesville. Going north, the village
to the right of the road contained few residences, but almost all of the
industrial buildings. Here was the warehouse, the office of the general
manager, a small depot, a post office, the laundry, the all-important ice
plant, the sawmill, the veneer plant, the lumber yards, the boilers that
supplied both power and steam, and, after the influx of population, a new,
but scarcely attractive, apartment hotel. Most of the colonists lived to the
left of the road. The village proper, with its few new homes and many
unpainted sawmill shacks, covered a sloping hillside and the pine woods
beyond. The village included two schoolhouses, a small park and baseball
diamond, a two-story hotel and dining room, the waterworks, a small
hospital or clinic, the store, a filling station, shoe and tailor shops, and,
in the thirties, a new tourist camp. The two most impressive buildings

46. *Llano Colonist*, Apr. 8, 1933, Apr. 30, 1932.
47. *Ibid.*, Sept. 27, 1930.
48. *Ibid.*, Jan. 10, 1931, Mar. 14, 1931.

were at the north of the village and near the highway. One huge, eighty-foot-square, concrete drying shed was converted into three lower sections —a theater, a cabinet shop, and a sweet-potato-drying kiln. The top was turned into a roof garden and dance floor. The other building was a smaller, two-story building used to house the printing equipment. Stretching for several miles to the west of the village were pine and hardwood forests, farms, and scattered dwellings. One road led westward to the Kid Kolony, to Pickett's home, and on to the main farm and dairy. Another led westward to an orchard, tree nursery, and the hog ranch. Despite the electric and water systems, Llano's streets remained unpaved and, in winter, were thick with mud. Most of the houses were small, unpainted, and heated with wood stoves. Bathrooms were rare.[49]

Well before the last surge of growth in the thirties, Llano was facing grave financial and governmental problems, but was always enjoying a busy and widely acclaimed social life. Before turning to these separate facets of Llano life, it is worth noting that in the thirties Llano set an endurance record not only among the cooperative commonwealth colonies but among all nonreligious communitarian colonies in the United States. Ironically, it established this record at a time when the belief in a future cooperative commonwealth had almost completely disappeared, and when it was slowly but surely dying even in the minds of all but a few of the Llano colonists.

49. See map in *Llano Colonist*, Apr. 7, 1934, and in many other issues. The description is in large part based upon a personal visit to the old colony site in 1959.

VI. Utopia and Authority

The Llano colony never solved the related problems of leadership and government. Its history was constantly marred by jealousy, factionalism, and even revolution. A communitarian society necessitates a high degree of organization, with vastly more rules and regulations than exist in a more individualistic setting. As in the case of the Hutterites, a community can become an efficient, fully integrated, corporate unit or, more likely, it can degenerate into a faction-ridden, completely inefficient, incoherent mass of conflicting opinions. As a rule, the more property held in common the greater the possibility of conflict. Without the authority of a total creed, only able leadership or a strong, even dictatorial, government can insure success. But these are very difficult to achieve in a highly idealistic and completely voluntary community. Most governments exercise authority over a relatively captive constituency, but at Llano the colony leaders always had to rely upon the voluntary support of the colonists. Even the most able policies could be opposed by a minority who were free to complain or, ultimately, to leave the colony. Thus it was an impossible task to hold the colony together without continuous friction.

Llano, in keeping with most past communitarian experiments in the United States, proposed to combine political democracy with a socialist economy. The implications seemed obvious. The scope of individual participation in public policy would be broadened, simply because the government would now own and direct all of the economy. The worker was to achieve his age-old dream—he would elect his own boss and own his own shop. The few distant, impersonal capitalists who had always monopolized the power of economic decisions (the most important decisions of all) would be replaced by all the people, acting either directly or through elected representatives. Of course, elected officials would exercise more power than in a capitalist society, but this power would be exercised for the electorate and not for small private groups.

When theory is translated into practice, problems always develop in a socialist colony. A poor choice by the electorate, or a mistaken policy by an official, can be much more disastrous than in a capitalist society where governmental decisions less often affect the economic sources of liveli-

hood. Could the mass of colonists be trusted to select the best officials
or to make the best policy decisions? Could a democratic government
ever achieve a highly efficient, integrated productive unit? Perhaps
experience would bear out the insight of Marx. Perhaps only a dictatorial
minority, with a clear grasp of colony ideals and economic actualities,
could be safely entrusted with the management of the young community.
But yet, without any ultimate sovereignty and without the power of
physical coercion, any minority would have to use persuasion to carry
out its policies in a socialist Llano.

In organization, Llano was always a corporation. Legally, its government was always exercised by a nine-member board of directors elected
annually by the stockholders. Since stock ownership was limited to two
thousand shares, and since all permanent members of the colony had to
become shareholders, the annual election was, at least on the surface, as
democratic as in any cooperative. Until 1923 the colonists always elected
Job Harriman as president of the board of directors, which gave him
virtual control over major policies. Yet, at least in California, the actual
direction of colony affairs was almost always delegated by the board to
various other governmental bodies. The directors were content to remain
in the background, serving mainly as a court of last appeal.

During the California years the exuberant colonists experimented with
several different systems of government, some of which ran concurrently.
From the beginning the board of directors appointed a superintendent to
manage the colony economy. This office became permanent, although
later designated as general manager. During most of the colony's history
there were also departmental managers or foremen working directly
under the superintendent. But this was only the beginning. In the first
year of Llano the colonists approved an elaborate constitution and in-
stituted a general assembly as the instrument of popular rule. The
general assembly (all over 18 voted) provided an outlet for discussing all
the pet projects and theories of both idealists and crackpots, gave the
many vocal members a chance to talk, forced one superintendent after
another to resign, permitted detailed public criticism and censure of
members, debated elaborate new constitutions or amendments, and made
endless laws that were rarely enforced. As many later remembered it, the
general assembly degenerated into a mass dictatorship, without conscience
or intelligence. To some, and particularly to those in positions of authority,
it seemed to be a sinister body, constituted for the purpose of colony
politicians, dissidents, spies, visionaries, and troublemakers. In the words

of one colony leader, it "was democracy rampant, belligerence unrestrained; an inquisition, a mental pillory, a madhouse of meddlesomeness and attempts at business, a jumble of passions and idealism—and all in deadly earnest."[1] The assembly met fortnightly, with uproarious sessions lasting to 2:00 A.M. Yet, despite endless quarrels and up to a dozen critical resolutions at each meeting, there was never any violence. To all those who later opposed the more dictatorial government in the colony, the much-lamented general assembly was remembered as a lost but desirable ideal.[2]

In early 1915 the colonists approved a revised constitution which established the most elaborate government ever attempted in the colony (or perhaps in any colony). In addition to the nine-member board of directors, the superintendent and foremen, and the general assembly, the constitution provided for a nine-member community commission or legislative body to make laws and to be in "charge of affairs." In addition, the general assembly elected a five-member (*sic*) tribunate (the executive branch), two censors (a board of survey), and two advocates (to protect the people).[3] This elaborate system did not last a year, but rather led to a reaction in behalf of simplicity and efficiency. By 1916 the actual administration was in the hands of the managers of the various departments, who met every evening in a type of industrial council. Each decision of the council automatically superseded the last; no records were kept and no official motions were entertained. In 1917 the general assembly solemnly voted to abolish the general assembly. The book-length constitution was burned, with only the declaration of principles being salvaged.[4]

The experiments in pure democracy gave outlet to, but did not eliminate the cause of, dissatisfaction within the colony. Many came to the colony expecting four dollars a day and a nice home. They found only a meager diet, a scarcity of even canvas homes, a commissary that could furnish only the bare necessities, endless hard work, and work credits that would never be redeemed. Some who invested a hard-earned

1. Ernest Wooster, "They Shared Equally," *Sunset Magazine*, LIII (July, 1924), 81.

2. Fred Hanover, "Llano Cooperative Colony: An American Rural Community Experiment" (unpublished M.A. Thesis, Tulane University, 1936), pp. 62–63; *Llano Colonist*, Jan. 28, 1933; "Colonists Clear and Plant Community Land," *Western Comrade*, II (Mar., 1915), 17.

3. "Colonists Clear and Plant Community Land," p. 17.

4. "Gateway to Freedom," *Western Comrade*, IV (June–July, 1916), 3; *Llano Colonist*, Jan. 28, 1933.

$1,000 in unrealized expectations were bitterly disappointed. Others were just as disappointed when the colony failed to give them a voice in its affairs or refused to adopt their own pet schemes. With the perspective of time, Job Harriman became a hallowed figure, with almost everyone willing to testify to his character, intelligence, and idealism. But it was he who received the brunt of the early criticism. In 1915 a dissident group organized a welfare league to resist the policies of the management. About a dozen had their work contracts canceled and were given only twenty-four hours to leave the colony, leading to the transposed title "Farewell League." Thirty-two members of the league resigned, accusing Harriman of being a dictator. It was this same group that complained to the California Commissioner of Corporations, leading to an embarrassing investigation and the necessity of reincorporation in Nevada.[5]

As disappointed colonists either resigned or were forced out of the colony, they reformed their welfare league in Los Angeles, directing a bitter tirade of propaganda against the colony. From 1915 on there was always at least one opposition group outside the colony, plus frequent organized revolts within. Since many of the early members of the welfare league wore bits of sagebrush for identification, the name "brush gang" was always used to designate all those who opposed the existing management. Fortunately, with time, the loyal colonists accepted the inevitability of such opposition and laughed as much as cried over the terrible doings of the "brush gang."[6]

After the fateful move to Louisiana in 1917, Llano lost most of its faithful members and almost died away in 1920. During these years of hardship, colonists usually left because of economic privation and not because of management policies. Some remained loyal to the Llano ideal, returning later when conditions improved. The only bitter struggle was with the Texas colonists, who were soon forced out of the colony. After this period of gloom, and after the reorganization in 1920, General Manager George T. Pickett assumed almost complete control over colony policies. From 1920 until the final liquidation of Llano in 1938, everything in Llano revolved around the personality and policies of this one

5. Ernest Wooster, "Bread and Hyacinths," *Sunset Magazine*, LIII (Aug., 1924), 59; Archie Roy Clifton, "A Study of Llano del Rio Community in the Light of Earlier Experiments in Practical Socialism" (unpublished M.A. Thesis, University of Southern California, 1918), pp. 48–49, 51, 64; Hanover, "Llano Cooperative Colony," p. 54.

6. Clinkenbeard Clews, "Llano—A Soul Laboratory," *The Internationalist*, VI (June, 1918), 12–13; *Llano Colonist*, Jan. 28, 1933.

man. In fact, to many people, Llano and Pickett were inseparable. Even in those periods when Pickett temporarily lost his controlling position, he still was the dominant figure. He was the most loved man and the most hated man in the history of Llano. He was either an inspired and self-sacrificing leader or an unfair dictator; either a saint in the religion of cooperation or a traitor to the whole socialist movement.

Pickett was born in Iowa in 1876, in a poor family that included six boys. After his father died on a new claim in Oregon, young Pickett moved with his mother to Falls City, Nebraska, where he eventually completed high school. As he remembered his childhood, he began earning his own way at eight years of age by selling garden produce, shining shoes, doing janitorial work, and, at fourteen, by working as a barber. He was always proud of this vocational training, using it to justify his own educational policies. As a boy he joined the Christian Church (as had Harriman), but later revolted against religion. He forsook a college education to become a baseball and football coach and to teach dancing and physical culture. This also was to be a lifelong interest. In his early twenties he left coaching and sold insurance in California, developing expert techniques in salesmanship and, in his estimation, was earning $1,900 a month when he gave up everything to join Llano in 1914.[7]

When Job Harriman founded Llano, Pickett was already a convinced socialist, living on a small farm near Fresno, California, where he and his close friend, Robert K. "Doc" Williams, had been planning a small cooperative colony. Pickett investigated Llano at Harriman's invitation and in behalf of a group of interested socialists at Fresno. His visit fired his enthusiasm—an enthusiasm that was never to waver. He, his first wife, and "Doc" Williams not only joined Llano, but almost immediately began proselytizing new members. Pickett was never again to make his home outside the colony or the old site of the colony.[8]

In California Pickett spent some time traveling about as a missionary for Llano, but soon became the principal educator within the colony. He formed a work gang of boys from seven to fourteen and used them to repair colony roads. Since only Pickett could be induced to assume the difficult task of managing these almost uncontrollable children, he was highly praised in the colony for his work. He soon acquired the title of director of physical culture and playgrounds, giving the children instruc-

7. Hanover, "Llano Cooperative Colony," Appendix A (no pages given); personal interviews with George T. Pickett in the summer of 1959.

8. Hanover, "Llano Cooperative Colony," pp. 94–95; *Llano Colonist*, Jan. 3, 1931.

tion in games, dancing, and physical culture when not directing their work activities. His Thursday night dancing class became a colony institution. Pickett slowly expanded his work with children into a unique educational endeavor. With the help of his wife, who worked with the girls, Pickett used the labor of children to establish a separate little colony, which offered the youngsters high adventure, constructive work, and instruction in various skills. The children built their own classrooms and living quarters, grew their own vegetables, and attended their own special classes. Unlike the regular county schools in the colony, the instructors at Pickett's school did not have to have teacher's certificates. Soon over fifty students were enrolled, combining a half day of classroom instruction with their actual work in their colony. Since Pickett liked goats almost as much as children, they too were moved to the children's colony, where they lent their name to the new institution. From then until the end of Llano in Louisiana, Pickett's special school was called the "Kid Kolony." Pickett loved his school almost as much as the colony, and often talked of resigning as general manager in order to develop a larger Kid Kolony for orphans. In Louisiana he always lived at, or near, the Kid Kolony and closely supervised its activities.[9]

Pickett rose to power in the Louisiana colony primarily because of his ability as a salesman, both within and without the colony. Just before he became general manager he saved the colony from disaster by a successful "begging" trip to the North. It was his enthusiasm and optimism that won him the important election in 1920 and which encouraged the last wavering colonists to remain in the colony. It was his organizational ability, plus his unexcelled role as a propagandist, that enabled the colony to progress in the early twenties. Pickett did not have the temperament for philosophical speculation and hated all theories. Yet he was very interested in economics and particularly in problems of human relations. A determined advocate of cooperation and economic justice, he was always quite flexible about the means to be used in achieving the new society. Although a socialist by conviction, he never tried to formulate a precise and dogmatic definition of socialism. During the same depression years that he tried to organize Louisiana for the Townshend Movement (even being

9. See the following articles by Robert K. Williams: "Snow Caps Greet Colonists," *Western Comrade, III* (Nov., 1915), 18; "Improvements at Llano," *Western Comrade*, III (Mar., 1916), 18; "A Trip over the Llano," *Western Comrade*, IV (June–July, 1916), 11–12. Also see Ernest Wooster, "What Two Years Have Wrought," *Western Comrade*, IV (May, 1916), 19; "Our Industrial School," *Western Comrade*, IV (Jan., 1917), 19–20; *Llano Colonist*, Aug. 3, 1929.

a candidate for Congress), he expressed open admiration of Huey Long and praised Franklin Roosevelt for moving as rapidly as possible toward a collective economy. If expedient, he could denounce communists in the colony and woo capitalists for monetary support. Although not a believer in Christianity himself, he always claimed the Golden Rule as the principal motto of the colony.

Pickett so loved power and responsibility that he had to be in the center of things. He could not bear subordinate roles. He was a small man in size (a little Napoleon said some), and had thin, sharp features. Yet his personality was almost irresistible. He could on occasion persuade even those who hated him, and all his foes respected his indomitable courage and his dogged determinism. He loved a good fight. He welcomed all disciples, and was happiest with children or with docile old folks. He would never tolerate those who challenged his power or defied his will. Pickett tended to view all the colonists as children, and himself as the great protector or father. He craved recognition and, when away from the colony, dressed and acted like a man of affairs. Even at the colony he had a privileged position, with better food, good clothes, and, ultimately, a very nice house. As many another socialist leader, he had a poorly concealed respect for men of wealth and power, for the "hated capitalists." Except for their "immorality," they were his type and his equal, unlike the faddists and theorists, the poor, broken, and meek old people, the pure idealists, the misanthropes and misfits who flocked to Llano. If these groups would work hard, obey, and be duly appreciative, Pickett welcomed them and rejoiced in his opportunity to help them. If they came with the idea of helping determine policy, George Pickett had no use for them. They were his enemies.[10] One visitor gave the following critical but perceptive characterization of Pickett:

He is an outspoken, democratic little man, kind to kids, old folks and hard-workers who don't complain. "I'd rather work with a bunch of morons," he says, "than with a lot of over-educated kickers." And obviously that's because morons are easiest led, for George honestly thinks he's leading them not only for their own good, but that of the world. He's sold himself on that. So while straining at molehills he makes heroic faces and Atlas-like shoulder shrugs as though he's actually moving mountains of competitive wrongs right off the face of this faulty old earth-ball, while the ancient and rusty co-operators stand on the sidelines and cheer, leaning on him quite naturally and wobbling only

10. Bob Brown, *Can We Co-operate?* (New York: Roving Eye Press, 1940), pp. 132–133.

slightly for fear somebody will snatch away the only support they have left. They are mostly tired socialists, wornout idealists, the static kind who call themselves "tired radicals."[11]

Although Pickett loved a position of authority, he was no hypocrite and no mere opportunist. His abilities would have insured him wealth and position in the bourgeois world that he condemned out of sincere conviction. As most successful politicians, he craved respect and even adulation, but at the same time felt a need to use his talents in behalf of a new, perfected social order. He was both a reformer and a savior. His Llano was more than a struggling, impoverished colony in the barren pine woods of Louisiana; it was a socialist version of the City of Zion. Here the first faithful, struggling saints had gathered; soon the whole world would emulate Llano, and Pickett, the savior, and all his loyal disciples, would receive their due honor, and Llano would complete itself as a glorious, cooperative heaven. As a savior, Pickett felt that no one could lead the flock as well as he. The burden of Llano, and thus the burden of struggling mankind for which Llano was the one symbol of hope, was on his shoulders. He gave all for Llano, and had no other love. He fought for Llano, and at times fought unfairly. The end was too great for one to be overly concerned with means. To him, Llano was a body, an organism, and George C. Pickett was its head. Without the head the body would wither and die. Pickett may well have been correct, for without his strong, even dictatorial, leadership, Llano might have died long before it did.

Pickett had some weaknesses that hurt the colony. He was not a good businessman or administrator, and never really claimed to be. The records of the colony were incomplete and misleading. Except for one occasion, and then only because of outside intervention, Pickett never allowed even a preliminary audit of the colony's finances. He avowed his distrust of all bookkeepers and kept many financial details secret, or else manipulated them to suit propaganda purposes. Many of his judgments were questionable from an economic standpoint. His decision to expand Llano by adding new units was the main reason for ultimate bankruptcy. At times he seemed more interested in developing the largest and most impressive possible number of industries rather than in developing prosperous industries. He tended to neglect agriculture, and spent needed colony funds on fantastic ventures, such as oil exploration. He was quite hasty and definite in some of his judgments of other people and thus,

11. *Ibid.*

following heart instead of head, accepted people who later hurt the colony or who were unable to make any real contribution. He was also a faddist, and pursued certain fads (purgative showers, dislike of heavy meats in the diet, and an interest in osteopaths and naturopaths) to the detriment of the colony.

Soon after gaining power, Pickett centralized all authority in the general manager (himself) and the board of directors. The only constitution was the vague declaration of principles. The GM (as the general manager was called in the colony) selected the foremen of the various departments and assigned the workers to their various tasks or departments. The daily work in the colony was planned in regular foremen's meetings. Although appointed by the board of directors, Pickett almost always dominated this body and, in addition, was always a member. The board was elected each October, with various members of the board automatically serving as department heads. This meant that it closely corresponded to an industrial council or a city commission. Legally, the board had to be elected by a quorum of stock, but after the move from California so many stockholders lost contact with the colony that a quorum was always an impossibility, despite requests for proxy votes by both Pickett and his opponents. Thus, as a court later affirmed, Llano had no legal board at all, since it was always elected by a small minority of the voting stock. Until Harriman left the colony in 1924, the board was a deliberative body that was able to exercise real control even over Pickett. After 1924 it always contained good friends of Pickett's, and thus was an instrument of his authority.

In spite of the centralization of power in Pickett, Llano was never a formal dictatorship, for the forms of democracy were retained. Yet, as in the Soviet Union, democracy was a one-party affair, in this case Pickett's party. The annual election was limited to full members, and thus excluded all recent arrivals who had not yet worked out their full amount of stock in the corporation (almost always one year). Very few of Pickett's enemies remained in the colony long enough to obtain voting rights, but these few always nominated an opposition slate of candidates. The election was held on a Sunday afternoon, with Pickett himself (although GM and a member of the board) always serving as chairman. The old board automatically stood for reelection, with additional nominations from the floor (either pro- or anti-Pickett). Voting was never secret, since Pickett insisted upon a "free and open" ballot. The votes were usually written on a piece of paper and could easily be checked for handwriting. Even if they wanted to, most members were afraid to vote against the Pickett ticket. At best, the colonists had only the freedom of selection from among the Pickett supporters, which was small consolation to those who disliked Pickett and his policies. In each election there tended to be a small turn-over in the board, but only among Pickett's friends, and, often, only as a reflection of changes that he himself desired.[12]

While Harriman was still the nominal head of the colony and in the early days of Pickett's rule, the general assembly was revived, but only under the admitted management of Pickett, who "stripped it of most of its power to damage the process of administration."[13] In 1921 a group of "pure democracy advocates" were given land for their own colony in order to get them out of Llano.[14] The general assembly was then dropped, but in its place Pickett substituted a weekly psychology meeting, which was probably his most effective technique of control. A mixture of a revival, a pep meeting, and a confessional, it demonstrated Pickett's insight into the secrets of leadership. He knew that colonists needed some type of assembly, regardless of the amount of power they exercised. Pickett usually presided at the psychology meeting, delivering inspira-tional talks on the ideals of the colony and occasionally working up so much enthusiasm that derelicts confessed their sins against Llano and the cooperative ideal. Others were brought under the power of deep convic-tion and freely contributed all their savings to Llano or, if visitors, made the final decision to become a colonist. At other times Pickett used the meeting to identify his enemies or to indict the colonists for their failures. He would confess even his own mistakes, permitted great freedom in the discussions, and probably enabled many colonists to work off their basic hostility. Yet, it was primarily the loyal members (loyal to Pickett) who were most conscientious in attending the meeting. Some colonists rarely or never attended, and on this basis were usually identified as anti-Pickett or lacking in the spirit of cooperation. With the absence of any churches, the psychology meeting was the nearest substitute.

Under Pickett Llano became a worldwide movement. Increasingly the very survival of the colony was dependent upon gifts and contributions from the outside. In attracting such support, Pickett had no equal, and it was in recognition of this ability that some idealistic colonists supported him despite their opposition to some of his policies. His main propaganda

12. *Llano Colonist*, Nov. 26, 1927, May 19, 1928, Oct. 26, 1929, Mar. 11, 1933.
13. *Ibid.*, Mar. 11, 1933.
14. *Ibid.*

instrument in the outside world was the colony newspaper—the *Llano Colonist*—which had suspended publication after the move from California, but was begun again in 1921 under the able editorship of Carl Henry "Dad" Gleeser. In addition to being a propaganda sheet for the colony, it became one of the better socialist newspapers in the United States. For several years Pickett personally wrote the most important column, the "Colony Diary," under the pseudonym of "Ye Lady Reporter." Although a day-by-day account of events at Llano, it ignored most of the inadequacies, glorified every success, justified all the actions of Pickett, roundly convicted all of Llano's enemies, and all in all gave a false impression to hundreds of idealistic readers. Yet it was (and is) fascinating reading. Even today it has its desired effect, casting a subtle spell of romance around what must have been a very unromantic colony. Many people, entangled in this spell, contributed money in answer to the continuous requests for aid in some all-important endeavor. Others became so enthusiastic that they came to Louisiana to join the colony. The diary was supplemented by full-page solicitations for either members or contributions, by endless offers to sell land or Llano products, and, at every crisis (Pickett loved a crisis and manufactured one at regular intervals), by front-page articles written by Pickett (or, some said, by his secretary in his name).

The centralized and authoritarian government lessened the possibilities of political factions or even criticism of policies but, with most other avenues of redress securely closed, invited open rebellion. The first revolution occurred in 1926 and 1927, and almost succeeded in deposing Pickett and destroying the colony. The rebellion began while Pickett was away from the colony on a vacation and business trip from July to September, 1926. The able colony postmaster, W. H. Burton, who had been a very close friend of Pickett's, led the revolt and was able to enlist a large anti-Pickett party from among disappointed colonists. After Pickett returned to oppose the rebels, a battle of hot words ended in the Louisiana courts. Burton led off with a $25,000 damage suit against Pickett for defamation of character. More important, another rebel, J. R. Allen, brought suit against the Llano del Rio Company in June, 1927, and succeeded in having a local court issue an injunction against the existing management and appoint a receiver. The general charge was that the corporation had never paid any dividends and that it was insolvent. The receiver took over in July, 1927, but decided to permit the colony to continue operating under his direction. Pickett lost all official authority in the colony, but declared himself a trustee for the Llano movement and solicited gifts to be made out in his own name. At the same time the colony appealed the decision of the lower court, hoping for a favorable opinion from the Louisiana Supreme Court.[15]

The suit against the Llano del Rio Company contained numerous charges, some serious and some ridiculous. In general, Pickett and the other board members were accused of misuse of funds, bogus mortgages, graft, prejudice of minority rights, misrepresentation of conditions in the colony, acts of immorality, default on repayment of funds deposited by stockholders, misuse of machinery and equipment, unprofitable ventures, false procurement tactics, and an unbusinesslike neglect of profits.[16] The accusers alleged that the colony had reduced workers to peons in behalf of the Gulf Lumber Company, and that colonists were poorly fed, wretchedly clothed, and housed in typhus-infested mill huts. The colony schools, with their program of half-work and half-study, had prostituted small children to the nefarious purposes of Pickett, and had further cheated them by employing nondescript teachers and then accepting their salary payments from the state. The most fantastic charges, and those most regretted by the lawyers who were fighting the colony, were those relating to immorality. According to the charge, colony leaders had "advocated the social practice commonly known as 'free-love'—the promiscuous relation of the sexes—the abolition of the family and home life; the regulation by a 'father' of the 'unattached' women of the community according to the demands of the sex desire..."[17] When the immorality charges were easily refuted, the case boiled down to a matter of poor management. On this point, the State Supreme Court, in February, 1928, found that the colony was solvent, in itself an indication of good management, that the colony was clearly a nonprofit organization and therefore not subject to all the businesslike practices of a profit-making corporation, and that the dissenting rebels knew these facts when they came to the colony and therefore freely took the risks involved. Thus the court ruled in favor of George T. Pickett and ended the receivership.[18]

The original injunction against the Llano management forbade the expulsion of any dissident members. Thus, a minor civil war waged in the

15. *Ibid.*, Nov. 26, 1927, Apr. 15, 1933.
16. *Ibid.*, Jan. 28, 1928.
17. *Ibid.*, Feb. 25, 1928.
18. "Allen *v.* Llano del Rio Co.," *Louisiana Reports*, CLXVI (1927–1928), 78–91; "Llano Receivership Reversed," *Cooperation*, XIV (Apr., 1928), 72–73.

colony even as the suit slowly made its way through the courts. New-comers to the colony were accosted by the rebels and, if possible, re-cruited against Pickett. The old management, which retained a loyal majority, was able to keep control of the newspaper, but complained about having to clothe and feed a parasitic group of traitors who were in the process of wrecking the colony. With near-violence within the colony, someone was arrested on trumped up charges almost daily, and the court costs rose alarmingly. Yet, for Pickett, such a major crisis was perfect cause for a fervid appeal for gifts. The *Colonist* carried on a con-tinuous campaign for money to pay the court costs and to save the Llano movement from its enemies. In pessimistic moments, Pickett thought beyond the possible end of the existing Llano, and appealed for funds to buy new land and start a new colony. Among the widespread support enlisted by Pickett, the most significant came from the neighboring town of Leesville, where 130 leading citizens signed a petition in behalf of the colony and the Pickett management. The petition stressed the fact that Llano was a real asset to the area, with its law-abiding, moral citizens. Cynics argued that the local support was based primarily on the lucrative legal fees paid by the colonists to Leesville lawyers.[19]

After the receivership, Pickett tried to rid the colony of critics within and to silence or refute the enemies without. In 1928 he announced that Llano was a monolithic community that required unity instead of com-plaints. He castigated new members for not submitting to order and authority and for not admitting their own mistakes. For the benefit of outside critics, he answered some widely circulated reports that Llanoites were without meat or adequate food, that trucks and machinery were either in poor repair or standing idle, and that the colony was burdened by too many older people. Pickett, a near vegetarian, denied any need for meat in the diet, blamed poor drivers for the truck situation, and praised the old people (they always voted for Pickett) for their needed and willing contributions.[20] Other critics accused Pickett of stock speculation (true), of secrecy concerning colony finances (very true), and for not permitting a constitution to protect the rights of colonists (in part true). Pickett argued that he had made $50,000 for the colony through careful invest-ment, that financial statements would only attract undedicated new colonists who would join only because Llano was a proved success, and that the only constitution Llano needed was the Golden Rule.[21] His

19. *Llano Colonist*, Nov. 26, 1927, Dec. 3, 1927, Dec. 24, 1927, Jan. 21, 1928.
20. *Ibid.*, Sept. 8, 1928.   21. *Ibid.*, Nov. 2, 1929.

somewhat evasive arguments were apparently accepted within the colony. While Pickett was away on one of his many speaking and fund-raising tours in 1931, loyal colonists and devoted friends around the world began contributing to a fund to build Pickett a new house, costing thousands and having the many conveniences befitting his contribution to the cooperative movement. After the house was eventually finished, and after Pickett made the expected protests about its cost, he, his second wife, and young son moved into the truly attractive home (unexcelled in the colony), located next to the Kid Kolony in a nice grove of trees.[22]

Some of Pickett's unpopular policies, plus the appearance of some rebellious, strong-willed young men in the colony, led to an organized attempt in 1932 to restore democracy to Llano. The situation developed in 1931. The *Colonist*, although heavily censored at all times, published a critical letter from a former colonist in order to give Pickett a forum in which to refute some nasty charges. The aggrieved former colonist, who had joined Llano in California and had lived in the colony for over ten years, had discovered on a visit to the Vernon Parish Court house in Leesville that Pickett, and not the Llano del Rio Company, was listed as the sole owner of the colony land. Shocked and angered at what seemed to be some type of fraud, he left Llano, tried to sell his colony stock, and charged that the colony had existed for years on untrue statements and unfulfilled promises in spite of the fact that Pickett had spent millions of begged and borrowed money. An embarrassed Pickett admitted that he had switched some of the land to his name during the receivership trial, and argued that the mortgage holders still preferred it that way. At this time he made no offer to restore the land to the corporation. Instead he made a fund-raising trip to the West and began a campaign for new colonies to care for the unemployed of the depression. This implied a great, national role for Pickett, but threatened a diversion of funds and supplies from the already impoverished mother colony. With this, the colony was ripe for rebellion.[23]

Ernest G. Webb was the principal leader of the new crusade for democracy. He came to the colony in 1931 from California, for the admitted purpose of writing articles about Llano for some newspapers in California. He became the head nurse in the colony infirmary, and began a clever, seemingly inoffensive crusade for popular participation in colony affairs. By the time his crusade had become unbearable to Pickett, he had

22. *Ibid.*, June 6, 1931; Brown, *Can We Co-operate?* p. 131.
23. *Llano Colonist*, June 6, 1931, Sept. 5, 1931, Nov. 7, 1931.

enlisted two allies. Meyer Tuber, who came to Llano with his family in 1930, dared voice his open opposition to the new units proposed by Pickett. Since he had paid his full $2,000 membership fee, and had used his own funds to construct one of the finest homes in the colony, he was a valuable recruit in the campaign against dictatorship. Tuber had invested his savings in the colony, was acknowledged to be an able worker, and apparently wanted to protect the colony against the ill-advised economic policies of Pickett. As a full member of the corporation, he was almost invulnerable to any legal attack, and thus continued to occupy his home and use it as a meeting place for the rebels. The other member of the triumvirate—Walter Groth—was hardly as distinguished. On entering the colony he avowed that he would not trust Pickett with a nickel. When asked to recant or leave, he simply joined with Webb. In March, 1932, Webb organized a colony welfare league for the avowed purpose of advancing the total welfare of the colony. In the organizational meeting, which even Pickett attended, the ever-popular Webb was elected president of the league. In his acceptance speech he declared that Llano was a democratic colony and that the welfare league would provide an avenue of expression for "all that wished to support the management."[24]

Within two months the welfare league was virtually a combined general assembly and colony labor union. It fought for free speech and voted against voluntary Sunday work except in a true emergency, threatening one of Pickett's favorite techniques for completing large work tasks. Pickett, as always, responded to any challenge to his leadership. Using his weekly psychology meeting as a counter forum, he emphatically rejected the idea of a popular assembly or of published financial reports. He threatened to take a "short" vacation for as long as a democratic government would last. He also rejected welfare league proposals for a secret ballot, arguing that this would lead to trickery and cheating in the "one big family" that was Llano. When Pickett openly condemned and threatened Webb and the league in July, 1932, Webb declared a war to the finish, forming a civil liberty bureau to get rid of the "most vicious, untruthful, and incoherent individual within the cooperative movement today."[25] Webb and Groth were officially expelled from the colony, were arrested three times for trespassing on colony property, and finally were forbidden further entry into the colony by a court order. As a result, the

24. *Ibid.*, Mar. 5, 12, 1932.
25. A Welfare League circular, dated July 15, 1932, in the personal papers of George T. Pickett, Newllano, Louisiana.

welfare league set up headquarters and a printing press in Leesville, captured the colony mailing list, flooded the colony and all Llano supporters with bitter anti-Pickett tracts, and even elected their own board of electors for the "true" Llano. They bravely entered their own slate of candidates in the October, 1932, election for the board of directors, although Pickett's forces easily won the election by a vote of ninety-five to thirteen. But it is important to note that, before the election, Pickett deeded eight thousand acres of land back to the corporation in order to allay all unjust suspicions and accusations. The most effective brush gang in the history of Llano was at work.[26]

The challenge from the welfare league led Pickett, for the first time, to declare his open support for dictatorship. He asserted that "there should be no MINORITY in such an organization or enterprise as the colony, for the reason that IT ITSELF IS THE MINORITY," existing within the shell of capitalism. In Marxian language, he demanded a solid, united front, a "solid phalanx," the "utmost loyalty." Minorities, he claimed, could only lead to opposition and attempts to overthrow the existing management. He felt that welfare organizations should construct things during free hours, but "all they ever do is criticize." Any disloyalty in critical times, he averred, was treasonable and could not be tolerated. There could be only one side to the colony, never two. One was either for or against the organization, and those against would have to straighten up or get out.[27]

Pickett argued that he was no dictator, but that he did manage affairs. In his terms: "I really believe that if I were a dictator we would be a greater economic success—in fact, I am sure of it. But I am not altogether working for that."[28] In 1933 he stated: "A dictator who directed the policies of an enterprise or a nation certainly produced better results by far than the rank and file of the people composing the enterprise or the nation."[29] He felt that few voters ever know what they are voting for. As the New Deal was inaugurated in 1933, Pickett voiced a hope that Roosevelt would become an industrial dictator, for only in this way could his will be worked out through Congress.[30]

The welfare league remained active through 1933 and 1934, maintaining its headquarters in Leesville and conducting an unending propaganda campaign against Pickett. This propaganda, plus the depression, virtually

26. *Llano Colonist*, July 16, 1932, Aug. 6, 1932, Oct. 1, 1932, Oct. 22, 1932.
27. *Ibid.*, July 16, 1932.   28. *Ibid.*, Aug. 6, 1932.   29. *Ibid.*, Jan. 28, 1933.
30. *Ibid.*, May 27, 1933.

ended all outside contributions to Llano, but did not alienate the colony from its loyal supporters in Leesville. A petition in support of Pickett and against the welfare league was signed by the mayor and most public officials in the city and parish.[31] And, in a final irony, the welfare league itself suffered from factionalism, with Ernest Webb being expelled. This led to a brush gang within a brush gang. At the colony, endless but unsuccessful efforts to expel all disloyal elements through legal means were abandoned in favor of direct action. Pickett suggested "that a committee of resolute, home-loving members would probably solve the matter and clear the colony of those whose purpose was destruction."[32] Meyer Tuber, whose home had remained the heaquarters of the welfare league within the colony, finally left Llano in 1933, but only after receiving a cash settlement from Pickett.[33]

Even as the welfare league was developing, Pickett was busier than before with his grandiose plans. In addition to new units and oil exploration, he engaged in a long, unsuccessful effort to win governmental support for Llano. This meant long trips to Washington and other parts of the country. As his interests expanded, he surrendered more and more of the actual administration at Llano to his subordinates. By March, 1933, he was talking of resigning as general manager in order to devote all his time to the total Llano movement. In September, he actually turned the direction of the colony over to a nine-member workers' council, headed by a long-time friend, Septer Baldwin.[34] This loosening of control came at a time when the colony was nearest complete destitution, and seething with resentment against outside expenditures by Pickett. The resentment was fanned, and then organized, by a growing number of new, younger members who flocked to Llano to escape the depression and who had no respect for Pickett or, in many cases, for the idealism of the cooperative movement. They came to Llano for what material comfort and security it could offer.

Pickett almost lost control of his colony in 1934. The young people in the colony wanted to commercialize the weekly dances, thus taking in enough money for lights, repairs, and decorations. They also had some hope of using modern dance music and possibly hiring outside orchestras, both of which were anathema to Pickett, who liked only old waltzes and the fox trot.[35] While Pickett was away from the colony, his new workers'

31. *Ibid.*, Jan. 6, 1934.   32. *Ibid.*, July 8, 1933.
33. Hanover, "Llano Cooperative Colony," pp. 106–107.
34. *Llano Colonist*, Mar. 18, 1933, Sept. 2, 1933.
35. Brown, *Can We Co-operate?* p. 207.

council approved a charge of 75¢ for all outsiders attending the Saturday night dances. When Pickett returned and protested, the council reversed itself and revoked the permission. In a mass meeting the colonists voted for commercialization by fifty-seven to thirty-seven. Pickett resigned in anger. Then a meeting of stockholders (fully paid up members) voted sixty-two to thirty-seven in favor of Pickett. With this, Pickett resumed his duties, but only after "the thirteen days that shook the colony" (as they were soon called) and only against the popular will. As a concession, he agreed to lease the roof garden to a group of colony and area youths, but only with a provision that the commercial dances not be sponsored by the colony.[36]

Just before the annual election of the board of directors in October, 1934, a group of colonists met in an angry mass meeting in protest against conditions and policies in the colony. Pickett, always up to any situation, stood up to the crowd and tried to answer all their charges—that he lived in the best house, that he was leasing the sawmill to a private firm, and that the community had not improved in several years. One irate colonist refused to express his feelings toward Pickett because "there were ladies present."[37] Yet when Pickett asked who wanted his job there were no takers. The old management won the election the next day, but a revolution was clearly in the making.

In March, 1935, Eugene Carl came to Llano from Pittsburgh. Only in his middle thirties, Carl was an accomplished bookkeeper, a World War I veteran, a cynic about human nature and women, and an extremely energetic and ambitious colonist. Having left a comfortable, well-paid position in a grocery chain, he was considered a fortunate addition to the colony. With Pickett's blessings, he took over the bookkeeping duties in the colony and was made the executive director of the colony, a new office created especially for Carl. With his education and exceptional ability, he quickly attracted a loyal following among the colony young people and the more recent arrivals. Apparently without the slightest suspicion on the part of Pickett, a new colony leader was finally in a position to lead a successful revolution.[38]

The revolt really began at a colony dance in April, 1935. When Pickett ordered the orchestra to slow the music, an angered young drummer, Henry Davis, protested and verbally insulted Pickett. Since Davis was an ex-convict on parole, he was advised to apologize to Pickett or risk being reported to his parole board. Whether or not Pickett really had any intentions of reporting him or not, the rumor to this effect soon spread through

36. *Llano Colonist*, June 30, 1934, July 7, 1934.   37. *Ibid.*, Nov. 3, 1934.
38. Hanover, "Llano Cooperative Colony," Appendix B (no page numbers given).

the colony. Some of the colonists met in a protest meeting and signed a petition to keep Pickett from sending Davis back to jail. Before the uproar ended, Pickett had to leave the colony on April 24 to go to Washington for some official business. The protest meetings continued, and plans were made.[39]

With the departure of Pickett, Eugene Carl assumed the leadership of the rebellious colonists, and was ably supported by Walter Robinson, a recent arrival, and by several of the older colonists. The actual revolt occurred on May Day in 1935, the twenty-first anniversary of Llano's founding and a holiday in the colony. At a large mass meeting, one of the rebels read a new constitution, called the "Llano Declaration of Freedom," which provided voting rights for all workers over eighteen. Then, with great enthusiasm, resolution after resolution was accepted by acclamation. The old management was deposed and a new board of directors elected. Realizing that this popular assembly might be illegal under the corporate charter, the rebel leaders solicited a resignation from all the old board members and, in a new mass meeting on May 3, reelected their new board of directors by a secret ballot. This vote was 132 to 17 in favor of the revolution and, therefore, against Pickett. Even Pickett's long-time friend, "Doc" Williams, went over to the new forces and was elected president of the board. Carl, as planned, became the general manager and assumed most of the responsibilities formerly held by Pickett. Sidney I. Foster, who had fought most of the colony's legal battles in the past, liked the new management and helped them conform with Louisiana laws. Most surprising, even George T. Pickett seemed to capitulate. When both Williams and Foster, in friendly letters, urged him to resign, he wrote from Washington: "Dear comrades: In conforming to what seems to be the desire of the colonists at Newllano, I am offering you my resignation from your Board of Directors and also as your General Manager. With best wishes for your future success, and hoping you continue the integral co-operative program. . . ."[40]

The new board of directors announced a complete new program for

39. The story of the revolt was always colored by the sympathies of the participants. The Pickett side is overstated in Sid Young, *The Crisis in Llano Colony* (Los Angeles: n.p., 1936). Beginning with the issue of May 25, 1935, the *Llano Colonist* was always in the hands of the rebels, and thus represented their point of view. Fred Hanover, a young sociologist who lived in the colony shortly after the revolt, tried to be objective in his "Llano Cooperative Colony," but was inevitably swayed toward the rebel version.

40. *Llano Colonist*, June 8, 1935. Also see Hanover, "Llano Cooperative Colony," pp. 126-127.

Llano. Although still advocating a cooperative commonwealth, they were most interested in making Llano an economic success and in raising the living standards of the ragged, malnourished colonists. They repudiated new units, abolished the Kid Kolony, withdrew all support from a struggling new unit in New Mexico, denounced begging as a means of support, announced a new policy of accurate records and full accounting, and tried to improve the basic industries, especially agriculture.[41] The new approach was less idealistic, but seemingly more businesslike. The new managers stressed the new deal at Llano, and the rise of a new democracy and a new freedom. Yet, such was the popular mandate that Carl had almost as much leeway in his policies as Pickett ever had in the past. The colonists were more interested in accomplishment—in food and clothing —than in freedom.

Within a month of the "glorious revolution," Llano was in the midst of a civil war. Pickett returned to the colony on May 21, and again declared his loyalty to the new management. But almost immediately he began secret meetings with his loyal supporters and, within a week, traveled to Baton Rouge to determine if the revolt had been legal. Assured by the State Attorney General that it was probably illegal, Pickett returned to the colony to reclaim his presidency. In a face-to-face meeting with the new officials he was rebuked in a battle of ugly words. On May 30 the new directors quoted Pickett's own words about the duty of a minority to cooperate or leave and, condemning both his past actions and present plotting, removed his rights and privileges, revoked his work contract, and ordered him and his wife to leave the colony.[42] Pickett entrenched himself in his new home and formed his own brush gang, even employing some of the lawyers formerly used by the welfare league. In a circular he claimed that the new directors were illegally elected, that some of them were not even colony members (some had not purchased two thousand shares of stock), and that they were betraying the early ideals of the Llano movement. Pickett was probably sincere in his belief that the colony was facing doom without his direction, but his attacks only helped destroy the colony, which was engaged in a desperate battle for economic survival.[43]

The main events in the Llano civil war (from May, 1935, to April, 1936) were either ridiculous or humorous to outsiders, but deadly serious

41. Hanover, "Llano Cooperative Colony, pp. 129–132; *Llano Colonist*, May 25, 1935.

42. *Llano Colonist*, June 8, 1935.   43. *Ibid.*, June 22, 1935.

to Llanoites. The highlights follow: On May 31, 1935, Pickett, at the point of a gun, refused to allow some colonists to inventory his household possessions, claiming them as his own. On June 24 Pickett won a court order to permit him to live on in the colony. After a brief truce, Pickett and some loyal friends "captured" the main offices of the colony on July 22 and refused to evacuate them. When Harold Emory, the new editor of a drastically altered *Colonist*, shoved a door in Pickett's face, he was arrested and charged with assault. In the afternoon Pickett's force was physically evicted from the offices, with deputies around to prevent any real violence. Pickett's group immediately filed warrants for the arrest of their opponents, gaily watching them go into Leesville to appear before a judge. While they were gone, Pickett's group regained all the important buildings. The counterattack came in the evening, when Pickett's smaller group was overwhelmed. One Pickett recruit fired wildly with his pistol, wounding an opponent in the leg. Many from both groups were arrested. Pickett faced two charges of assault. Every colonist who came to Pickett's aid during the long day of warfare quickly lost his colony job and was evicted if possible. On the following morning all the utilities were disconnected at Pickett's home. The resulting trials in the parish courts were correctly described as "a farce." The first phase of the war ended without a winner.[44]

The next phase of the war was decided by a Leesville court in answer to a suit filed by Pickett to eject the new board of directors. The court ruled in September, 1935, that the new board was unlawfully elected and therefore not a legal board. But, at the same time, the court ruled that Pickett's old board of directors was equally illegal, since it had not been elected by a majority of the voting stock (an impossibility since most stockholders had been lost after the move from California). In such a circumstance, possession was ten-tenths of the law. The board in control had as much right to Llano as the deposed board.[45]

In October the new management was overwhelmingly reelected, but colony warfare continued. Pickett and about twenty supporters continued to hold secret meetings and to issue dire warnings that the colony was on the way to certain ruin. Now that he was no longer head of the colony, Pickett finally told the real truth about the poor food, tattered clothes, and lack of fuel, conditions that had existed for years. A Pickett ally

44. *Ibid.*, July 27, 1935, Aug. 3, 1935; Young, *The Crisis in Llano Colony*, pp. 48–49, 57–58, 61–63; the (New Orleans) *Times-Picayune*, July 23, 24, 1935.

45. Hanover, "Llano Cooperative Colony," pp. 128–129.

claimed that the colony had fallen to a "Communist coup" and a group of oil speculators. In letters to various mortgage holders, Pickett asked for the power of attorney in order to save some of the colony land when the new management drove the corporation to bankruptcy. The new managers moved the farm operations away from the western part of the colony (next to Pickett's home and virtually under his control) and twice disconnected Pickett's electricity. In both cases, Pickett swore out warrants, but to no avail. Whether faked for propaganda reasons or not, a shot was fired into Pickett's home and, according to his charge, narrowly missed him. Someone else apparently drove nails into his automobile tires, almost causing what could have been a fatal wreck.[46]

Even as delighted newspapermen reported and exploited the civil war in Llano, the colony itself struggled for its financial survival. This time the struggle was hopeless. In April, 1936, a Leesville court, in behalf of a group of creditors, appointed a receiver for the bankrupt colony. This, in effect, ended the civil war and transferred all management to the court and the supervising receiver. In the next two years there was a real attempt on the part of all factions to cooperate with the receiver and thus somehow earn profits and retire debts. In these last days Pickett once again became the central figure.

46. Young, *The Crisis in Llano Colony*, pp. 64–65, 68–69, 72–75; Letter from Pickett to the Rev. Eli and Mary Beers, Aug. 28, 1935, in Pickett papers; *Llano Colonist*, Sept. 7, 1935, Sept. 14, 1935, Dec. 21, 1935, Mar. 7, 1936.

VII. Not By Bread Alone

Llano colony, which never attained a stable government or a profitable economy, was blessed from its very beginnings with an active, challenging, and highly satisfying social and cultural life. From its founding in California, Harriman and other leaders had emphasized both the economic and noneconomic rewards of cooperation. As good socialists, they never repudiated material rewards. They believed these not only could be produced in greater quantities by cooperative endeavor but, more importantly, could be equitably distributed, thus drastically raising the living standards of all. Along with the increased production, they hoped to provide or promote organized and noncommercial forms of recreation, free entertainment, artistic endeavor, access to or participation in cultural events, and a new, cooperatively orientated educational system for both children and adults. Unlike the Hutterites, the socialists at Llano had few inhibitions concerning forms of art or recreation. While the spiritual-minded Hutterites were achieving complete material success with practically no social and cultural endeavor, the material-minded Llanoites were always facing imminent bankruptcy or starvation, yet were enjoying what even the best Marxists referred to as an uplifting spiritual experience.

Llano was never a totalitarian colony. Unlike in the Hutterite *Brüderhofs*, no all-encompassing ideology was ever prescribed for its members, and only the most nebulous form of socialism was ever preached in the Llano gospel. Even this was not binding on members, who were only required outwardly to cooperate in the practical affairs of the colony. Hard work and acquiescence in the policies of the management (or just the latter under Pickett) would assure anyone a good standing in the community, regardless of whether they were "Holy Rollers," communists, or anarchists. Only non-Caucasians were excluded, and these only for reasons of expediency. Thus Llano became a refuge not only for the unemployed and those who had lost out in the competitive world, but also for faddists and nonconformists, for radicals of every shading, for quacks and erratic geniuses, and for sensitive dreamers and soaring idealists. The oppressive, stultifying, enforced orthodoxy of most "democratic" small towns and villages was entirely lacking in Llano.

Although usually under a dictator and politically unfree, Llano was a "liberal" community, never fearful of those with strange ideas or odd behavior. It was, in fact, a whole community of nonconformists. Those who, with all sincerity, pointed so often to the freedom of Llano were not contradicting the critics who denounced Pickett's dictatorship; they were only stressing the freedom of thought and expression that they found at Llano, often after a lifetime of fleeing from intellectual loneliness, hostile criticism, or social ostracism. To some, a sympathetic understanding or even a tolerant, good-natured acceptance of their most fervent beliefs was worth much more than a political vote. Besides, on the outside their dissenting votes in behalf of some relatively unknown, small party candidate had been so completely, hopelessly ineffective as to be meaningless.

The tolerance and liberalism of Llano was both a strength and a weakness. It certainly helped to insure a colony of interesting people with widely varying talents and abilities, and with high social sensibilities. All of life was present, with all its possible color and joy and tragedy. There were stimulating conversations, esoteric fads, impossible dreams, absurd panaceas, noble aspirations, selfless sacrifices, and pathetic failures. But this very tolerance was an economic hindrance. Individuals were freely admitted to the colony without any reference to their possible economic value. No rigid screening process was ever used in order to eliminate those who were poor prospects for either physical or ideological reasons. Perhaps even more important, relatively few colonists ever so wholeheartedly accepted the vague goals of Llano as to make them the motivating factor in their endeavors. Most colonists came to Llano to acquire something, whether economic security, satisfying friendships, or a peaceful escape from an unfriendly world. Again a comparison will illustrate the problem. In the Hutterite villages, every colonist must wholeheartedly accept a clear, precise set of religious truths and social values. Every child is indoctrinated with this ideology from the age of two. Deviation is extremely rare. The ideology provides the rationale for every human endeavor, and sanctions the continued existence of their communal society. Although democratic in their political organization, the Hutterites live in a closed, albeit a very humane, society. If Llano had been able to sponsor and enforce a set, specific secular ideology capable of exciting religious zeal and fervor, and of motivating dedicated hard work, it might have prospered. If the ideology could have been propagated through propaganda and education, political democracy would have been possible without any risks of early dissolution, for the will of the community would have been as one will. Finally, if such an ideology had prevailed, entrance to Llano would have been limited to selected converts, real diversity would have been impossible, and the social life, at least to an outsider, would probably have seemed prescribed, unimaginative, and dull.

Undoubtedly much of the social attractiveness of Llano was based on the more intangible aspects of colony life and not on the institutionalized forms of diversion. Visitors usually commented on the endless conversation in the evening, particularly at the hotel. The discussions ranged far and wide, from mysticism to Marxism, from phrenology to Einstein. Since the colonists were a cosmopolitan group, coming from all parts of the United States and from many European countries, they could recount endless adventures, some true, many fancied. The *Colonist* frequently noted private parties celebrating birthdays or other occasions. One attraction of such private gatherings was the refreshments, usually purchased by a colonist with outside resources, and containing delicacies that were rarely or never served within the colony. The women were required to work for eight hours a day, but apparently had plenty of time for gossip either while working in groups or while at rest. Even the political battles and the financial hardships strengthened the bonds of friendship, as only shared adversity can. The fact that almost everyone else shared your poverty, your poor clothes, your inadequate food, made poverty a cohesive rather than a divisive factor.[1] The older folk, after their innocuous tasks were completed, could dabble in their gardens, once again indulge in youthful pursuits, and above all share their reminiscences. In the words of a visitor: "About the colony when darkness falls, may be heard the squeak of the fiddle, the plunk-plunk of the banjo, the call of the cornet, the mournful sob of the trombone, and the wailing of the mouth organ. In the morning one may see the bachelor pruning the grape vines near his cabin, or training the rose that is a living symbol, perhaps, of some sweetheart of the long ago."[2]

Many of the free-time activities at Llano became standardized and institutionalized. Park and play areas were developed in both California and Louisiana. The colonists maintained some type of swimming pool

1. Fred Hanover, "Llano Cooperative Colony: An American Rural Community Experiment" (unpublished M.A. Thesis, Tulane University, 1936), pp. 158–159; Bob Brown, *Can We Co-operate?* (New York: Roving Eye Press, 1940), pp. 84–86.

2. Hanover, "Llano Cooperative Colony," p. 159.

(or hole) at each location, and organized a baseball team in Louisiana. Sunday picnics were common, both for children and for the whole colony. During one period, both young people and adults attended special "social evenings" under the urging of "Doc" Williams. These socials included card games, singing, music by an orchestra, square dancing, and refreshments. For these occasions, outsiders were excluded, the best dress was demanded, and baby-sitters were provided. The young people had social outlets at school, and on two different occasions organized special youth clubs. In the booming days in California there were numerous hobby clubs and organized athletic teams. Even at the isolated rice ranch, a handful of colonists gathered to play cards in the evening. Almost all holidays (including Christmas) were celebrated with special dinners and parties. The one big holiday of the year was May Day. For this founder's day and world socialist holiday, the colony spent weeks in preparation. The colony buildings were decked out in bright (particularly red) colors, guests were invited from all around, industrial exhibits were shown, a miniature track meet was staged, in some years the baseball team played an outside opponent, a large dinner was served in the cafeteria, and all this was followed by a gala dance in the evening.[3]

Llano never neglected activities of a cultural nature. Throughout most of the years in both California and Louisiana, Sunday afternoon was reserved for an open forum on various intellectual or controversial subjects, many connected with the theories behind cooperation. Sunday evening was reserved for a cultural program in the colony theater. Here the fare was varied in subject and merit. Some programs were purely musical, with vocal and instrumental performances by both colony adults and children. Periodically, plays were produced, after weeks of rehearsal and the dedicated efforts of a few interested directors. Most of the plays were amateurish; none were written by colonists. On other evenings there were recitations by children, amateur contests, group or choral singing, spelling bees, and mimics and other types of comedy. In Louisiana the colony owned a movie projector and showed free movies either on Sunday or on any free evenings. The movies were silent films borrowed from anyone who would lend them at small expense, and were usually documentaries or travelogues supplied, with plenty of advertising, by large corporations. In California the colony had an art studio and, for a period, enjoyed the instruction of a talented sculptor. In Louisiana the

3. "Colony Celebrates Anniversary," *Western Comrade*, III (May, 1915), 15–18; *Llano Colonist*, Nov. 19, 1927; June 6, 1931, May 10, 1930.

colony had little contact with the fine arts except in the very active and highly valued colony orchestra. Pickett stressed Llano's future role in creative art, but admitted that, except for music, the colony would have to postpone any active role until a more prosperous future. An occasional painter visited in Llano, but none remained for more than a few weeks. The colony made extensive use of socialist and proletarian literature and music, but added little to either. In the tradition of the IWW and other labor movements, they borrowed a few traditional Christian tunes and added the words of the Llano gospel. Typical of this borrowing was the Llano Jubilee Song, composed by "Dad" Gleeser:

1. We've gathered at Newllano for honest industry
   To work for one another and thus to make us free;
   Our light is on the hilltops for all the world to see,
   For Llano's marching on.

Chorus: Gloria, Gloria Hallelujah
   Gloria, Gloria Hallelujah
   Our Light is on the hilltops for all the world to see
   For Llano's marching on.

2. Let's demand a year of Jubilee to make all people free,
   Money slavery abolish for all eternity
   The Golden Rule be practice of all humanity,
   For Llano's marching on.

3. A world-embracing brotherhood, mutuality, good cheer
   The long-foretold millennium, we want to help bring near,
   Want plenty and abundance for all the world to share,
   For Llano's marching on.[4]

The Llano colonists were always ready to boast of their fine library, which ultimately contained over five thousand volumes and was considerably larger than most small-town libraries in the thirties. In Louisiana it was housed in a separate, two-story building and was always staffed by at least one full-time librarian. Its selection was very unbalanced, since the books had all been donated, but it did excel in the field of socialist and radical thought. Reading was enthusiastically encouraged, while visitors marveled at the intellectual depth of the most-read books.[5] The varied

4. *Llano Colonist*, Apr. 30, 1932. Also see Ernest Wooster, "Bread and Hyacinths," *Sunset Magazine*, LIII (Aug., 1924), 21; "Colony Development," *The Internationalist*, VI (June, 1918), 10, 37.
5. Hanover, "Llano Cooperative Colony," pp. 171–172.

articles in the *Llano Colonist* supplemented the library resources. Few rural people had access to a weekly newspaper as varied and educational as the *Colonist*, which featured news of cooperative groups around the world, the somewhat slanted news items of the Federated Press, book reviews, and special articles on psychology, philosophy, literature, and economic theory.

Above all, the colonists at Llano danced. Beginning with the first settlement in California, the weekly dance was the major social event of Llano, and was always freely open to outside visitors.[6] The colony orchestra was used for the dances, and was partly developed and always favored for this reason. The big dance was always held on Saturday night, but in California this did not preclude Tuesday dances for children and dancing instruction on Thursday. Pickett played in the colony orchestra and provided free dancing lessons before each Saturday session, thus assuring that everyone could dance well enough to enjoy the occasion. Both round and square dancing were enjoyed, with the young people always aspiring for newer steps and a faster tempo than allowed by Pickett. In Louisiana the dances were first held in the dining hall of the hotel, but later were moved to a new, spacious, unencumbered dance floor constructed on the roof of the largest of the concrete drying sheds. Roofed, carefully floored, and eventually enclosed for winter heating, this roof garden was acclaimed the best dance floor between New Orleans and Shreveport. The dances and other social affairs were acknowledged to be clean and wholesome by all visitors, and attracted many young people from Leesville. This free entertainment helped develop the friendship of local neighbors that soon distinguished Llano from almost all other radical community experiments.

In many ways life in Llano was similar to that in any other small town or village. Most families lived in separate dwellings, ate at their own table even though the food came from the cafeteria, reared their own children, practiced their own religion if they had any, sent their children to schools, had close friends, and worked for approximately forty-eight hours a week. Although they lived within the colony, they could leave anytime they wished. When off work, colonists traveled to Leesville, visited outside neighbors, or attended nearby church services. There were no fences, no guards, and no checking in and out. The boundaries of the colony were never distinct; a few colonists were housed more than two

6. "Co-operative Colony Shows Rapid Growth," *Western Comrade*, II (Dec., 1914), 16–17.

miles from the community center. Although colony life had to be more routinized than that of a normal village, there was little of the discipline and rigor of a military camp. Most colonists observed the regular meal schedule and the prescribed working hours. Other than this, the utmost diversity and individuality prevailed.

Although very low even in the twenties, the living standard at Llano was generally above that of the rural South. Usually little more than a shack, almost every colony home had free electricity, a daily delivery of ice, and, if near the main village, running water. New families simply moved into any vacant house of their choice, and thus permanently escaped the clutches of a landlord. The electricity was generated by the colony, and often used even for cooking. A few new homes had bathrooms, but these were the exception. Most homes were unpainted, generally in poor repair, and heated by wood stoves. Yet, considering the free utilities and the cultural opportunities, few farm families then had as much. But almost any farmer did have better food and clothing than the colonists, particularly after the beginning of the depression.[7]

Llano always included a disproportionately large number of men and of old people. Most females of marriageable age were married, while there were always large numbers of bachelors and widowers. Also, many married men came to the colony alone, allegedly awaiting better conditions in the colony before bringing their wives. Some wives found it almost impossible to adjust to colony life, and thus moved back to relatives or parents. Young girls in the colony were at such a premium that they always had plenty of suitors. Colony marriages were celebrated with great fanfare and rejoicing. Since many elderly people invested their savings in Llano, and in effect came there to retire, there were frequent funerals, but those were observed with little fanfare. Unless they had requested it, colonists were buried without religious services. They were usually interred in the colony cemetery, which was tended by one of the older men.

To the largely Protestant, or even fundamentalist, citizens of Leesville, the most appalling aspect of Llano was its lack of churches and of any organized religious life. The Llano colonists did nothing to agitate the problem of race, were usually law abiding and moral, and were a definite economic asset to the city and parish. The people of Leesville, as in the typical Southern town or village, were quite tolerant of political and economic radicalism. Thus the religious issue was the major point of friction between Llano and its neighbors. It was never important enough

7. Hanover, "Llano Cooperative Colony," pp. 144–145.

to destroy a tolerant acceptance or, in some cases, a basic sympathy (a few local farmers became colonists). Many people in Leesville still remember Llano with real affection, despite its one peculiar and, to them, almost unbelievable deficiency. Even some colonists left rather than rear their children in what they believed to be a heathen community.[8]

In California almost all colonists were members of the Socialist Party and were either avowed atheists or agnostics. In these years the hatred of organized religion, of the "opiate of the people," was clearly enunciated in the colony literature. One colonist asked: "Would you have us continue the practice of building hundred thousand dollar edifices in the name of the carpenter, and mortgage the soul, the conscience and the honor of those who 'worship' there to the money lenders of the community?"[9] After the move to Louisiana the militant unbelievers were joined by a growing number of religionists, some from the extremely orthodox or spiritualistic sects, such as "Hard Shell" Baptists, the Church of God, and Theosophists. The official policy of the colony was to exclude all churches, but to permit religious freedom to all colonists. Pickett permitted ministers to preach in the colony, and claimed that Llano was not opposed to religion or the Bible, but was rather trying to follow true religion in practice. Of course, to Pickett, the one true religion was integral cooperation, with the organized churches usually in the hands of the wealthy and a source of dissension and disunion in the ranks of men. The *Colonist* continued to carry many articles damning superstition, organized religion, and abstract theology. Yet the colony wooed Christian socialists and cooperators. Whether as a good propaganda tactic, or as a sincere statement of belief, Pickett often acknowledged a "Supreme Intelligence."[10] After the population influx of the depression, the irreligious complexion of Llano almost disappeared. In 1935 there were only sixty-five avowed nonbelievers or nonattached adult colonists, as compared with eighty-two Protestants, three Catholics, and two Jews.[11]

One compromise with religion was made in 1932. Dr. Samuel Irwin, a former Methodist missionary and a Christian socialist, came to Llano in order to establish a small Christian cooperative commonwealth. He lived at Llano while he constructed a small Christian colony about three miles south of Newllano. His small colony, which was often ambitiously

8. Brown, *Can We Co-operate?* p. 98.
9. Albert James, "The Church and Llano," *Western Comrade*, III (Nov., 1915), 22.
10. *Llano Colonist*, Nov. 26, 1927, Apr. 28, 1928, Oct. 6, 1928.
11. Hanover, "Llano Cooperative Colony," pp. 177–178.

referred to as Unit Number Three (the rice ranch was unit two), included a large, two-story log house, a dormitory for up to eight people, a small cabin in the woods, and a barn. He planned, but never completed, an orphanage and a school. His colony was used as a home for elderly, retired ministers and missionaries, but apparently never contained more than a half-dozen colonists at any one time. Dr. Irwin was a welcome addition to the Llano movement. Not only did he lend respect to it, but he was available for colony weddings and funerals. In a quite unique and unofficial way, he became the colony chaplain. He believed in both God and Llano, and thus was perfectly qualified.[12]

In the Llano propaganda, no part of the colony was as often praised as the schools. In the colony view, they were always drastically superior to anything on the outside. In California the state supported a public elementary school within the colony. On its part, the colony supported Pickett's industrial school or Kid Kolony, a day nursery, and, after 1915, a highly publicized kindergarten. The founder of the kindergarten, Prudence Stokes Brown, had studied under Dr. Maria Montessori in Italy, and advertised her Llano experiment as the second Montessori school in California. The kindergarten children rode to an improvised building in automobiles and were described as models of good behavior. In fact, one group of kindergarten children traveled to Los Angeles as living exhibits of the Montessori method.[13]

In Louisiana the school system was organized around George T. Pickett's educational ideals. These, in order of importance to him, were good health, industrial proficiency, better human relationships or co-operative habits, and the acquisition of knowledge and the ability to think for oneself. He wanted to forget diplomas and go in for proper development. To him, most teachers were exceptionally narrow-minded, able to impart well-memorized lessons but incapable of inspiring real thinking.[14] To implement these ideas, Pickett established a unique, vocational-type school program at both the elementary and high school level. All students from grade one through eleven attended classes for a

12. *Llano Colonist*, June 25, 1932, Oct. 15, 1932. Most issues of the *Colonist* after 1932 contained some news from the "Christian Unit." I also gathered some interesting excerpts from the present owners of the Irwin Colony.

13. "Colony Celebrates Anniversary," *Western Comrade*, III (May, 1915), 19; Archie Roy Clifton, "A Study of Llano del Rio Community in the Light of Earlier Experiments in Practical Socialism" (unpublished M.A. Thesis, University of Southern California, 1918), p. 40.

14. *Llano Colonist*, Jan. 2, 1932.

half day and worked the other half. The State of Louisiana approved this unorthodox arrangement and paid to the colony the salary for two teachers (the teachers always came from the colony and therefore did not receive any of the pay). The colony selected all its own teachers, and always had at least five or six. The qualifications of colony teachers varied immensely, from an Oxford graduate at one time to people barely qualified to teach vocational subjects. Many critics argued that the vocational training was only a ruse for the use of child labor, citing as evidence the many unskilled tasks performed by the youngsters. Yet some industrious boys learned printing, mechanics, and sheet-metal work.[15]

Pickett was most interested in preschool children. He felt that most mothers were not qualified for their task of child rearing, and that mothers should be replaced by a nurse-teacher as soon as they could be induced to surrender the child. In desiring to replace the family by the community, Pickett was simply following the footsteps of most communal societies. Both the Hutterites and the Kibbutzim of Israel insist upon community nurseries. Pickett hoped that the colony nursery could provide the proper nutrition, teach early habits in cooperation, and begin a program of character building. By the first grade, the child would be ready for a part-time work program, and thus ready to help make the schools as nearly self-supporting as possible. He always dreamed of bringing orphans to Llano and of using them to demonstrate the merit of his educational philosophy. The colony nursery was established in a grove of hardwoods about one mile west of the main colony, and was a part of the Kid Kolony, which also contained the first three elementary grades. The Kid Kolony occasionally accepted children as young as eight months, although two was the usual age for beginners. In normal times there were about fifteen to twenty preschool children at the Kid Kolony. Each morning a colony bus hauled the young tots away to their colony, and then returned them to their working parents in the evening. Located next to the dairy barn, the Kid Kolony had two school buildings, a kitchen and dining area, two apartments for teachers, and a hundred-acre farm with apple trees, a garden, horses, chickens, tools, and milk goats, all cared for by teachers and students. At one time the small children even organized a strike. Pickett, who always lived at or near the Kid Kolony, described it as his miniature integral cooperative community.[16]

Apart from its educational goals, the nursery and kindergarten program

15. Hanover, "Llano Cooperative Colony," pp. 166–169.
16. *Llano Colonist*, Apr. 14, 1928, Jan. 11, 1930, Mar. 5, 1932.

was important in freeing mothers for the work teams in the colony. Only mothers with small babies were exempt from daily tasks, since each woman was supposed to work forty-eight hours each week even as the men. Perhaps few mothers agreed with the sentiments of Theodore Cuno, the venerable benefactor of the colony and its accepted sage. He saw the real merit of the Kid Kolony in the fact that it relieved parents of the "insufferable company and anxious care of their children, who from the very day of birth are a burdensome nuisance, except perhaps, at playful moments; our educational system being somewhat of a defense of the comparative quiet and order of adult life against the comparative noise, racket, untidiness, inquisitiveness, fitfulness, shiftlessness, dirt, destruction and mischief, which are natural to children and conducive to making them healthy, active and vigorous."[17]

Pickett firmly believed that education should continue for a lifetime, and thus always encouraged some type of higher education for the colony. Not himself a college graduate, he was always suspicious of most colleges and seemingly resented the highly educated individual. He recommended that parents not send their children to the recognized colleges and universities, where they would only learn capitalistic ideas day after day. Instead, he asked parents to take advantage of the unique and very practical educational advantages of Llano. Pickett always viewed Llano as a demonstration, and thus felt that residence and work in the colony was about the best education available. After the departure of the Commonwealth College, numerous other rather pitiful attempts were made to create some formal program of higher education for adult colonists. In 1928 Professor Lowell H. Coate came to Llano to plan and direct a junior college, and actually gave courses in 1928–1929. The *Colonist*, optimistic as ever, advertised for students to take advantage of the new cooperative college. The so-called college courses were offered on three evenings of the week, and included such subjects as psychology, English, mathematics, and health. The hastily assembled faculty of six included the colony's registered nurse, a past high school teacher with no degree, a mathematician who had taken only nine college courses, and one colonist with a Bachelor of Science degree. At one time Pickett was listed as a faculty member. Coate was a graduate of Taylor University in Indiana, possessed the B.A. and B.D. degrees, and had been president of a college in Idaho. During the day he supervised the high school program. After one year he left the colony to teach in Los Angeles, only

17. *Ibid.*, Jan. 2, 1932.

to return again in 1932. Coate was replaced by a Professor Hewerdine, who came from Minnesota to teach in high school and head the college program. Acknowledged by all to be an excellent teacher, he quarreled with Pickett and left the colony in anger. Some adult courses were continued, but were rarely referred to as being on the college level.[18]

The effectiveness of the education at Llano was generally proven by the success of the many young people who left the colony, but the very fact that so many young people left proved that the schools did not strengthen the Llano movement. The very process of education created among the young a desire for a better and more exciting life than could be obtained in the colony. The educational system stressed cooperation, but except for the part-time work was not essentially different from progressive schools outside the colony. There was no intense ideological indoctrination that might have influenced the children to remain in Llano. There was no real attempt to isolate the children from the outside world and its influences. In fact, the Llano teenagers were remarkedly normal. Unlike their security-conscious parents, they were ready to get from life the best it had to offer and were very much influenced by the glitter and promise of a capitalistic society. They usually decided that their future was not in Llano. It was too much a colony of defeated individuals, of acutely sensitive idealists and escapists, of old people searching for a home, and was not a colony of youth and adventure.[19]

The real flavor of Llano was not so much in its institutions as in the unique individuals who came to the colony, and particularly in those who came to stay permanently. Actually, most who came did not stay long. Only a minority could adjust to the new way of life; many came for only selfish reasons and soon wore out their welcome. Others were dedicated, but could not accept the dictatorship of Pickett or the poor food and housing. Only a few colonists were both converted to the religion of cooperation and, at the same time, able to practice it. Yet, flock to Llano they did, particularly after the depression. They came from "every cranny in this cracked old world, all sorts, college professors, beachcombers, trained nurses, expert mechanics, lady barbers, writers, stowaways, reformed preachers—in this social ark there is a sample pair of every class and kind."[20] They came down the highway from Leesville, "casting fearful glances back, their toes thrusting through broken leather, their

18. *Ibid.*, Sept. 8, 15, 22, 1928, Oct. 26, 1929, Dec. 28, 1929, Jan. 25, 1930, Mar. 1, 1930, July 23, 1932.
19. Brown, *Can We Co-operate?* p. 192.   20. *Ibid.*, p. 84.

noses popping out of sidedoor Pullmans, seeking escape and a hideout for a while. Like stoned dogs they flee to this social haven for a moment's refuge in which to lick their sores and bruises."[21] The doors of Llano were seldom closed to those in need, even though the depression hoboes usually stopped for only a few days in their wandering, and even though many repaid their hosts by criticism or worse.[22]

Although estimates of the number of people who came to Llano and then left run as high as ten thousand, the number was undoubtedly much less. Although only a few (less than ten) colonists from California remained in the colony until the thirties, about thirty of the sixty-five who backed Pickett in the low period of 1920 were still in the colony in 1929. In the same years approximately 554 others had lived in the colony, with 141 still there. After the depression even the management could only guess at the number that came and left, although many stayed so briefly they were really visitors. Some unemployed men took advantage of the generosity of the colony to spend a winter and then left with spring weather.[23]

The recruitment propaganda in the *Colonist* was very effective in luring prospective colonists, but tended to obscure the realities of Llano and thus invite early disillusionment. One typical recruitment notice promised the following:

Dear Friend: HOW WOULD YOU LIKE to live in a Community where you had no House Rent to pay; NO BOARD OR GROCERY BILLS to meet each week or month; NO FUEL OR LIGHT BILLS presented to you every 30 days; NO WATER BILL harassing you every quarter; NO DOCTOR OR NURSE BILL, and indeed, no funeral bill, should this sad fate befall you or your dear ones; NO CHARGE FOR DANCING to the music of a good orchestra on one of the finest floors in Louisiana; ... WHERE EVERY EFFORT [will be] MADE to place you in the job or position that you like best or can function best in, and ... WHERE YOU ARE AN EQUAL OWNER of everything on these odd thousands of acres of Llano Colony. ...[24]

In addition to security and tolerance, to free ice and laundry, some pleas for membership stressed the "cozy little shingle cottage with vines and roses [really an old lumber shack], hop-toads along my walks in the cool of the evening, wood to burn winter nights in a jolly little stove com-

21. *Ibid.*
22. See Robert Whitcomb, "The New Pilgrim's Progress," *Atlantic Monthly*, CXLVII (May, 1931), 548.
23. *Llano Colonist*, Oct. 5, 1929.
24. Hanover, "Llano Cooperative Colony," Appendix D.

panion."[25] The subordinated stress on plain food and hard work was scarcely noticed by the idealist, at least not until he arrived in the colony.

Another effective technique for attracting colonists was the frequent use of testimonials. Beginning in the *Western Comrade* in 1916, and continuing all the way down to the thirties in the *Colonist*, periodic "Why I came to Llano" statements were featured, with the more literate colonists contributing highly idealistic, dedicated (and most likely well-edited) words of praise about Llano and the cooperative movement for which it was the vanguard.[26] The statements were all fascinating documents. One colonist came not only to help "solve the ills and troubles of mankind," but to escape compulsory vaccination.[27] Others came to escape the new slavery of wages, to solve the problems of human relationships, to re-establish the communism of the early church, to escape religious persecution, to advance socialism, and to satisfy their curiosity. One exuberant colonist wrote a ten-verse poem as his testimony. A couple from West Virginia gave the more typical response. They came "to demonstrate to a sick world that cooperation is or may be made more conducive to human health and happiness than competition and selfish individualism. . . . We are traveling along the Llano way which will by and by lead us and the world into the Cooperative Commonwealth, the Brotherhood of Men, where war and fratricidal strife shall tear and rend the race no more."[28]

Llano was a haven for esoteric faddists, with some unorthodox behavior more the rule than an exception. Most of the fads concerned health. There was always a large number of vegetarians, and even a few colonists who would not harm, let alone eat, animals. Pickett preferred naturopaths to orthodox physicians and supervised the construction of a special shower bath for "blood washing" and cleansing the system of all impurities.[29] The *Colonist* carried numerous articles by a Walter Siegmeister, Ph.D., who advocated not only vegetarianism but complete sexual abstinence except for that necessary for procreation. He believed this regimen would abolish sickly, deformed children and create a super race. He railed against poisonous vaccine (pus of a sore on a cow), against meat and all starchy foods, against cooking in such dangerous metals as aluminum, against the manifold evils of tobacco, and against

25. *Llano Colonist*, Sept. 1, 1928.
26. These began in the *Western Comrade*, IV (Sept., 1916), p. 29.
27. *Llano Colonist*, Apr. 21, 1928.
28. *Ibid.*, Apr. 21, 28, 1928.   29. *Ibid.*, Apr. 19, 1930.

the artificial, dangerous climate of the temperate zone. He hoped to found a tropical utopia in the near future.[30]

A Dr. Kimmel lived in the colony for several years and propagated his own distinctive type of medical quackery. His well-advertised panacea was a special homemade antiseptic suitable for any illness if used in conjunction with a special diet and manipulation.[31] The *Colonist* carried numerous articles on the "science" of phrenology. One expert used phrenology to prove the untrustworthiness of capitalists and to give advice about marriage and family problems.[32] The colony, at one time or another, contained Theosophists, Rosicrucians, and convinced but nonpracticing nudists. One arrival in 1930 wanted to restore the natural Garden of Eden, and had actually tried to do so without success. He wanted to form an Eden Group to live in complete tune with the laws of nature in order to enjoy "peace, harmony, joy, a heaven on earth." But since no one else could live up to his ideas, he came to Llano with assurance that no one would prevent him from at least following his own food habits. Incidentally, his Garden of Eden was to have included only live, vegetable food, unclothed sunbathing, daily exercise, and bathing in fresh water. He believed that the only evil was sickness, which was usually caused by eating dead foods.[33]

Some of the most important and best-loved colonists were excessively "normal" in their behavior. One of these was Septer Baldwin, who was usually on the board of directors and who successfully managed the rice ranch for several years. Equally indispensable was Ole Synoground, a pugnacious, strong Swede from South Dakota, who had had two years of mechanical engineering in college, experience in a farm cooperative, and who was an expert carpenter and construction engineer. He doggedly worked for Llano through all the crises, and at the expense of one arm that he lost in one of the numerous colony accidents. His wife, equally dedicated, operated the colony laundry for years.

A colony mainstay was Carl Henry "Dad" Gleeser, the eloquent, fervid editor of the *Colonist*. An old man, he was born in Hanover, Germany, in 1855, prospected in Australia, came to America to work with the Knights of Labor in the Colorado mines, published a labor journal in San Francisco in the nineties, and lived in Kansas City before coming to Llano in 1921 with a $3,500 contribution. Short, bald, energetic, "Dad" Gleeser was a born nonconformist in politics and religion. Although over seventy, he danced with the girls every Saturday night, wanted to live forever, and got up every morning at 4:30 to eat his raw food breakfast, take his gymnastics, and "coach his subconscious."[34] Another mainstay was the affable "Doc" Williams, who was able to afford an automobile, who directed many of the social affairs, and who practiced his osteopathy both within and without the colony. One permanent fixture was kindly, elderly "Dad" Thomas. For years the oldest member of the colony, he puttered in his garden, cared for the cemetery, and lived in his "white rose cottage."[35]

Many very talented people either visited or lived awhile at Llano. An eccentric artist and radical, Ed Merrill, came to the colony from California, directed a special colony bee unit in south Louisiana, and eventually settled on a private farm near the colony. He was a master at tricky blackboard drawings, professed an orthodox Marxism, had been a leader in the IWW, and had a daughter who was an organizer for the Communist Party. He published his own little newspaper or magazine— *Homo Sapiens*—at irregular intervals.[36] For over a year, Mack and John Rust were at Llano, using colony funds to perfect their now-famous cotton picker. In 1930 Pickett agreed to finance up to twenty of the first pickers, with a promise of one-half the net profits on all future sales. For some unexplained reason, the Rust brothers left the colony and Pickett lost his interest in the machines.[37] Another talented colonist was Sidney Lloyd Young, who migrated to Llano from Welwyn, England, to become the most vocal supporter of George T. Pickett. Young was a talented writer, sending a series of highly favorable letters about Llano back to England. He contributed to the *Colonist* and his family took an active interest in the colony theater.[38]

The radical fringe always included its colorful characters. Theodore Atworth had survived six former utopian colonies before coming to Llano. He wore a beard, tried to look like Karl Marx, pushed a wheelbarrow around the colony as he planted shrubs, and carried with him a design for a model village. More radical was Harry Weatherwax, a former Communist Party organizer who viewed Llano as a rather pathetic "Golden Rule Republic," but who stayed for the social life.

34. *Ibid.*, Apr. 19, 1930.
35. Brown, *Can We Co-operate?* pp. 116–117.   36. *Ibid.*, pp. 155–167.
37. Hanover, "Llano Cooperative Colony," pp. 182–183; *Llano Colonist*, May 10, 24, 1930, Feb. 21, 1931.
38. *Llano Colonist*, July 11, 1931.

When he married he asked for a divorce coupon when buying his license, and wrote "red" for his color. He was a professional comic, dressing in different costumes for every party. He gave a completely irreverent blessing before meals, in the vein of: "O Santa Claus, we thank thee for the bountiful appetite that thou hast bestowed upon us, with which to devour the food that we have gone out and worked so like hell to produce." He ended his popular skits with: "Yours for the Revolution, H. C. Earwax, Collector of the Infernal Revenue of Yah-no Colony, Fleasville, Vermin Parish, Lousyana."[39]

A few colonists came with the purest of ideals and the most sincere and abiding belief in the future of the cooperative commonwealth. Their faith never wavered; their devotion was equal to every ounce of their strength. Esther Allen symbolized these, the best of colonists. A registered nurse, Miss Allen came to Llano in 1924 from New York City, leaving behind twenty years of friends and associations. Her father had dreamed of universal brotherhood, and from him she absorbed the same dream, finding in her middle years a happy, natural, and unencumbered life at Llano. She had discovered life in modern New York to be a selfish, planless enigma, but lost herself in the cooperative way, looking forward to, and working for, a world-embracing, universal, coordinated plan for all men. Her idealism was almost lyrical: "It is not at all difficult for me to believe that in a little while now, a few generations of intelligent cooperative living, our race will enter upon a life that would be altogether wonderful to us, could we but anticipate it. [It will be] beyond anything we can now dream of, or desire. . . . At Llano, while we are keeping our ties on earth, we are winging our thoughts to the stars."[40] An aging, grey-haired, increasingly deaf spinster, Esther Allen was a true nun in the service of cooperation, a loyal, sensitive, romantic angel of mercy who gave full devotion to her cooperative religion.[41]

Theodore Cuno was the sage of Llano. He was the philosopher of cooperation, the wisest of colonists, a man of broad experience and of an unbelievably diverse number of interests. With a brilliant and a free mind, he wrote the best and least inhibited articles in the *Colonist*. Coming to Llano in 1919 as the leading benefactor of the colony, and always the financial crutch behind George T. Pickett, he was always treated with respect if not with reverence. He said exactly what he thought on any

39. Brown, *Can We Co-operate?* p. 88. Also see pp. 121–122, 172–173.
40. *Llano Colonist*, Apr. 26, 1930.
41. Brown, *Can We Co-operate?* p. 69.

issue, and personally compensated for the trite fads, pseudo-science, and barren clichés of so much of the *Colonist*. He was a catholic scholar who, by surrendering his books when he had read them, was practically the sole contributor to the colony library. In appearance he was unforgettable, with a handsome face, long, flowing white hair and beard, and white garments or robes. He stood erect as a soldier and, into his eighties, swam during the summers. He was a champion pinochle player and, as an avid stamp collector, he helped form the American Philatelic Association.

From a tangle of his own reminiscences in the *Colonist*, Cuno's life can be partially reconstructed. He was born in 1846 in Westphalia, Germany, and was seventy-seven years old when he and his wife came to the colony (his wife died in 1925). As a youth in Germany he was trained as a mechanical engineer, and then traveled throughout Europe as an industrial designer. In 1864 he joined Marx's International Workingmen's Association and attended the last session of this First International at The Hague in 1872, representing the city of Düsseldorf. Here he met Marx and Engels and acquired their autographed photographs. In his travels to Berlin, Vienna, Brussels, and Milan he told workers that they were being robbed by capitalist thieves. His organizational work for Marxism led to six jail sentences and expulsion from six countries. While living temporarily in Milan, reveling in its beauty and art, he formed that city's first local of the International Workingmen's Association. It was visited by Garibaldi, whom Cuno knew personally, and only finally abolished by Mussolini. In Milan Cuno met his wife, an American singer performing in Italy. In about 1873 Cuno came to the United States, where he worked for radical socialist causes and later reported for and edited the *New Yorker Volkzeitung*. As a reporter, he was at the scene of the Homestead and Pullman strikes, analyzed the work of the Knights of Labor, became acquainted with three presidents (and particularly with Chester A. Arthur), and amassed a comfortable amount of money and property for himself. When he came to Llano in 1919, he was easily the colony's most famous citizen except, possibly, for Job Harriman.

Apart from his fervent belief in the future of Llano, Cuno had few illusions. He was a determined materialist and hedonist, a born rebel who courageously thrust aside all conventional opinion and looked at the world with a refreshing or a shocking originality, and a scholar who read voraciously in all fields. He gave talks using Bertrand Russell as a text, talked on love as an attractive force in the universe, traced Christianity back to the Essenes, analyzed secret societies from the cult of Isis to the

Knights of Labor, condemned the Russian departure from true Marxist principles, warned against the future danger of the "Yellow race," and chatted endlessly and intimately about Karl Marx, his family, and Engels. He believed none of the Marx family knew how to handle money; as a result they were not alive to help the continuing socialist movement. A complete liberal on the race question, he believed that segregation would end with the death of capitalism, and had considered marrying a Negro on the recommendation of Marx. He authored informative articles on Darwin's theory of evolution, biochemistry, Greek mythology, morals and religion, European art, the crudity of American life, great literary masterpieces, psychoanalysis and Freud, Neanderthal man, the role of chromosomes and genes in heredity, sex education, the loyalty of dogs, Brook Farm (he knew most of the members) and other communal experiments, and on women. He hated American Puritanism, desired nudity at least for athletic contests, collected a gallery of famous reproductions, and quite frankly admired beautiful women, particularly when they wore few clothes. He elevated the *Colonist* by his analysis of world events and his astute predictions about the future. He spent his last years with the Pickett family, was increasingly afflicted with kleptomania, and unexpectedly died on March 24, 1934. Perhaps fortunately, he was spared the agony of seeing his beloved Llano fall prey to revolution, civil war, and economic bankruptcy.[42]

42. This material on Cuno was selected from dozens of issues of the *Colonist*, particularly from 1928 through 1932. Some interesting observations about Cuno were contributed by George T. Pickett in an interview in the summer of 1959.

VIII. But Then There Was No Bread

A bankrupt Llano colony was liquidated in 1938 because of complete economic failure. This bankruptcy was anticlimactic, for the colony had been in financial trouble throughout nearly every moment of its existence. The bitter factional struggles were never mortal; the failure to earn its own way inevitably was. The reasons for financial misfortune were in part external, since the depression of the thirties destroyed many formerly sound corporations, and Llano del Rio had never been sound. But the main reasons for failure were internal, and therefore deserve careful analysis.

In theory, a fully cooperative or collective economy should be more productive and support a higher living standard than a privately based economic order, particularly in the area of agriculture. Cooperation in production and marketing means large units, which permit the utilization of the most efficient machines, encourage a division of labor according to skills, and, unlike a private corporation, give the worker a share in both ownership and profits and, therefore, again in theory, the same incentive to work efficiently as he would have on his own farm or in his own shop. Whether the members receive their returns in private wages and dividends or in community services as at Llano, the living standard in either case is dependent upon the amount of the total production. In order to achieve a high production, a cooperative must respect the prerequisites of successful economic endeavor. It must have adequate capital, expert management, proficient laborers, and an efficient organizational structure. Llano had none of these. In addition, if a cooperative eschews wages or any rewards based specifically on the amount contributed by a member-worker, and instead adopts the principle of "from each according to his ability and to each according to his needs," the problem of incentive increases. The worker must then completely identify his interests with the community as a whole, or work because of some noneconomic incentive.

In California, Llano survived financially because of the steady influx of new members who were required to purchase stock in the corporation. Each family head had to make a cash payment of $1,000 for himself, and lesser payments for his wife and children. This capital was used to buy the land, construct the colony facilities, and begin a large number of

167

industries. Yet the colony was obviously completely dependent on agriculture, with almost all of the industries only providing services to the colonists. The land was best suited for pear production, but orchards require several years for development. The gardens and livestock provided only part of the subsistence needed. As a result the colony was quickly overpopulated, could scarcely provide the most vital necessities for incoming families, and soon faced complete bankruptcy as the water supply proved inadequate. Without an adequate economic base, the elaborate organization of working crews, the admittedly hard work by some colonists, and the steady growth of colony buildings, were all practically useless. Unlike Pickett, Job Harriman was not willing to rescue the colony by appeals for donations and gifts, and thus made the decision to move to Louisiana. In the final accounting, the California colony lost almost all the invested capital, leaving the Louisiana colony with some transported equipment, some small parcels of land, a small debt of about $17,000, and with all payments to be made on the Louisiana land.

In Louisiana the colony barely survived from 1917 to 1920, depending mainly upon gifts for survival. After Pickett became manager in 1920, various small industries were established and the colony, with a constant stream of small gifts and loans, was able to remain solvent throughout the twenties. From a purely financial standpoint, this was the one normal period in Llano history. The taxes and the payments to the Gulf Lumber Company were sometimes delayed, but were always paid, even though this meant selling some of the outlying land, or even mortgaging the land already purchased in full.[1] In addition, the rice ranch was purchased in 1922, and some scattered portions of land in several southern states were accepted as payments for colony membership.

Unfortunately, Pickett never kept complete financial records for the colony, and it is therefore impossible to determine how much the colony gained from each individual industry and how much from memberships and gifts. One bookkeeper in the colony reported membership receipts of $41,000 in 1922, $24,000 in 1923, and much smaller amounts in 1924 and afterwards. As the number of new members declined, the colony adopted a new policy of holding the membership fee in trust for one year, and returning it in full to any member who decided to leave the colony or to anyone who could not be accepted as a permanent member. This unpredictable drain on colony resources did not increase the number of

1. *Llano Colonist*, Oct. 29, 1927.

recruits, and was modified in 1931 and dropped altogether in the next two years.[2]

Pickett admitted that the colony had a good income for the first time in 1927, since the earlier efforts had been directed toward a good foundation of new industries and machines. In his terms, Llano had been investing for its workers the income that Wall Street always stole from industry.[3] Because of the successes in 1927, he argued that the colony would not dare publish a financial statement, but that many debts were paid and that the colony owed only about 10 per cent of what it owned.[4] In the receivership case in 1928, the Louisiana Supreme Court found Llano to be solvent, although making no annual profits. Based on incomplete records, it found debts of $146,054.06 and assets estimated at $521,694.87. Yet there was an operating deficit for 1926 and much of the colony land was mortgaged to members of the board of directors.[5]

The main asset of the colony was its land, although most of it was cut-over pine forests too poor for profitable farming. The land always provided much of the subsistence for the colony, but was never developed and farmed at anywhere near its capacity, since Pickett tended to emphasize other types of enterprises. Even five hundred acres of good farming land, intensively utilized, would have served the colony far better than its approximate fifteen thousand acres of submarginal land, and would have cost no more at the beginning. Apart from extensive vegetable gardens and a dairy that was never large enough to supply the colony's milk needs (only twenty cows being milked in prosperous 1929), the farm provided some truck for sale in the better years, furnished peanuts for candy-making and for peanut butter, and occasionally supplied other salable products, such as eggs, cotton, and nursery plants and trees. The best farm, by far, was the rice ranch, located seventy-five miles to the south in Jefferson Davis Parish. With excellent land, a large farm home, and a huge pump for flooding, the ranch produced large quantities of rice, some extra garden crops, and earned money by pumping water for other farmers. Unfortunately, the ranch was usually poorly managed and understaffed, and was always bled for the benefit of the mother colony. Even in such a normal year as 1927 some of its rice land was rented to

2. A. James McDonald, *The Llano Co-operative Colony and What It Taught* (Leesville, La.: n.p., 1950), p. 50.

3. *Llano Colonist*, Oct. 29, 1927.   4. *Ibid.*, Oct. 13, 1929.

5. "Allen *v.* Llano Del Rio Co.," *Louisiana Reports*, CLXVI (1927–1928), 78–91; Fred Hanover, "Llano Cooperative Colony: An American Rural Community Experiment" (unpublished M.A. Thesis, Tulane University, 1936), p. 114.

local farmers because of a lack of help. Few colonists wanted to live at the ranch, with its hard work and its lack of an active social life. But the ranch was the best agricultural asset the colony ever had, and in most years insured the colony of at least a rice diet.

The largest monetary income in the colony was from the ice plant, which developed a large market in Leesville and kept several men busy either at the plant or on delivery trucks through the warm months. In the twenties a winter income was derived from the manufacture of sweet potato crates and from the sale of unfinished lumber. The colony store profited from sales to visitors and to the few colonists with outside incomes. The salaries of the two school teachers and the postmaster were guaranteed sources of revenue. The tailor and shoe shops, laundry, print shop, guest rooms in the hotel, and filling station and garage all brought in small sums of money. Yet, in 1930, all of these industries brought in only slightly over $30,000. Operating expenses exceeded this income. In fact, every major enterprise lost money in that year. Even when supplemented by gifts or loans, the annual money income of the colony could not have been much over $50,000 in any one year, and this for from two hundred to three hundred people. After 1929, the colony survived only because it slowly used up all its accumulated capital.[6]

Although there are no statistics for proof, there can be little doubt but that the economic problems of Llano were due not only to the lack of capital, poor land, and managerial mistakes, but also to the inefficient use of labor. The colony always had a disproportionate number of older people, either totally retired or able to perform only small tasks. By 1935 nearly 45 per cent of all colonists were over forty-five (as compared to 21 per cent for the United States). Only 20 per cent of the colonists were in the most highly productive age bracket (twenty to forty-four). Because of poor diets, there was much illness, particularly in winter months. In addition to all this, there was always the brush gang—the dissatisfied colonists who refused to work because of disagreements with the management. Visitors always discovered some colonists who worked as little as possible, while the *Colonist* constantly condemned certain individuals and groups for lack of zeal and hard work. The noticeable lack of motivation on the part of some colonists resulted from a lack of identification with the community, from despair and loss of hope in the colony's future, from a lack of energy which resulted from a low protein diet, and from a lack of individual incentives or rewards for exceptional effort. The solid core of loyal colonists, who worked more than the required eight

6. *Llano Colonist*, Mar. 7, 1931.

hours a day, and who were highly motivated by their own idealism, were all too often engaged in nonproductive enterprises (secretarial, teaching, librarian), or in strictly service facilities (laundry, kitchen, commissary). In the twenties valuable machinery was constantly out of use because of insufficient labor, yet the school and printing plant were always completely staffed. The colony was fragmented by too many tiny industries (up to fifty), and was handicapped by the amount of time used in organizing the various work gangs.[7]

In 1930, as the depression began to be felt throughout the country, Pickett was able to retire the colony debt to the Gulf Lumber Company, but only with great difficulty. The company, desiring to get what it could from the colony, agreed to cancel all debts, interest, and mortgages for $25,000, a greatly reduced sum. This meant a clear title on all colony land and the acquisition of the final eight thousand acres included in the original option. Since the new acreage was poor, cut-over land, and since it was soon encumbered with unpaid taxes, the directors of the Llano del Rio corporation never accepted it for the colony. As a result it remained in Pickett's name until the final liquidation, when creditors forced it into the corporation. In order to raise the $25,000 Pickett launched his most fervent campaign for gifts, but could raise only $2,200. Because of the advancing depression, this was still larger than any subsequent gifts, but hardly helped in the over-all campaign. By the sale of land and new memberships, Pickett raised only $9,200. He was able to borrow $5,000 from the Rev. Eli Beers, a West Coast minister who eventually loaned $10,000, or all his life savings, believing the colony to be safer than the banks (it was not, for Beers lost all his money). The Columbia Conserve Company of Indianapolis, a large cooperative organization, loaned a final $10,000 without a mortgage, but only after a thorough investigation of the colony. Their preliminary and necessarily incomplete audit (the first ever made) showed assets of only $220,910.12, yearly losses in operations, and growing liabilities (excluding stock) of $153,651.41. The company considered a working agreement with Llano, but wanted complete control over management, which Pickett rejected. The company recommended a reorganization, careful bookkeeping, and surplus production through greater efficiency.[8]

The earliest effect of the depression on the colony was a drastic increase

7. *Ibid.*, Nov. 9, 1929; Hanover, "Llano Cooperative Colony," pp. 148–152, 173–176.
8. McDonald, *The Llano Co-operative Colony*, p. 54; Hanover, "Llano Cooperative Colony," pp. 133–136; *Llano Colonist*, Feb. 28, 1930, May 10, 17, 1930, Jan. 24, 1931, Feb. 14, 28, 1931, June 22, 1935.

in membership and a suggestion of growth and prosperity. Suddenly Llano was desirable to many unemployed families, who responded to Pickett's promises of free rent, free groceries, free fuel and lights, free medical attention, and free entertainment. By May of 1930, every facility was full, with new, temporary frame cottages being rushed to completion by voluntary work crews. The colonists began the long, drawn-out construction of a new hotel to house approximately one hundred of the waiting applicants. In the same year, the first five or six permanent homes were completed, but almost always with some subsidy from the future occupants. The depression practically cut off all free gifts, destroyed most markets for colony products, and attracted a less dedicated, more selfish, less radical, and less docile membership. Although conditions in the colony seemed better than ever when contrasted with the outside, the real level of living in the colony declined steadily after 1931.[9]

With the election of Franklin D. Roosevelt in 1932, Pickett turned to the federal government for aid to Llano, arguing for the next three years that the colony provided a model for efficient relief and rehabilitation and thus deserved governmental support. Although the colony had been reported on by the Department of Labor, it had been ignored by other governmental agencies. But with the growth of a depression back-to-the-land movement, and a new interest in land settlement and colonization for relief purposes, the colony was more widely publicized and praised than ever before.[10] Pickett jumped at a chance to use Llano as a model for a large colonization program. With the help of a former Wisconsin state senator, he drew up a proposed bill and persuaded Senator Morris Shepperd of Texas to introduce it into the United States Senate in April, 1933, as "Senate Bill 1142, The United Communities." The bill was widely discussed by Llanoites, fervently advocated in the *Colonist*, and, in the mind of Pickett, was always on the verge of passing. He defended it in Washington to the point of physical illness, connected it with one of his new fads, technocracy, bemoaned its opposition by Henry A. Wallace, and tried to place the colony on its best behavior to avoid any possible embarrassment to the bill. The Senate Bill proposed to create a federal

9. *Llano Colonist*, May 31, 1930, Jan. 24, 1931, Aug. 1, 1931.

10. United States Department of Labor, Bureau of Labor Statistics, "Llano Co-operative Colony," *Monthly Labor Review*, XXXII (May, 1931), 1134–1136; the (New York) *Times*, Jan. 29, 1933, IV, 3; Alva W. Taylor, "No Poverty in Llano Colony," *Christian Century*, L (Apr. 26, 1933), 571; W. L. Newman, "Is There Any Hope for the Unemployed?" *American Federationist*, XL (Feb., 1933), 171–173.

corporation to establish several united relief communities all over the United States. Not only were they all to be modeled on Llano, but Llano was to become the first of the colonies. Obviously, Pickett hoped to direct this corporation and turn his Llano into a national movement. The bill was, surprisingly enough, debated before the Senate Committee on Agriculture and Forestry, with Pickett as the sole witness, but, like several similar bills, was never reported from the committee. Even as it was considered, the Division of Subsistence Homesteads was established in the Department of the Interior and began the construction of thirty-three small, cooperatively oriented, widely distributed communities. Llano was ignored.[11]

Even as he continued to lobby for Senate Bill 1142, Pickett tried in other ways to get some of the money being so freely appropriated by the New Deal. In one case he succeeded. The colony was unable to pay its short-term debts to a wholesale grocery chain in 1933. As a result the parish sheriff bound the colony assets and planned a sale of the two most valuable buildings—the ice and power plants. Pickett, thoroughly cornered, raved and ranted against the creditors, admitted that the colony might be on the verge of failure, and then went to Washington. When he could get no help from the Reconstruction Finance Corporation, he turned to Louis Howe, the administrative secretary to President Roosevelt. Howe was sympathetic and called Senator Huey Long of Louisiana, instructing him to straighten out the situation. With Long's backing, Pickett received a loan from the Federal Farm Loan Bank, saved the colony, and allowed that Howe was the right man to see in Washington. Desperate for money to repay this loan, he temporarily lowered the membership fee to $500 and tried to revitalize agriculture.[12]

In 1934 Pickett spent much of his time in Washington, seeking aid of any sort. He offered to turn Llano over to the Division of Subsistence Homesteads and donate his leadership without a salary, but the division rejected all of his offers after one of their officials visited the colony. Ironically, an appeal for relief loans to the division was rejected by Dr. William E. Zeuch, the old enemy of Pickett and former head of Commonwealth College, who was then a cooperative specialist for the Division of Subsistence Homesteads. Stressing that Llano had been in the relief

11. Senate Committee on Agriculture and Forestry, *Hearings on S. 1142, the United Communities*, 73rd Cong., 1st Sess., 1933, pp. 1–31; U.S., *Congressional Record*, 73rd Cong., 1st Sess., 1933, pp. 1172–1174; *Llano Colonist*, Mar. 25, 1933, May 27, 1933.

12. *Llano Colonist*, June 10, 17, 24, 1933; July 15, 1934.

business for twenty years and was then caring for hundreds of unemployed people without compensation, Pickett appealed to Harry
Hopkins of the Federal Emergency Relief Administration and to Jacob
Baker of the Federal Surplus Commodities Corporation, asking to "line
up with the Federal Government" in a constructive relief program.
Again, the government was not interested in joining with Llano. Pickett,
with great publicity back in the colony, became one of three members of a
National Committee on Self-Help Co-operatives, but his committee was
only encouraged, not supported, by the government. Nonetheless,
Pickett had great hopes for a truly national movement, and began to
prepare his colony for outside aid, lining up foremen and workers and
listing needed machinery and equipment. Yet no money was forthcoming
and Pickett was desperate. Meanwhile, the National Recovery Administration codes raised the prices on products purchased by the colony,
while tightened Securities and Exchange Commission regulations forced
Pickett to withdraw the colony from its listing with the Federal Trade
Commission and stop selling all stock membership. Since the colony was
officially solvent or even prosperous, none of the colonists were eligible
for individual relief. Despite Pickett's efforts, Llano was a New Deal
orphan.[13]

Even as Pickett wooed the federal government, he began some daring
and expensive programs at the colony. In 1932 he reversed a long-
standing policy and, in cooperation with outside speculators, began
drilling for oil on colony lands. With his usual enthusiasm, Pickett
predicted the greatest oil field in the United States and began advertising
for interested investors. Several colonists protested the oil policy,
claiming that oil-rig workers were receiving preferential treament. An
infuriated Pickett denounced all opposition at such a critical period and
avowed that he was going to have peace if he "had to fight for it." In
June, 1932, the drilling commenced, with the first object being gas and
not oil. Pickett planned a cracking plant for the colony and a fleet of
cooperative trucks to distribute the new wealth. The drilling was slow, the
breakdowns often, and the original excitement and anticipation slowly
lessened. Yet, almost every colonist hoped against hope for a great
windfall, for Pickett now admitted that the colony was completely broke.
In less than a year the drill bit broke in the well and the first attempt had

13. Hanover, "Llano Cooperative Colony," pp. 121–124, 138; McDonald, *The
Llano Co-operative Colony*, p. 67; *Llano Colonist*, Jan. 20, 1934, Feb. 10, 17, 24, 1934,
Apr. 28, 1934.

to be abandoned. Under the direction of "Doc" Williams, two more hopeless attempts were made in 1933 and 1934. The investment was completely lost, and Vernon Parish remains to this day one of the few Louisiana parishes with no appreciable production of either gas or oil.[14]

It was also in 1932 that Pickett finally launched a long-awaited policy of expansion, or of new units. This drive for additional colonies, coming at a time of greatest financial weakness, did more than any other one thing to destroy the parent colony, and was the most fatal managerial decision ever made by Pickett. Some believe that he anticipated a complete collapse of the competitive economy and, therefore, felt that the loans he negotiated would never have to be repaid. Actually, Pickett had long dreamed of turning Llano into a national movement, but never had he had the means for expansion. In 1930 he predicted colonies in every state, and as immediate goals talked of complete self-sufficiency through a wheat unit in the North, a tropical fruit unit in the South, iron and coal units in mining areas, and a cotton and woolen plant for Llano.[15] He argued that several small units were more efficient than one large one, and that they could make a better demonstration of the Llano way. By 1931 he was campaigning for several new colonies to care for the unemployed, and even had architectural plans readied. Hardly an issue of the *Colonist* ignored the new obsession of Pickett.[16] Meanwhile, the rice ranch, the small Christian settlement, and even a sawmill site about ten miles from the colony were designated as units, giving an illusion that the expansion was already under way.

The first major expansion came in 1932, when the colony acquired a small citrus farm near Fremont, Texas. Ole Synoground, probably Pickett's most loyal supporter and an invaluable colonist, settled on the new unit with a few other colonists, taking with him the needed supplies. Synoground later purchased the site himself when the colony could not meet its payments. Also in 1932, Pickett negotiated a purchase contract with the Federal Farm Bank for a huge sugar plantation in Terrebonne Parish, to be paid for in twenty years by means of the actual farm production. The plantation, near the Gulf Coast of Louisiana, included 2,700 acres and over twenty houses, yet sold for only $50,000. Despite hard work by some of the colonists, little sugar cane was produced the first

14. *Llano Colonist*, June 11, 25, 1932, July 2, 1932, Sept. 3, 1932, Feb. 4, 1933; Bob Brown, *Can We Co-operate?* (New York: Roving Eye Press, 1940), pp. 209–210.
15. *Llano Colonist*, Mar. 8, 1930, May 17, 1930, Feb. 14, 1931.
16. *Ibid.*, Sept. 5, 1931, Nov. 7, 1931.

year. As a result the Federal Farm Bank canceled the contract in December, 1932. The colonists then moved to another sugar plantation near Jeannerette in Iberia Parish which purportedly had more land, more houses, better transportation facilities, and could be purchased at lower terms. For some unexplained reason, this contract was never completed and Llano was permanently out of the sugar business.[17] Individuals closely connected with Llano attempted to establish small units at Magdalena, New Mexico, in Arkansas, and in northern Louisiana, but none of these temporary settlements were financed with colony funds.[18]

The most ambitious and the most disastrous new unit was established in the Gila River Valley of New Mexico. The Gila unit, as it was always called, was purchased in February, 1933, at a total cost of $100,000. Pickett made the deal with the Bassett Land and Live Stock Company, which held a $35,000 mortgage on the property. In close cooperation with the land company, Pickett obligated the Llano del Rio Company not only to pay Bassett its $35,000, but to pay the owners of the property (an Armstrong family) a total of $65,000, beginning with $12,000 in 1933, $10,000 in 1934, and the balance at $4,500 annually. The $35,000 debt was easily postponed, but the Armstrongs were determined to collect their payments when due.[19]

Despite these unbelievably large financial commitments by an already impoverished colony, Pickett managed to obscure the financial details and to make the deal sound like a glorious bargain. As he described it, the Gila property included 3,500 acres of land (two thousand in cultivation), a huge, hotel-like community house, several small houses, barns, warehouses, offices, an ice plant, dairy, laundry, and a factory building. The farm was stocked with one hundred dairy cows, one hundred Herefords, two hundred hogs, one hundred horses and mules, stored feed, a flour mill, and several trucks and cars. [20] With the purchase, colonists left from Llano to occupy this veritable heaven on earth, taking with them truckloads of badly needed supplies and exciting the envy of a majority of Llanoites, who had scarcely enough to eat themselves. Quickly the Gila unit became an adjunct of Llano, contributing news items to the *Colonist* and apparently copying most of the parent colony's institutions.

The Gila colony did not even begin to meet all its financial obligations.

17. *Ibid.*, Mar. 12, 1932, May 7, 1932, Jan. 14, 1933.
18. *Ibid.*, Jan. 9, 16, 1932, Oct. 22, 1932.
19. Hanover, "Llano Cooperative Colony," p. 118.
20. *Ibid.*, pp. 118–119; *Llano Colonist*, Oct. 29, 1932.

In the first two and one-half years it paid only $4,878.37 cash on its scheduled payments of approximately $32,000, completely defaulted on its taxes, and all this in spite of the sale of some of the colony land. After the seizure of the colony rice crop in 1933, the Armstrongs gave the colony a clearance for the first payment, but after a default on the $10,000 payment for 1934 sued the Llano del Rio Company, asking a local New Mexico court to forfeit the contract and evict the colonists. The colony assets were frozen in December, 1934, and in the next March all food supplies were cut off from the destitute colonists.[21]

Pickett, who was almost as attached to Gila as to the parent colony, fought a hopeless battle to save the unit, arguing that it was a war of the poor against the bankers (the Armstrong claims were held by a New Mexico bank). Pickett believed that the Gila unit should have been credited with up to $22,000 for work accomplished, and wrote emotional appeals to congressmen, the Reconstruction Finance Corporation, and the Resettlement Administration. Rushing back and forth between Gila and Llano, Pickett received what must have been a very reluctant vote of confidence at Llano in March, 1935, and then returned to Gila to attend a court trial. Because of inflammatory articles in the *Colonist*, he was arrested and convicted of contempt for trying to pressure the court. The sentence of six months was suspended, but court costs were added to the almost continuous drain of money. Pickett was in Washington in a final bid to save the Gila unit when the Llano colonists revolted against his leadership on May 1, setting up a new colony government. Eugene Carl and the new leaders repudiated all new units and, except for an attempt to recover the colony investment, deserted Gila to the "wolves." The Gila colonists were completely dispossessed and, being Pickett supporters, were not welcomed back to Llano. The small payments of money plus all the supplies sent from Llano were completely lost. By this time the financial situation at Llano was beyond redemption.[22]

Even before the revolt in 1935, living conditions at Llano were at a subsistence level. From 1930 on visitors had been appalled at the ragged clothing of the colonists. By 1935 many adult colonists were without shoes, while shirts and trousers were often so torn and ragged that individuals were embarrassed around visitors. When someone died,

21. Letter, William R. Warner to G. T. Pickett, Feb. 16, 1935, in the personal papers of George T. Pickett; Hanover, "Llano Cooperative Colony," pp. 118–119.

22. McDonald, *The Llano Co-operative Colony*, p. 41; *Llano Colonist*, Mar. 16, 1933, Apr. 6, 1935.

there was always an eager competition for the extra pair of shoes. The old sawmill shacks were no longer kept in good repair, with many colonists fighting a losing battle against leaking roofs, sagging doors, and falling porches. Small family gardens were increasingly abandoned because of poor fences, which would not turn the wandering hogs and cows of colony neighbors (Vernon Parish was then an open range). In the winter colonists had to scavenge at ever-increasing distances for their firewood. The food situation was most critical. The steady diet of rice, sweet potatoes, and rare servings of meat led to malnutrition and frequent illness (a typhoid epidemic ravaged Llano in 1935). A home economist analyzed the Llano diet in 1935, finding it deficient in calcium and most vitamins. It included few vegetables, milk products, fruit, or eggs. The colony dairy had declined to ten cows for over four hundred people. The average Llano family consumed only $4.89 worth of food weekly, which was $2.00 less than the amount approved for Federal Emergency Relief Administration clients. The colonists were almost unanimous in their belief that they ate better before coming to Llano. Of course, a minority of colonists had some outside income and were able to supplement the diet of the dining hall. A few others had subsistence gardens. The over-all plight of the colony was vividly demonstrated at the traditional Christmas party of 1935, when, for the first time, only children and adults over sixty received the meager bags of fruit and candy. The other hopeful colonists were "bitterly disappointed," although many were too ill even to attend the party.[23]

The new management that replaced Pickett in 1935 applied themselves most directly to the economic problem. Denouncing begging as a means of raising money, they revived the crate industry, tried to revitalize agriculture, began a system of complete bookkeeping, and as a result were able to ward off a host of hungry creditors. Some of the more urgent and immediate debts were paid, but there was nothing left for an improved living standard. By 1936 a large number of the older colonists had departed, some because of loyalty for Pickett, but others because of a loss of hope in the future of the colony. Yet, most visitors and observers agreed that the new management was improving conditions and that a profitable economy might not be too far in the future. At this juncture, old injustices overtook the colony and destroyed it.[24]

23. Brown, *Can We Co-operate?* pp. 64, 119–120; Hanover, "Llano Cooperative Colony," pp. 143–146; Robert Whitcomb, "The New Pilgrim's Progress," *Atlantic Monthly*, CXLVII (May, 1931), 548; *Llano Colonist*, Jan. 6, 1936.

24. *Llano Colonist*, Nov. 16, 1935, Dec. 21, 1935, Mar. 7, 1936.

In the early thirties Pickett stopped returning membership fees when an applicant left, or was forced to leave, within his first year of residence. This was a rank injustice to many elderly couples, who came to Llano because of gross misrepresentations and who often invested their life savings for membership. But to Pickett it was a necessary injustice, for the colony rarely had any money to refund memberships. In May, 1933, a Leesville lawyer and embittered former colonist, A. James McDonald, brought suit against the Llano del Rio Company in behalf of an old man, Albert Schmidt, who asked for a return of $520. Quickly McDonald added other former colonists to his suit, bringing the total to $4,262. This suit was decided against the colony in July, 1934, but in the meantime Pickett had either mortgaged or "sold" all the colony assets, in most cases to his best friends within the colony. McDonald therefore asked the court in January, 1935, to appoint a receiver and to set aside two of the mortgages in order that his clients could collect. A state moratorium law (a pet of Huey Long's) postponed any action until March, 1936. At that time the new management agreed to accept a court-appointed receiver without a legal fight. The colony manager, Carl, was immediately appointed and bonded, only to be challenged by Pickett and other creditors of the corporation. Most of the old, deposed board of directors held first and second mortgages on colony property. The local judge then selected a new receiver from among four names, two submitted by Pickett and two by the new colony managers. The judge favored the new management and, in April, 1936, appointed a Leesville druggist, Richard Pollard.[25]

As receiver, Pollard decided to maintain the colony in the hope of profitable operation. He officially ended the revolution by consulting with both Pickett and Carl, appointed the ever-popular "Doc" Williams as his colony representative, and asked for united effort. May Day in 1936 was a solemn occasion, with fear beneath the cries of harmony and the expressed hope that, after twenty-two years, Llano would yet go on to spread the idea of a cooperative commonwealth. Even as May Day was celebrated, the last oil well was abandoned and the oil venture discontinued. In the fall and winter of 1936–1937 the colony began to disintegrate. So many old members left that, by spring, the *Colonist* admitted that few capable workers remained, but that there were plenty of old, dependent people and laggards. Fortunately, with the receivership, individual colonists were eligible for federal relief payments or employment. As the last industrial enterprises closed down, the

25. McDonald, *The Llano Co-operative Colony*, pp. 64–68; *Llano Colonist*, Apr. 4, 18, 25, 1936.

colonists began farming their own small subsistence plots. Only two colonists remained at the rice ranch, which was leased out to neighbors until it was foreclosed by the Federal Land Bank. Meanwhile Pickett, again acting for colony creditors, challenged the financial report by Pollard and sued the receiver for damages. Pollard resigned and was replaced by Dwight Ferguson, a Leesville lawyer who was only slightly more acceptable to Pickett.[26]

After the appointment of Ferguson, Pickett was able to regain a position of leadership, and thus presided over the final death of his beloved colony. As the end neared, most of the young leaders of the earlier revolt left the colony for outside jobs. Pickett once again gave his pep talks, took over personal direction of the farm and tried to inspire hope by recalling the desperate situation in 1920. Nonetheless, most of the farm had to be leased to neighbors, the *Industrial Democrat*, a colony-owned parish weekly, was sold in May, 1937, and the ice plant and store continued operations only because Pickett spent his own money to support them. Pickett even regained control of the *Colonist*, resurrecting the diary and making some final pleas for financial gifts. He reinstituted the psychology meeting, condemned once again the old revolution, and worked with the few able-bodied colonists in the fields. But his desperate pleas went unanswered, the diesel engines for ice and power were running only part-time, the school closed for the first time in twenty-three years for lack of teachers, and, by September, Pickett was purchasing ice in order to maintain his loyal customers. By October, 1937, all was lost. The diesels were through, Pickett's personal credit was exhausted, not one industry was active, and there was no common food. Pickett asked about those interested in starting a new colony and carried out some devious plots to save some of the colony land.[27]

The last *Colonist* appeared on December 9, 1937, after a lapse of over a month. In it Pickett admitted complete defeat, and at last accepted the inevitability of liquidation. At that time Pickett still hoped that the mortgagees (primarily his loyal friends) could pay off the McDonald creditors and then foreclose their mortgages, receiving clear titles to the assets of the bankrupt corporation. They could then pool their land and reform the colony under a new corporation. There was also one other hope. The colony site was investigated by the Farm Security Administration, which briefly considered it as a site for a cooperative farm com-

26. *Llano Colonist*, Apr. 25, 1936, May 3, 1936, Feb. 6, 13, 27, 1937, Apr. 24, 1937.

27. *Ibid.*, Mar. 20, 27, 1937, May 15, 1937, June 5, 12, 1937, Aug. 21, 1937, Sept. 4, 11, 1937, Oct. 30, 1937.

munity similar to ones already established at Lake Dick, Arkansas, and Casa Grande, Arizona. Neither hope materialized, since the several creditors had priority claims on the colony assets and could set aside as many mortgages as necessary to safeguard their claims. Thus, Pickett's final testimony in the last *Colonist* was also, unknown to him, a type of salutation to the Llano colony:

I am thoroughly convinced that Heaven on earth will never be built until human beings build it. I believe there is a Supreme Intelligence that can be brought to play through human agencies that can and eventually will build that Heaven on earth. You and I have the power within ourselves to make our existence worth while for society as a whole; and, after the time I have spent in the Llano Movement, I cannot see any place in the world where I can go and offer myself more opportunity for doing something worthwhile for society and at the same time bring into my life more real happiness than is to be found working with my fellowmen in an integral cooperative movement such as we have.[28]

The actual liquidation of the colony occurred in 1938 and 1939. The court first ordered the sale of assets in March, 1938. In a resulting auction in June, the Bassett Land and Livestock Company bid in the total property in order to try to protect its note of $35,000 against the corporation, but was unable to make payment and complete the sale. Then, in a series of sales that led to endless controversy and litigation, the receiver sold all the colony land and improvements to local citizens by private negotiation. The prices received were unbelievably low, even for the depths of the depression and in spite of the justified fear of unclear titles. In the belief of many mortgage holders, the receiver and court was only interested in accumulating enough money to pay the McDonald clients and to cover the court and receiver costs. The whole townsite of Llano, including seventy-five buildings, was sold for only $6,650.00; the industrial plants brought only $7,200. One unit of forty acres, with two residences, two barns, and a swimming pool, sold for only $250. The total received for all assets was only approximately $40,000, which barely covered the judgment creditors, past tax bills, and the costs. The mortgage holders lost all. Of course, many of them were former colonists who unfairly acquired their mortgages, but a few were innocent outsiders like the Rev. Eli Beers.[29]

28. *Ibid.*, Dec. 9, 1937.

29. Letter from Gerald Weatherly to John R. Hunter, July 7, 1947, in Pickett papers; McDonald, *The Llano Co-operative Colony*, pp. 68–69; John B. Pollard, "Report on the Llan Del Rio Co. of Nevada," a mimeographed report by. the State Farm Debtor Supervisor for the State of Louisiana, Feb. 25, 1939, pp. 1–6.

The actual liquidation was, at least in part, in accordance with Pickett's own plans. Back in 1937 he had attempted some complicated legal maneuvers to try to save some colony land. He made a private bargain with a local hardware dealer, J. H. Anderson, who had already aided Pickett by paying back taxes on about eight thousand acres of pine land that Pickett claimed as his own (the court never agreed). According to the agreement, Pickett was to collect all notes and mortgages against the corporation and then turn them over to Anderson, who in turn would buy the colony property in a tax sale. Pickett hoped to acquire the mortgages at a reduced value, and to pay for them with stock in a new Llano corporation. In exchange for the mortgages and thus a free title to the land, Anderson promised to deed the colony land over to Pickett in exchange for all timber rights (actually worth more than the land). In the actual liquidation, Anderson's company, the Anderson-Post Hardware Company, paid $17,042 for the largest portion of the colony land, but never turned it over to Pickett, since Pickett was never able to collect all the mortgages and did not have any money to pay the receiver costs. Anderson later claimed that he would have been willing to fulfill his part of the bargain anytime within one year if Pickett could have raised any funds, which he was never able to do.[30]

After Pickett failed in his last attempt to save any of his colony, he charged that the liquidation had been one great conspiracy between the receiver, the State of Louisiana (as represented by two local judges), and the Leesville businessmen, such as Anderson, who practically stole the colony in a privately negotiated giveaway. In 1947 Pickett, in the name of the old corporation and abetted by lawyers, finally filed a $13,500,000 damage suit against Anderson-Post Hardware, other purchasers, and the state. Pickett contended that this sum represented the true value of the former colony in 1947, since land values had soared in the area after the construction of Fort Polk in 1939 on lands adjoining the colony. Both the lower courts and the United States Fifth Circuit Court of Appeals rejected the contention of Pickett, and in so doing upheld the integrity of the Louisiana courts. A hopeless appeal to the United States Supreme Court for a writ of certiorari was rejected in 1951, but nonetheless Pickett still talked vaguely about new legal moves to regain his stolen colony.[31]

The Llano colony, like some hardy but very ill and emaciated old man,

30. Letter, Gerald Weatherly to John R. Hunter, July 7, 1947, Pickett papers.
31. The complete file of legal documents concerning these suits are in the Pickett papers.

died slowly and agonizingly from 1937 to 1951. But the Llano movement, the dream of a future cooperative commonwealth, did not die with the mother colony. Pickett remained the leader of what now became a purely spiritual movement, which as such escaped the factions and bitterness of a practical movement. Even the Llano del Rio Company was continued as a more or less honorary club of old people with gradually lengthening memories. George T. Pickett was president, and there was no one to challenge his leadership. Many of the elderly and most devoted colonists lived on at Llano after the liquidation, paying a negligible rent for their shacks and living from relief payments. Esther Allen, the "nun of co-operation" and by then old in the service of a lost cause, wrote to a friend in 1940: "I pay two bucks a month for my little cabin and fifty cents for light and water. And I eat—sometimes."[32]

In California a group of former colonists continued the Llano movement into the post-World War II period, even publishing a mimeographed *Llano Colonist* which hopefully followed the court battles and contained beautiful memories of the old colony. Walter Millsap editorialized in 1947: "Get this straight, Llano Colony was the only group of people in the whole Western Hemisphere that was daring enough to try and learn the basic laws that govern a better system of co-operative economics. We people of Llano Colony, compared to many other communities of a like size, were more peaceable, more industrious, more attentive to our own business, less meddlesome with other people's affairs, more kindly disposed toward our neighbors than many others, and we were, on the average, better citizens in every way."[33]

George T. Pickett was able to salvage a little land at Llano and constructed on it a small, never-completed bungalow. He continued to keep his goats, lost his second wife, suffered a severe stroke, but mainly spent his time and effort in his fruitless attempts to regain the colony. Until his death in 1962, he lived alone in his increasingly dilapidated, unpainted house on a site near the old Kid Kolony and also near the empty site of the nice new home constructed for him by the colonists, but later moved away to Leesville. Pickett lived a hermit-like existence, with only his memories and his goats for companionship. His house was packed with scattered records and memorabilia from the colony. Increasingly feeble, Pickett could scarcely care for himself in his last years. In 1959, emaciated and near death, his memory was slowly fading. Events many years past

32. Brown, *Can We Co-operate?* p. 231.
33. *Llano Colonist*, Sept. 2, 1947 (mimeographed, in Pickett papers).

were recalled as happening only yesterday. Thus, his precious colony was not something that ended twenty years before, but only in the last year or the year before that.[34]

Pickett mellowed with age, and eventually had no real animosity toward any of his former enemies. When visited in 1959, his eyes still shone with the old fire, particularly when he had an opportunity to talk about the colony. He was then quite disturbed that his lawyers were not proceeding any faster on his lawsuit (then eight years in the past), and proudly proclaimed himself the president of the Llano del Rio Company. His futile ambition was to regain the colony and use it as an old people's home, supporting the colony by the old-age pensions of the members. Pickett hesitated to go back into the main part of the colony, and explained this fear as a desire to keep the "conspirators" guessing about his next move. He assumed that all the purchasers of Llano property were in deep fear of losing it to him in an early lawsuit. Pickett welcomed all questions about the past, and remembered day-by-day events in the colony with a crystal clarity that directly contrasted with his vague forgetfulness of events after the colony died. In a real sense, Pickett died in 1938 with his colony. Or perhaps, conversely, the colony did not die in 1938, but only in 1962 with Pickett.

The main colony buildings are still standing at Newllano. As late as 1959 the warehouse still faintly reflected the words: "Llano Co-operative Colony." The hotel, the heart of Llano in Louisiana, and the roof garden, scene of so much dancing and gaiety, then looked very much as they did twenty years earlier. But the roof garden was a storage warehouse and the hotel had been turned into cheap, rented apartments. The ice company, long operated by a private company, was idle. Many of the motley frame houses were gone; others were occupied by laborers. When touring the colony and identifying old landmarks, it was almost unbelievable that over two decades had elapsed since the liquidation.

It is easy to sympathize with the few remaining colonists who still live at Newllano, or who occasionally return to the scene of so much of their past endeavor. No one who remained at Llano for any considerable time was able to resist its subtle attractiveness. But eventually there will be no one left to remember. The loyal alumni are shrinking in number. Soon only historians will be able, vicariously, to join the colony, to share once again in the Llano dream, to enjoy the friendship of so many fascinating people, to suffer with them the privation and discouragement, and to

34. Personal interviews with George T. Pickett in the summer of 1959.

join them as they drowned their sorrow, their hunger, their squalor in the Saturday night dance. Only the most sympathetic historian will be able to recreate the exhilaration of a May Day, when, at least for a brief moment, all the colonists were convinced that the Llano way was really the way of the future.

Perhaps a dying Pickett, sitting for endless hours on his back porch, watching the evening fall over the pine trees that once guarded his thriving colony, was the last person who could truly revisit Llano, and see as clearly as ever before the work gangs dissolving, the buses discharging the children from the Kid Kolony, and the gathering at the hotel for supper. Until the end, his world was always inhabited by Llano personalities, by Cuno in white robe, by "Dad" Gleeser of the *Colonist*, by Esther Allen with her rosy optimism. The cooperative commonwealth had shrunk to one lonely man.

Epilogue

The Hutterites and the Llano socialists illustrate two heretical extremes in our conventional society. By the standards of their critics, the Hutterites are too religious, too authoritarian, too strict and joyless, and too lacking in art and culture. The Llano colonists were too irreligious, too avowedly secular, too materialistic, too undemocratic, too naive and idealistic, and too nonconformist. Both groups joined in the common heresy of communal property, in their desire for either perfect obedience or perfect institutions, and in their vigorous condemnation of the encircling, outside world.

The heretic may or may not be dangerous; he is always a revelation. Fortunately, at least for their own survival, neither the Hutterites nor the Llano colonists were ever so powerful or influential as to pose any real threat to the majority society, despite the ambitious hopes of Llano or the early missionary fervor of the Hutterites. But for many of the individuals who had contact with either of the two groups, there was a threat to the individual's sense of security. If he took either Llano or the Hutterites seriously, his basic assumptions and dearest values were not only challenged, but, by the very contrast, for the first time fully recognized and clarified. His reaction might range from conversion or a fascinated admiration to bitterness and vindictive condemnation. To many casual visitors and even to most neighbors, Llano was too pathetic, too much a freak, to be taken seriously, and thus was interesting and little else. Few serious observers of the Hutterites could remain aloof or merely curious. This in part accounts for the greater intensity of local resentment against the religious and passive Hutterites and the calm local acceptance of the radical, irreligious Llanoites.

Heresy originates either in apostasy or reaction, or in both. An individual who begins a heretical movement may follow the path of the first colonists at Llano, who rejected their own former society, their own past values, and espoused a new social order. In other cases he may imitate the Hutterites, who tenaciously clung to traditional values long beyond their almost universal rejection, refusing to adapt themselves to the gradual changes in the surrounding society. Because of such unique institutions as common property, the Hutterites originated in a type of mild apostasy even in an age of religious and social chaos. Yet, in 1528, they actually accepted most of the institutions and mores of their age, and tenaciously clung to them through four centuries. Mild heretics in their origin, they slowly became even more heretical from the viewpoint of their neighbors. The most radical apostate cannot bequeath his apostasy to later generations, but only his heresy. Even though his descendants may continue, or even enlarge, his heretical protest, they have never broken with the orthodox and thus risk a loss of the early fervor of revolt. It is probable that heresy born of apostasy is much less likely to survive over long periods than the heresy slowly evolved in reaction.

Usually the heretic is more worthy of close study than the alien. He always rejects some of the dominant values and institutions of his society, often with the vehemence of one embittered or angry, or with the dogmatism of one who feels vastly superior. The alien is only a casual observer who is expected to be different. Only the heretic can become a traitor. Thus, unlike the alien, the heretic serves as a valuable social barometer. Even though overamplified and extreme, his heretical protest often anticipates grave crises that are developing in the majority society. He, with his sensitivity and anger, his orthodoxy and dogmatism, vividly demonstrates existing injustice, inconsistency, immorality, superficiality, and false complacency. It is true that a study of alien cultures also reveals a great deal about one's own, at least by contrast. But rarely can it reveal as much about ourselves as a close scrutiny of our own dissidents. In some cases, our own heretics may be related to, or even part of a movement that, in another nation or society, has already achieved dominance and thereby ceased to be heretical. In this case it has immediate practical relevance, insofar as we have to deal with the other society. Even when a heresy is so totally esoteric as to seem virtually irrelevant (and this is rare), it may still be interesting enough for serious study. In all cases it demonstrates one way of coping with the human predicament, and a way usually typified by extraordinary adventure and the highest of ideals.

The Hutterites represent a living protest to most aspects of modernity in America. They merge the simplicity of a past, communal agrarianism with the certainty of a medieval religious authoritarianism. In a "progressive" country, their complete communities are both limited and enriched by unbending traditionalism. Although the Hutterites have freely sacrificed such luxuries as art, competitive rewards, intellectual freedom, and assertive individuality, their communities are increasingly attractive in the mid-twentieth century, as attested by a growing number of converts or imitators. Although they never promise ideality or worldly happiness, the Hutterites offer a means of escaping from the burdens of economic insecurity, from the perils and anxiety of having to choose among conflicting values, and from the fearful complexity and disorder of urban life. Other orthodox religions, as well as secular creeds, offer the same intellectual certainty, but never the same degree of economic security and the same rustic simplicity.

Total Christianity is rarely attempted in the twentieth century. The Hutterites do attempt it, and in so doing represent an affront, a reproach, or a challenge to all who want to remain completely in the Christian tradition. The Hutterites find in Christianity a completely encompassing creed, and try to shape all aspects of their life by its demands. Unlike most Christians, even including most other orthodox ones, they are very close to the literal, nonrationalized faith of the Hebrews and of the first Church at Jerusalem. Lacking an elaborate theology, they lack not only intellectual subtlety but also excuses. They base their society on a literal, unquestioning reading of Scripture, on a straightforward interpretation of Christ's concept of brotherly love and the Kingdom, and on an attempted imitation of the practices of the earliest churches. As such, they permit no compromises, prescribe a rigid, inflexible, and virtually impossible standard, and never permit theological abstractions to preempt the place of obedience. As a result, the total authority of creed and church are very nearly realized in practice. Hutterites are only free to accept or reject the creed; to be or not to be a Christian.

The Enlightenment never influenced the Hutterites. They still see a foreboding world and a finite mankind. The affirmation, the secular hopes of the eighteenth century were always rejected as illusions. Yet, few other Christians were unaffected. To a certain extent, almost all have followed the secular lures of the modern world. But not the Hutterite. He remains an extremist, a fanatic, a reactionary. He abides by a narrow and inflexible authority. He firmly believes that he has access to revealed and eternal truth. On the basis of this, he condemns the secular world and all those who compromise with its temporary but illusory pleasures. Other orthodox churches espouse a total creed, but, except for a few small sects, always find ways of adapting their creed to the changing world and thus manage to retain their large membership. Few would dare prescribe complete community, denounce all luxuries, demand complete pacifism, and suffer all types of persecution. Most Christians (and most humans) try to have the best of two worlds, and thus are only paatial citizens of both. To these people, the Hutterites are very disturbing. If, apart from doctrinal issues, Christianity is really so very demanding, so total, so illiberal, so strict and narrow, many modern men would have to reject it. The same lessons are applicable to secular creeds, such as Marxism. The Hutterites demand an unwanted choice between alternates. They push men toward untenable extremes, force them to face undesirable inconsistencies, and show them the illusion of tolerant, good-natured compromise.

To those who advocate an open society, who repudiate any authoritarian ideologies, the Hutterites are more frightening than challenging. Perhaps they have the most attractive of creeds, but it is still an illiberal one which leaves scant room for individual choice. Since their particular ideology is mild and passive, and since their communal villages are benevolent and humane, they offer no great threat to the surrounding, professedly liberal society. They do not even have missionaries, and their economic system is probably worthy of serious study. But in spite of this they propagate their inflexible creed among their own impressible youth, forever denying them the freedom of knowing and, perhaps, choosing another type of life. Believing that they have the Truth, the Hutterites necessarily define education as indoctrination and attempt, as near as possible, to isolate themselves from external influences. To liberal critics, the Hutterites are effectively enslaved by archaic, obviously false, and dangerously absolute concepts.

The success of Hutterite indoctrination is a frightening commentary upon the possibilities of other, less humane, secular totalitarian societies of our day. These have the means of even more effective isolation and indoctrination. Perhaps in a few generations they can achieve the same results, and with less and less force. Then they can claim, as do the Hutterites, that all choices in their society are "voluntary" and that all decisions are made by a "democratic" majority. At the very least, and again to the consternation of some, the Hutterites have proved the possibility of molding and conditioning human beings to fit various economic and social patterns. They have lived communally for so many generations that it is the normal and accepted pattern. The individualistic outside is the abnormal, the new, the strange, the fearful, the sinful, and, to some youth, the glamorous.

The Marxist dream of a governless, classless, noncoercive, but fully authoritarian communism has come closest to realization with the

Hutterites. Accepting the authority of God's word instead of Marx's interpretation of an historical process, and operating within the confines of a church instead of a party, the Hutterites have no coercive laws, no judges, no courts, and no prisons. They absolutely refuse to use the coercive weapons of surrounding political organizations. Yet, so far, they have enforced a complete orthodoxy, proving the possibility of total-itarianism based on persuasion, careful indoctrination, and virtual isolation. Conformity and performance is achieved through self-discip-line, a sense of communal responsibility, and a fear of social disapproval or ostracism. The only weapons against nonconformity are informal ones, such as neighborly scrutiny and admonition, ministerial advice, public disapproval or censure, or, ultimately, the religious ban. There is some evidence that noncoercive, para-political methods of control are slowly replacing State controls in the Soviet Union, although the State always provides a latent threat of force. In the same vein, the fear of future damnation is, to the Hutterites, a source of latent coercion. Yet, with no existing instrument of practical, political control, several Hutter-ite colonies are helplessly unable to cope with deviant behavior and open irresponsibility among the youth, a deviance caused in large part by a loss of the former almost complete isolation from conflicting outside values. When the authority of the ideology is rejected, and when the social approval of the community is no longer valued, the totalitarian society requires coercion for survival. Effective isolation (by geography or by careful insulation through travel restrictions, controlled education, and slanted news) seems to be a prime necessity for any mild totalitarianism, as many Soviet theorists have argued.

The nonauthoritarian, "liberal" critic of the Hutterites (or of any totalitarian society) must, if he is consistent, not only deny the complete validity of any total creed, but also of any absolute authority, however limited in scope. He must speak as an epistemological skeptic or agnostic, who denies to man any ultimate certainty in any realm. This does not mean that he must be a complete relativist or subjectivist, for he may find objective, factual criteria for tentative but workable judgments. It is a serious mistake to make "objective" synonymous with "absolute." Thus, such a critic must be aware that when he condemns the Hutterites he comes close to condemning a vast majority of men who, warranted or not, accept an unchanging, absolute, and usually religious creed for some areas of their life even if not for others. Most men are absolutely certain about some things. If, like John Dewey, the liberal condemns even this limited reliance on authority, he probably has no real reason for expecting a "liberal" society in the near future, if ever. On the other hand, when he almost necessarily accepts an alliance with those who are incompletely but partly "emancipated," he seemingly condones their dualistic outlook, which usually can be analyzed into some type of basic inconsistency. It is ironic, but probably true, that a degree of superficiality, of unknowing inconsistency, of expedient practicality instead of logical rigor, of unrecognized hypocrisy or intellectual dishonesty, is often conducive to moderation, tolerance, social acceptability, and political success, all of which the simple but consistent Hutterites reject. If the liberal is willing to accept these dubious "virtues" as being the only *practical* alternatives to totalitarianism, he merely condemns the Hutterite for being *too* religious, for being *too* consistent, and for being *too* honest, for what separates the Hutterite from other religious groups in our society is the scope rather than the content of his religion.

In spirit, the Llano colony was far removed from the Hutterites. The total movement for a cooperative commonwealth was inspired by a dream of utopia, of a heaven on earth. By a change in economic institutions, by the realization of cooperation, mankind would be able to abolish all selfishness, discord, and exploitation. In a sense, the institutional change would open the way for human perfection in much the same way that the Holy Spirit was supposed to enable the Hutterites to live a life of perfect obedience. Unlike the Hutterites, who expected only a few converted men to separate themselves in Christ's Church and, through God's aid, overcome their basic selfishness, the Llano colonists were inspired by the hope of a universal, cooperative society, encompassing all of a basically unselfish and good mankind. If the Hutterites set too high a standard for the separated Christian, the Llano colonists were certainly too naive in expecting all men, without divine aid, to become perfect citizens of their great community. Their naive expectations were never fulfilled, and Llano became a pathetic example of idealistic but frustrated reform, of heroic but largely wasted endeavor.

As radical but nonviolent reformers, the leaders of Llano were very American and completely modern, although a bit too optimistic to be contemporary. Sometimes painted in the coldly rational terms of the Enlightenment, sometimes in the fuzzy romanticism of the nineteenth century, sometimes in the bitter, apocalyptic vision of Karl Marx, utopia lies glimmering and beckoning just beyond much of modern history. No matter when perfection will finally appear, or what means are needed for its achievement, any belief in inevitable progress is utopian, for in such a world all ideals are ultimately realized. Actually few men have ever been under the illusion that utopia has ever been achieved, except in beautiful fictional descriptions. No colonist ever described Llano as being a utopia. But they did expect it to become a utopia, and tried to mold it according to their own ideas of what must typify a perfect society. The utopians at Llano expected an early but at first a geographically limited realization of perfection through nonviolent methods. The Marxists expect an early, universal realization through violent methods. The moderate and less optimistic reformer expects only partial realization of his ideals in limited areas and by means of compromise. All join in following some vision, in pursuing some ideals.

Just as the Hutterites, the Llanoites were almost always simple men. With two or three exceptions, there were no intellectuals connected with Llano. The colony did not sponsor any clear ideology to justify its aspirations. They had no fictional Utopia to copy, and thus were vague on ultimate goals. The nebulous quality of their ideals related them to most Americans. At Llano the desires for economic security, education, some luxuries, social opportunities, entertainment, or, in summary, happiness, were in no way heretical. The colonists were heretical in rejecting certain other widely accepted values, such as religious faith, and in desiring to achieve their ends by a radically different economic and social arrangement. Lacking a clear ideology, and always permitting or even encouraging wide variations of nonpolitical belief and practice, Llano could not offer the same intellectual certainty as the Hutterites, and because of practical failures, could never offer even the same economic security. It did offer a great deal more nonpolitical freedom, more entertainment and luxuries, and more diversity. For most Americans in the twenties and thirties, it was more appealing than the orthodox *Brüderhofs*.

Llano dramatized many of the insurmountable problems, dilemmas, and paradoxes that face all radical reformers. When dreaming gives way to working, when abstract theories are translated into practical action, the first dilemma appears. The reformer, such as Job Harriman, usually attracts his disciples by stressing the relatively vague advantages to be offered in his small heaven. For example, most Llano colonists welcomed a new order, fervently desired economic security, believed in cooperation, hailed the end of competition, and joined the early colony. But inevitably each colonist defined security and cooperation in his own, distinctively personal way, and many were soon disappointed when the new society did not meet each of their particular expectations. If such dissatisfaction is general, any reform effort will soon end in complete failure. More often, as at Llano, various individuals became dissatisfied with different aspects of the new order and created small, embittered factions that sometimes split off to try to build their own utopia. In their words, they were now going to build the true community; they would have real cooperation and security, and not the pseudo-varieties developed in the great betrayal.

Although most utopian reformers are moved by humane impulses, their behavior may often be characterized by either extreme dogmatism or by a callousness to human values. To be human it is necessary to have positive value commitments, to feel that, on some questions, we are right and those who disagree with us are necessarily wrong. It is also necessary at rare times to act on this judgment by forcing another person to conform to our view (the alternative may be our own conforming). The most idealistic reformer will usually have a clearer, better-justified set of values than most men. Just as Pickett in the last years of Llano, he will also be quite certain of the ultimate rightness of these values, whether they are insured by God, reason, nature, or only experience. Enraptured by his noble ideals, impatiently awaiting the coming heaven, he may well be contemptuous of those deluded individuals who disagree with and oppose him. Heightened idealism almost always invites heightened zeal and dogmatism. The dilemma is almost inescapable. Thus radical reformers (not radical philosophers) are often the most repelling of individuals—narrow, single-minded, abstract, cruel, harsh, unrelenting, unforgiving, and inhumane.

At Llano, the cooperative commonwealth was always defined in terms of democracy and complete economic cooperation, and rightly so. These concepts were at the heart of the ideal. Yet, in practice, the more thorough the reform attempted the greater the likelihood of dictatorial government and economic compulsion. Here again the dilemma is complete. Even when a reformer restricts his efforts to one small area, only a few leaders at first ever completely accept or even fully understand the guiding ideals, particularly when they involve really significant changes in the habits, values, and institutions of the people involved. Thus, relatively few at Llano understood the demands of cooperation. The majority simply awaited the expected satisfactions, whether economic or social. Only in rare, completely homogeneous villages, such as the Hutterite *Brüderhofs*, is complete ideological agreement possible. Only here can radical changes be both democratic and successful. In most cases, if more than a minority attempt to share in the defining of goals and in the selection of means, no thoroughgoing reform is possible, but only the opportunistic patching, the many less than perfect or, to many, less than moral compromises that typify most reform programs in democratic countries. But this the dogmatic, righteous idealists at Llano could never accept, and the early, democratic colony was soon enervated and almost destroyed by endless "brush gangs," by warring factions each too right to compromise or to cooperate.

But if a few men (or one man) who have seen the same truth, who know the one path, are able to exercise almost complete, efficient, dictatorial power, significant and even revolutionary changes can be effected. The coercive techniques may be subtle; the paternalism may be benevolent; but the process cannot be democratic, unless democracy be defined in terms of the real, although unknown, wishes of the population, or, more beguiling yet, in terms of a truth as yet grasped by only a few but applicable to all. In either case the people are forced to be democratic and made to cooperate in spite of themselves. Pickett soon learned this lesson, and applied it vigorously at Llano. He had a type of logic on his side. Are not wise dictators needed to interpret and implement the Truth in behalf of the people? Does Christ need even a cabinet to help him rule the New Jerusalem? If the philosopher kings know and follow the truth, what better government can be conceived? Should the bureaucratic expert refer his noble but complex plans to the untutored masses? If heaven is to be democratic, it will not include human beings. If heaven includes humans, it will not be democratic, or else it will quickly cease to be heaven.

The utopian, perhaps more than anyone else, is faced with an irresistible urge to concentrate on the ideal, on the end in view, and either to forget or completely subordinate means. The more wonderful heaven is, the more it seems to justify any means for its early achievement. It is true that most radical reformers conceive of man in the most idealistic and optimistic terms. It is true that their efforts are in behalf of greater human happiness. But to them man is all too often only an abstraction, for man, as they describe him, is not the existing and imperfect creature, but rather a perfected member of the future utopia. This abstract and perfect man demands all their sacrifice and devotion, while the existing creature becomes only a means of benefiting the abstraction. Imperfect, and therefore expendable, he may be sacrificed if necessary. He has no deserved rights, even though abstract man is completely free. The basic liberal faith of the West, at its best, has fortunately always assured the rights of existing, imperfect man who is, to use Kant's term, an end in himself and never just a means. This evaluation of man is more a statement of faith than of fact. Empirically, many men obviously deserve no rights and have no worth. Like animals, they could be used as a means or destroyed as a nuisance. The reformer, so very sensitive to the short-comings of his fellow men, may quickly reach this conclusion. But sincere, idealistic, he transfers all his loyalty to the men that someday will live in his great and heavenly community. Only they are worthy of his respect.

The ultimate dilemma of all utopian reformers springs from their fervid but mistaken belief that the ideal can become real. An ideal is, by its very nature, unachievable. The idea of a perfect community, although vague at best, is no illusion, but it is only an ideal, an imaginative insight. Ideals are certainly powerful, literally moving mountains at times, but they are, and remain, ideals. The great community will not, in some near or distant future, by some evolution, revolution, or miracle, cease to be what it has always been, an ideal, and become real. When you define its details, map its streets, chart its institutions—when you build it—you destroy utopia and erect only an imperfect city. Reformers often see heaven; architects rarely; contractors never. The glorious cooperative commonwealth always becomes an existing and tarnished Llano. This does not preclude a Llano from having distinct advantages and desirable institutions. It may really benefit from the insight of the reformer. Nor does it prevent some future inhabitant of the colony from reacting against its manifest imperfections and suggesting that it be replaced by a true community, which he will describe in terms more appealing by far than the existing reality. Here, fortunately perhaps, the lesson of history is never learned. Not even a thousand failures will prevent the lonely soul from dreaming of a great community, or prevent the multitudes from following him in his quest, quite sure that this time they will succeed.

Llano, and any other such ambitious and tragic an endeavor, can only teach a paradoxical lesson to contemporary man. It is a lesson of fear, for radical reform is dangerous. But it is also a lesson of courage, for we yearn for high and noble adventure. However much we fear the dedicated and committed crusader, the true and fanatic believer, we are even more afraid to be without them, for they come so close to the very essence of man. To lose them completely might be to lose man completely. In our age most men have only a chastened faith in heaven, but most of us are reluctant to relinquish heaven completely. We all believe the perfect community is an impossibility, yet at times most of us would like to help build it.

Perhaps the voice of worldly wisdom can safely brand all great reformers as at least naive and unrealistic, if not actually intolerant and dictatorial. In our sophisticated world the term "reformer" is no longer very respectable. But we dare not denounce reform; even more, we dare not avoid some of it ourselves. To refuse to lend our efforts in behalf of our ideals is, admittedly, to escape most of the real tragedy of life, but it is also to escape most of the responsibilities and most of the rewards of life. If man, in his twentieth-century sophistication, becomes too tolerant to have ideals, too afraid of the impossible to try to attain it, too democratic to exert forcible moral leadership, then only irony can describe the long pilgrimage of civilized man. From his primitive but blissful ignorance he will have traveled only a large circular route that leads to the more enervating ignorance of complete cynicism. Even wisdom, if taken to the extreme, leads to absurdity. No one at Llano could be accused of being too wise.

A Note on the Sources

The two basic sources for all Hutterite history before their migration to America are their own two chronicles or history books. The old chronicle was first published with Hutterite funds in Vienna in 1923. Edited by Rudolph Wolkan under the title of *Geschichtsbuch der Hutterischen Brüder*, it was printed in contemporary German. In 1947 a German linguist, A. J. F. Zieglschmid, carefully edited and published the old chronicle in its original form, based on the extant manuscript in a South Dakota colony. It was entitled *Die Alteste Chronik der Hutterischen Brüder*, and was published by the Carl Schurz Memorial Foundation in Philadelphia. Zieglschmid followed this editorial work by publishing, this time in contemporary German, *Das Klein-Geschichtsbuch der Hutterischen Brüder* in 1947. In addition to the small chronicle, which was written in Russia by the Hutterite leader, Johannes Waldner, this volume contains various other source materials collected by Zieglschmid in what became a true labor of love. These two imposing volumes contain not only an account of Hutterite history, but also much of the Hutterite doctrinal writings.

The one great source for Hutterite doctrine is the confession by Peter Riedemann, which is still accepted by Hutterites as an authoritative statement of their beliefs. First published in 1565 as *Rechenschaft unserer Religion, Lehr und Glaubens, so man die Hutterischen Nennt*, it was translated into English by Kathleen E. Hasenberg and published in London in 1950 as *Account of our Religion, Doctrine and Faith, Given by Peter Riedemann of the Brothers Whom Men Call Hutterians*. This one all-important source can be complemented by Peter Walpot, *True Surrender and Christian Community of Goods, From the Great Article Book by Peter Walpot, 1577*, trans. Kathleen Hasenberg (Bromdon, Bridgnorth, Shropshire, England, 1957); Paul E. Gross, trans. and ed., *The Defence Against the Prozess at Worms on the Rhine in the Year 1557* (Lethbridge, Alberta, n.d.); Peter Hofer, *The Hutterian Brethren and Their Beliefs* (Starbuck, Manitoba, 1955); Paul S. Gross, *Who Are the Hutterites?* (Pincher Creek, Alberta, 1959); and by *Die Lieder der Hutterischen Brüder* (Scottdale, Pa., 1914).

An enormous amount of both primary and secondary material has been written concerning the Anabaptist movement in general, and the early Hutterites in particular. Even before the Hutterite chronicles were rediscovered by modern scholars, European historians were unearthing, collecting, and publishing other Hutterite manuscripts and were exploring the whole Anabaptist movement at the time of the Reformation. The best bibliography of this literature is in Zieglschmid's *Klein-Geschichtsbuch*. Many of the articles written by the two leading twentieth-century Anabaptist scholars, Johann Loserth of Austria and Robert Friedmann of the United States, have been published in the *Mennonite Quarterly Review*, which contains a large number of scholarly articles on all phases of Hutterite history. The various articles on the early Hutterites by Robert Friedmann have been collected in one volume, *Hutterite Studies*, ed. Harold S. Bender (Goshen, Ind., 1961). Several excellent, summary articles on the Hutterites are included in the four-volume *Mennonite Encyclopedia* (Hillsboro, Kan., 1955–1959). The standard account of Anabaptist history in English is Charles Henry Smith's *The Story of the Mennonites* (3rd ed., Newton, Kan., 1950).

Although unknown or ignored by most students of American communalism, the Hutterites have attracted an increasing amount of interest in the twentieth century. The notes of this study include references to approximately one hundred different secondary books and articles. Yet there is no adequate history of the Hutterites. An American Mennonite scholar, John Horsch, published a rather unperceptive but accurate study entitled *The Hutterian Brethren, 1528–1931 : A Story of Martyrdom and Loyalty* (Goshen, Ind., 1931). It only provides a bare summary of Hutterite experience beyond 1774 and in many places only paraphrases or quotes lengthy excerpts from the Hutterite chronicles. Many chapters are simply copied from an unpublished M.A. Thesis: David E. Harder, "The Hutterian Church" (Bethel College, 1930). An earlier M.A. Thesis—George J. Zimmer, "Huter's Religious Communism" (Yankton College, 1912)—contains the first perceptive account of Hutterite institutions in the American colonies.

The best of several lengthy articles on the Hutterites was written by an American political scientist: Bertha W. Clark, "The Hutterian Communities," *Journal of Political Economy*, XXXII (June and Aug., 1924), 357–374, 468–486. Although less accurate in detail, Norman Thomas provides a good view of Hutterite life in "The Hutterian Brethren," *South Dakota Historical Collections*, XXV (1951), 265–299. A glowing but very summary account of Hutterite history was published in pamphlet form by the European convert, Eberhard Arnold, who died before completing a more detailed history. The pamphlet was published at Ashton Keynes, England, in 1940 and entitled *The Hutterian Brothers: Four Centuries of Common Life and Work*. The most recent, the most perceptive, but also the most rambling description of contemporary Hutterite life is in another unpublished M.A. Thesis: Victor J. Peters, "All Things Common: The Hutterites of Manitoba" (University of Manitoba, 1958).

The social scientists have discovered the Hutterites and subjected them to their research techniques and procedures, all to the benefit of historians. In 1943 Saul M. Katz completed a socio-economic study of the Hutterites, "The Security of Co-operative Farming" (unpublished M.A. Thesis, Cornell University). Lee Emerson Deets, a sociologist, lived in the Hutterite colonies and published an excellent study: *The Hutterites: A Study in Social Cohesion* (Gettysburg, Pa., 1939). In 1950 and 1951, a team of sociologists and psychiatrists used a special grant from the National Institute of Mental Health to survey the mental health of the Hutterites, a uniquely isolated group. This survey, unprecedented in its thoroughness, was published as: Joseph W. Eaton and Robert J. Weil, *Culture and Mental Disorders: A Comparative Study of the Hutterites and Other Populations* (Glencoe, Ill., 1955). The same research led to a personality study, Bert Kaplan and Thomas F. A. Plaut, *Personality in a Communal Society: An Analysis of the Hutterites* (Lawrence, Kan., 1956), and to a demographic survey, Joseph W. Eaton and Albert J. Mayer, *Man's Capacity to Reproduce* (Glencoe, Ill., 1954). In Canada, the Saskatchewan Division of the Canadian Mental Health Association conducted a more limited and less thorough study in 1953. Entitled *The Hutterites and Saskatchewan: A Study of Intergroup Relations*, it was published in mimeograph form at Regina.

Llano del Rio has received (and possibly has deserved) only a small fraction of the scholarly interest lavished on the Hutterites. Thus the main sources for any history of Llano are the surviving records and publications of the colonists. Beginning with its founding in 1914, the colony owned and sponsored a monthly socialist journal, the *Western Comrade*. The journal was moved to Louisiana in 1917, was changed to the *Internationalist* in 1918, but then had to suspend publication as the colony declined and almost failed. Every issue of the *Western Comrade* carried at least one article on Llano, tracing in great detail the growth and successes of the colony in California, but neglecting most of the failures. It was in this journal that Job Harriman expressed his ideas about socialism and his hopes for Llano. Other excellent, firsthand accounts of the California and early Louisiana colony were written by the one-time general manager, Ernest Wooster. In his *Communities of the Past and Present* (Newllano, 1924), he features a summary account of Llano and includes an introduction by Harriman. Wooster also wrote a series of three articles on Llano for *Sunset Magazine*, LIII (July, Aug., Sept., 1924).

In the desperate years from 1918 to 1921, the colony suspended all publications. But with the return of prosperity in 1921, the colony began its weekly newspaper, the *Llano Colonist*, which was published continuously from then until the fall of 1937. Unfortunately, only a few numbers of the *Colonist* before 1927 have survived. After 1927, George T. Pickett kept a complete file and graciously loaned it to the Louisiana State University Library for microfilming. Without these newspapers, the story of Llano in Louisiana could never have been told in any detail. In fact, the *Colonist* remains the one all-important source for the whole history of the colony, since it frequently included historical articles or reminiscences about the colony's founding and early years. This weekly newspaper, with its day-by-day diary, its detailed description of colony work and events, its gossip, its sketches and characterizations of colonists, its appeal for members or gifts, provides what in all probability is the most intimate view of life in a communitarian colony ever vouchsafed non-members or later generations of historians. This newspaper source is complemented by the mass of unorganized personal records collected by George T. Pickett. Unfortunately, only a few items in the Pickett papers relate to the "lost" period from 1918 to 1921. Also, the Pickett papers may not be preserved by Pickett's son and only heir.

The three small books written about the Llano colony are each biased and limited in scope. A. James McDonald, a Leesville lawyer who spent some time at Llano before quarreling with Pickett, wrote a short account in order to explain his own actions in helping to destroy the colony and in order to expose what he believed to be the duplicity of Pickett. Entitled *The Llano Co-operative Colony and What It Taught* (Leesville, 1950), it provides several valuable insights into the financing of the colony and also some needed information about the complicated legal maneuvers that led to liquidation in 1938. During the depression, a Marxist journalist, Bob Brown, lived awhile at Llano and later published a flippant, half-comical account of his visit: *Can We Co-operate?* (New York, 1940). It provides some accurate description and some perceptive character sketches, but little else. After the overthrow of Pickett in the revolution of 1935, a fanatically loyal Pickett supporter, Sid Young, wrote and published a bitterly partisan account entitled, *The Crisis in Llano Colony* (Los Angeles, 1936).

A few magazine articles were written on Llano, especially in the early thirties, but almost all of these drew their information either from Pickett, from colony publications, or from carefully conducted tours of the colony. Thus the articles usually painted a falsely optimistic picture. The same optimism colors Pickett's 1933 testimony before the Senate Committee on Agriculture and Forestry, *Hearings on S.1142, the United Communities*, 73rd Cong., 1st Sess. On the other hand, a series of critical articles appeared throughout the twenties in *Co-operation*, the official organ of the Co-operative League of America, whose officials so despised Pickett that they could never acknowledge anything good about the colony. In partial compensation for these biased articles, Robert V. Hine, in *California's Utopian Colonies* (San Marino, Calif., 1953), devotes one excellent, balanced chapter to Llano in California.

Even as in the case of the Hutterites, some of the most balanced studies of Llano were completed by M.A. candidates. Archie Roy Clifton, in his "A Study of Llano del Rio Community in the Light of Earlier Experiments in Practical Socialism" (unpublished M.A. Thesis, University of Southern California, 1918), accurately described the matured California colony, but was overly optimistic about the colony's future prospects. By far the most valuable and complete contemporary analysis of Llano was made by Fred Hanover, an M.A. candidate in social work at Tulane University. He visited the colony just after the revolution of 1935, utilized interviews and personal history statements, reconstructed an accurate history of the colony, and tried to evaluate its strengths and weaknesses. His resulting, unpublished thesis, "Llano Cooperative Colony: An American Rural Community Experiment" (Tulane University, 1936), was necessarily based on the conditions in the colony as he found it. Since 1935 was a depression year, and since the complexion of colony membership had changed so rapidly after 1932, the conclusions drawn by Hanover rarely apply to the colony during the more normal twenties. This lack of perspective, plus a normal tendency to rely on the existing management, only slightly detracts from the only noteworthy study to be made of Llano during its twenty-five-year history.

Acknowledgments

Most of the research for this monograph, including a trip to the Hutterite colonies of South Dakota, was financed by the General Research Board of the University of Maryland. It was aided immeasurably by the information and advice so generously provided by the Reverend David Decker of the Tschetter Colony, Olivet, South Dakota, and by the late George T. Pickett of Leesville, Louisiana.

Index